Lecture Notes of the Institute for Computer Sciences, Social Informatics and Telecommunications Engineering 363

More information about this series at http://www.springer.com/series/8197

Lianyong Qi · Mohammad R. Khosravi ·
Xiaolong Xu · Yiwen Zhang ·
Varun G. Menon (Eds.)

Cloud Computing

10th EAI International Conference, CloudComp 2020
Qufu, China, December 11–12, 2020
Proceedings

 Springer

Editors
Lianyong Qi ⓘ
Qufu Normal University
Qufu, China

Xiaolong Xu ⓘ
Nanjing University of Information Science
and Technology
Nanjing, China

Varun G. Menon ⓘ
SCMS School of Engineering
and Technology
Kerala, India

Mohammad R. Khosravi ⓘ
Persian Gulf University
Bushehr, Iran

Yiwen Zhang ⓘ
Anhui University
Hefei, China

ISSN 1867-8211   ISSN 1867-822X (electronic)
Lecture Notes of the Institute for Computer Sciences, Social Informatics
and Telecommunications Engineering
ISBN 978-3-030-69991-8   ISBN 978-3-030-69992-5 (eBook)
https://doi.org/10.1007/978-3-030-69992-5

This Springer imprint is published by the registered company Springer Nature Switzerland AG
The registered company address is: Gewerbestrasse 11, 6330 Cham, Switzerland

Preface

We are delighted to introduce the proceedings of the 10th edition of the European Alliance for Innovation (EAI) International Conference on Cloud Computing (CloudComp 2020). This conference brought together researchers, developers and practitioners around the world who are leveraging and developing cloud systems technology for high-performance and intelligent computing in cyber-physical environments. The theme of CloudComp 2020 was "Cyber-Physical Cloud Systems: Theories, Problems and Applications".

The technical program of CloudComp 2020 consisted of fourteen full papers, including two review papers and twelve original research papers at the main conference tracks. The conference proceedings book has been organized within four general areas of Cyber-Physical Intelligent Computing, Secure Cloud Systems and Cloud-Based Privacy, Cloud-Based IoT Architecture, and Cloud Computing Applications such that all fourteen papers were allocated to them. In the first track, four papers around the importance of cyber-physical computing and artificial intelligence in cloud systems, servers and industrial environments are presented. In the second track, there are three research papers with a serious focus on security and privacy in cloud systems and databases. The third track contains three research papers regarding cloud-based internet of things (IoT) services. And finally, the last track introduces four papers focused on different aspects of cloud and centralized computing applications such as human-computer interaction and medical systems.

We deeply would like to thank all of our technical committee members and reviewers who helped us to organize the conference under the difficult circumstances of the COVID-19 pandemic. Also, the contribution of our participants is highly appreciated and we hope to have all of them at the next meeting of CloudComp. Finally, a great thanks to all the EAI staff and managers for their constant support is essential.

We strongly believe that CloudComp 2020 has provided a good forum for all researchers, developers and practitioners to discuss all scientific and technological aspects that are relevant to cloud systems and cyber-physical computing.

Lianyong Qi
Mohammad R. Khosravi
Xiaolong Xu
Yiwen Zhang
Varun G. Menon

Conference Organization

Steering Committee

Chair

Imrich Chlamtac — University of Trento, Italy

Members

Xuyun Zhang — Macquarie University, Australia
Guanfeng Liu — Macquarie University, Australia

Organizing Committee

General Chair

Shangguang Wang — Beijing University of Posts and Telecommunications, China

General Co-chairs

Houbing Song — Embry-Riddle Aeronautical University, USA
Lianyong Qi — Qufu Normal University, China
Qiang He — Swinburne University of Technology, Australia

Technical Program Committee Chairs

Dong Yuan — The University of Sydney, Australia
Haipeng Dai — Nanjing University, China
Shaohua Wan — Zhongnan University of Economics and Law, China
Kaijian Xia — China University of Mining and Technology, China

Web Chairs

Guanfeng Liu — Macquarie University, Australia
Shancang Li — University of the West of England, UK
Xiaolong Xu — Nanjing University of Information Science and Technology, China

Sponsorship and Exhibit Chairs

Xianzhi Wang — University of Technology Sydney, Australia
Fei Dai — Southwest Forestry University, China
Qi Liu — Nanjing University of Information Science and Technology, China

Publicity and Social Media Chairs

Jia Wu	Macquarie University, Australia
Mehdi Elahi	University of Bergen, Norway
Nabil El Ioini	Free University of Bolzano, Italy

Workshops Chairs

Lina Yao	The University of New South Wales, Australia
Ling Jian	China University of Petroleum (East China), China

Publication Chairs

Mohammad Khosravi	Persian Gulf University, Iran
Yiwen Zhang	Anhui University, China

Local Chairs

Guangshun Li	Qufu Normal University, China
Wanchun Dou	Nanjing University, China
Maoli Wang	Qufu Normal University, China

International TPC Members and Advisors

Varun G. Menon	SCMS School of Engineering and Technology, India
Pooya Tavallali	University of California, Merced, USA
Wenmin Lin	Hangzhou Normal University, China
Yingjie Wang	Yantai University, China
Wanchun Dou	Nanjing University, China
Hongning Dai	Macau University of Science and Technology, Macau
Hongsheng Hu	University of Auckland, New Zealand
Hao Wang	Norwegian University of Science and Technology, Norway
Xuyun Zhang	Macquarie University, Australia
Haolong Xiang	University of Auckland, New Zealand
Mahdi Abbasi	BASU, Iran
Yirui Wu	Hohai University, China

Contents

Cloud Computing Applications

Cyber-Physical Intelligent Computing

Knowledge Graphs Meet Crowdsourcing: A Brief Survey

Meilin Cao, Jing Zhang(✉) ⓘ, Sunyue Xu, and Zijian Ying

School of Computer Science and Engineering, Nanjing University of Science and Technology,
Nanjing 210094, China
`1527449673@qq.com`, `{jzhang,320127010185}@njust.edu.cn`,
`834391247@qq.com`

Abstract. In recent years, as a new solution for hiring laborers to complete tasks, crowdsourcing has received universal concern in both academia and industry, which has been widely used in many IT domains such as machine learning, computer vision, information retrieval, software engineering, and so on. The emergence of crowdsourcing undoubtedly facilitates the Knowledge Graph (KG) technology. As an important branch of artificial intelligence that is recently fast developing, the KG technology usually involves machine intelligence and human intelligence, especially in the creation of knowledge graphs, human participation is indispensable, which provides a good scenario for the application of crowdsourcing. This paper first briefly reviews some basic concepts of knowledge-intensive crowdsourcing and knowledge graphs. Then, it discusses three key issues on knowledge-intensive crowdsourcing from the perspectives of task type, selection of workers, and crowdsourcing processes. Finally, it focuses on the construction of knowledge graphs, introducing innovative applications and methods that utilize crowdsourcing.

Keywords: Crowdsourcing · Human computation · Knowledge graphs ·
Knowledge mining · Ontology construction

1 Introduction

The concept of crowdsourcing was first proposed by Jeff Howe back in 2006 [1]. He pointed out that crowdsourcing was different from outsourcing. Crowdsourcing is the practice of assigning tasks of an organization or company to a non-specific crowd through network platforms. Crowdsourcing solves problems at a lower cost by tap-ping the potential talents in the crowd. As a novel solution to the acquisition of information and knowledge, crowdsourcing has been widely adopted by many disciplines to facilitate their development, such as business intelligence [2], computer vision [3], software engineering [4], information retrieval [5], machine learning [6], biomedical research [7], health science [8], and so on.

Nowadays, the complex knowledge has be represented as a graphical structure, which is called Knowledge Graphs (KGs). The concept was first put forward by Google in 2012,

L. Qi et al. (Eds.): CloudComp 2020, LNICST 363, pp. 3–17, 2021.
https://doi.org/10.1007/978-3-030-69992-5_1

where the new things were applied to its search engine. The introduction of knowledge graphs strengthened the semantic capability of the search engine, making a query search the contents in the level of domain knowledge instead of simply literally matching the strings in Web databases [9]. Knowledge graphs emphasize entities and their relations rather than strings. Similar to resource pages, knowledge graphs need to be built first, then stored, and finally applied.

The construction of knowledge graphs is inseparable from the participation of humans. Comparing with employing domain experts, introducing crowd workers in the construction and refinement of knowledge graphs is cheaper and fast. However, because of the low quality of non-expert workers, the core problem of crowdsourcing is to optimize the matching of tasks and workers and improve the user experience. Furthermore, when crowdsourcing is applied to the knowledge graph creation, it involves a process of extracting human wisdom. Undoubtedly, knowledge-intensive crowdsourcing may be more complicated, where production and utilization of large-scale knowledge will form an ideal cycle, and human wisdom will continue to promote the operation of this cycle.

In this paper, we first briefly review some basic concepts of crowdsourcing and knowledge graphs, especially focusing on the knowledge-intensive crowdsourcing and the construction of knowledge graphs. Then, we discuss three issues on knowledge-intensive crowdsourcing from the perspectives of task type, se-lection of workers, and crowdsourcing processes. Finally, we review some innovative applications and methods in knowledge graph creation where crowdsourcing was utilized.

2   Basic Concepts of Crowdsourcing and Knowledge Graphs

In this section, we briefly review some basic concepts of crowdsourcing and knowledge graphs.

2.1   Characteristics of Crowdsourcing

As a well-known fact, the definition of crowdsourcing was first proposed in 2006 by Jeff Howe [1], a journalist at the Wired Magazine. However, as early as 2005, a Chinese scholar Feng Liu had created a word "witkey", standing for "the key of wisdom", to denote the crowdsourcing business model from the perspective of computer technology [10]. Estellés-Arolas et al. [11] summarized as many as 40 different definitions of crowdsourcing. These definitions describe crowdsourcing from different perspectives. Through the comparison and analysis to these definitions, we can come to some basic characteristics of crowdsourcing:

- Participatory online activities;
- Crowdsourcing tasks usually solve complex problems that are difficult to solve individually;
- Distributed problem-solving mechanism.

According to these characteristics, the definition of crowdsourcing can be as follows: crowdsourcing is a kind of participatory online activity, which solves the task that the machine intelligence alone is difficult to complete by integrating machines and humans on the Internet.

Knowledge-intensive crowdsourcing is a particular kind of crowdsourcing applications as a bridge between the human brain and machines under the scenarios of exploiting and exploring knowledge. Knowledge-intensive crowdsourcing is recognized as one of the most promising areas of the next generation crowdsourcing, mainly because it plays a key role in today's era of knowledge economy [12]. Knowledge-intensive crowdsourcing has some particular characteristics:

- Diversity of tasks and data. The types of tasks include annotation, classification, ranking, clustering, etc., and the types of data include images, text, structured information, etc. The difficulties of the tasks are also different.
- Diversity of crowd workers. The expertise, educational background, intention, and dedication of crowd workers are different.
- The quality of tasks is difficult to evaluate because of the open nature of crowdsourcing and the absence of ground truth. It is also difficult to measure workers' confidence. Moreover, the cost of evaluation itself is rather high.

The main participants of crowdsourcing include task requesters and task completers (also known as workers). The workflow of task requesters usually includes four steps as follows: 1) Design crowdsourcing tasks; 2) Release the crowdsourcing tasks and wait for the results; 3) Filter the results according to predefined rules for quality control; 4) Integrate results and pay the workers via platforms. The activities of workers include: 1) Select crowdsourcing tasks within their interests and also according to their qualifications; 2) Accept the tasks; 3) Perform the tasks; 4) Submit the answers and get the payments.

2.2 Applications of Knowledge-Intensive Crowdsourcing

During the past decade, researchers and engineers developed various applications that belong to the category of knowledge-intensive crowdsourcing. In this section, we use a few very different examples to illustrate its huge practical value.

- Collaborative editing. As a free and open online encyclopedia, Wikipedia is a well-known crowdsourcing application in the world. It has accumulated more than 3 billion words and numerous knowledge items through crowdsourcing. It will be a huge project to formalize this huge knowledge network into a knowledge graph.
- Urban planning. In urban planning activities home and abroad, the practice of crowdsourcing to encourage public participation has become mature [13]. The Nexthamburg website [14] provides a planning platform for the public in Hamburg, Germany. Each participant participates in the planning and construction of the city's future development by voting, contributing ideas and participating in forums, and further carries out resource crowdfunding on the stadtmacher platform to help realize the public's planning scheme. Similar examples include Mindmixer [15] and Openstreetmap [16] in the United States, and "Zhonggui Wuhan" in China [17] (https://zg.wpdi.cn/).

– Healthcare and Medicine. In recent years, crowdsourcing has also been increasingly used in health science and medical research [18]. Cooper et al. [19] described Foldit, a multiplayer online game, by combining player inputs to determine whether players of the online game MalariaSpot could accurately identify malaria parasites in digitized thick blood smears.

– Marketing. Enterprises can use crowdsourcing to complete marketing related tasks, mainly focusing on product development, advertising and promotion, and marketing research [20]. Dasgupta et al. [21] used a crowdsourcing research website (StreetRx) to solicit data about the price that site visitors paid for diverted prescription opioid analgesics during the first half of 2012. These crowdsourced data provide a valid estimate of the street price of diverted prescription opioids.

– Online learning. In [22], the crowdsourcing method was used to construct Chinese semantic relevance dictionary. Hong et al. [23] combines the incentive mechanism of crowdsourcing with online question-answering technology to simulate teachers' questioning in the real classroom and applies it in MOOC.

2.3   Basic Concept of Knowledge Graphs

The definition of knowledge graph in Wikipedia is as follows: A knowledge graph is the knowledge base that Google uses to enhance its search engine function.[1] In essence, the knowledge graph is a kind of structured semantic knowledge base, which is used to describe concepts and their relationships in the physical world in symbolic form [24]. Knowledge graph is usually designed as a large-scale semantic web, which is composed of entities, concepts and other nodes and attributes, relationships, types and other edges. It is a collection of a large number of triples. Each triplet is composed of subject, predicate, and object.

Triple is the general expression of knowledge graphs [25]. There are four basic types of knowledge tuples:

– <entity, relationship, entity>. E.g., <Mcrosoft, founder, Bill Gates> ;
– <entity, attribute, attribute value >. E.g., <Microsoft, founded time, 1975> ;
– < entity, is-a, concept >. E.g., <Mcrosoft, is-a, listed companies> ;
– <child concept, subclass-of, parent concept>. E.g., <lised company, subclass-of, company>

At present, a number of knowledge graphs have been created for different purposes, such as open domain knowledge graphs (Freebase [26], Dbpedia [27], Wikidata [28], and YAGO[2]), vertical domain knowledge graphs (Linked Life Data[3] and ConceptNet [29]), and Chinese knowledge graphs (Xlore [30] and CN-Dbpedia [31]). Table 1 summarizes the characteristics of some knowledge graphs.

---

[1] https://en.wikipedia.org/wiki/Knowledge_Graph.
[2] https://yago-knowledge.org/.
[3] https://linkedlifedata.com/.

Table 1. Overview of some popular knowledge graphs.

KG name	Start year	Dependent resources	Scale
ConceptNet	1999	Crowd intelligence	28 million RDF triples
Dbpedia	2007	Wikipedia + Expert knowledge	3 billion RDF triples
YAGO	2007	WordNet + Wikipedia	4,595,906 instances
Freebase	2008	Wikipedia + Domain knowledge + Crowd intelligence	58,726,427 instances
Wikidata	2012	Freebase + Crowd intelligence	42.65 million entries
Xlore	2013	Crowd intelligence	16,284,901 instances

2.4 Construction of Knowledge Graphs

Current construction methods of knowledge graphs are usually based on information extraction in open domains. The construction processes of knowledge graphs typically include three stages [32]: 1) Knowledge extraction, which extracts useful data for business from the original raw data sources; 2) Knowledge fusion, which generally involves knowledge cleaning, entity alignment, and other related processes; 3) Quality evaluation, which judges whether the outcomes meet the predefined requirements. Having a high-quality knowledge graph, we can further carry out knowledge reasoning on it and mine hidden knowledge.

Knowledge Extraction. Knowledge extraction is the primary work of constructing knowledge graphs, including entity extraction, relationship extraction, and attribute extraction [33]. 1) The commonly used entity extraction methods include rule- and dictionary-based, statistical learning-based, and open domain-based extraction methods. Based on the statistics of the characteristics and laws of Chinese place names, Shen et al. [34] sum up the algorithm of Chinese place names, and put forward the reliability probability of word formation and place name continuation to balance the recall and accuracy. Zheng et al. [35] introduced a method of entity recognition based on corpus, extracted and analyzed the frequency of Chinese surname and given name words on the basis of large-scale corpus, and then combined with the rules of context information to determine the place name. Lin et al. [32] proposed a maximum entropy algorithm based on the dictionary, making the recall and accuracy of entity extraction above 70%. Table 2 shows the existing entity extraction methodologies with their advantages and disadvantages. 2) Relation extraction techniques usually can be categorized into template-based methods, lexicon-driven methods, and machine learning-based methods [36]. 3) In terms of attribute extraction, Yang et al. [37] proposed a heuristic attribute extraction method based on rules. Guo et al. [38] used conditional random fields (CRFs) and support vector machines (SVM) to construct collaborative classifiers for attribute and attribute value extraction. In the open test, the accuracy of the collaborative classifier reached 84.4%, and the recall reached 82.7%.

Knowledge Fusion. Knowledge fusion is an important step in the process of knowledge graph construction. After knowledge extraction, the original knowledge can be

Table 2. Entity-extraction methodologies with their advantages and disadvantages.

Methodologies	Advantages	Disadvantages
Rule-based	High accuracy and recall rates can be achieved on small datasets	As the size of a dataset increases, the construction time of the rule set becomes longer and the portability gets worse
Statistical model-based	Little dependence on language and good portability	The correctness of statistical methods and the reliability of statistical sources have a greater impact on the results
Machine (deep) learning-based	Directly take the vector of words in the text as input, without relying on artificially defined features	The implementation techniques are more complicated

obtained. Due to the wide range of knowledge sources in the knowledge map, the quality of knowledge is uneven, the knowledge from different data sources may be repeated, and the correlation between knowledge is not clear enough. Thus, knowledge fusion must be carried out [25]. Knowledge fusion is a high-level abstraction of knowledge organization mode. Key techniques include entity disambiguation, coreference resolution, etc. Entity disambiguation refers to the elimination of different meanings of the same entity. Tan et al. [39] proposed a NED algorithm combining entity linking and entity clustering for entity disambiguation. Ning and Zhang [40] proposed a hierarchical clustering method based on heterogeneous knowledge base to solve the problem of entity disambiguation, and used the Hadoop platform to cluster entity information objects extracted from Wikipedia. Coreference resolution refers to the elimination of the same meaning of different entities. Wang et al. [41] proposed a coreference resolution method based on a decision tree, which combines statistics and rules, and uses rules to filter examples with attribute conflicts. Their method achieved a successful elimination rate of 82.59%. Peng and Yang [42] introduced a maximum entropy model to resolute coreference. By training the model, the problem of common reference resolution is solved, and the improvement is significant.

Knowledge Evaluation. After building the knowledge graph, we need to evaluate the scale and quality of the knowledge map. Mendes et al. [43] proposed a framework for quality assessment, namely Sieve, which has been integrated into the Linked Data Integration Framework (LDIF). Using the Sieve, users can flexibly design their own quality assessment standards. Fader et al. [44] manually annotated entities and relationships in 1000 sentences, and used the results as training sets, and then used the logistics regression model to evaluate the quality of the results. In addition to Sieve, Zaveri et al. [45] also listed dozens of frameworks for knowledge evaluation, and comprehensively reviewed various methods used for quality assessment, and clarified the differences between these methods.

3 Key Issues on Knowledge-Intensive Crowdsourcing

This section briefly reviews three key issues on knowledge-intensive crowdsourcing from the perspectives of tasks, workers, and crowdsourcing processes.

3.1 What Tasks are Suitable for Crowdsourcing

For the purpose of saving budget and time, people generally select the most important tasks or tasks that machines cannot handle but humans are easy to complete to post them on the crowdsourcing platforms. In the process of creating knowledge graphs, crowdsourcing can hand over the task of entity matching and ontology matching. Wang et al. [46] elaborated on the problem of using crowdsourcing for entity matching. Unlike the existing methods (publishing all candidate pairs to the crowdsourcing platform), they studied the relationship between candidate pairs and transferring relationships to reduce overhead. For example, if the entity pairs o_1 and o_2 match, and o_2 and o_3 match, then (o_1, o_3) does not need to be posted on the crowdsourcing platform to make an inference, since the matching of o_1 and o_3 can be obtained automatically. Zhang et al. [47] explored how to use crowdsourcing to reduce the uncertainty of pattern matching (that is, to find the correspondence between the elements of two given patterns). They used probability calculation to locate the correspondence that mostly needs to be determined by crowdsourcing and then judged which group has the highest corresponding probability. Lin et al. [48] studied the application of crowdsourcing in knowledge graph cleaning. They proposed an algorithm to measure which edge to clean would maximize the uncertainty of the system, thereby increasing the time and cost of crowdsourcing. Mo et al. [49] proposed a novel pairwise crowdsourcing model to reduce the uncertainty of top-k ranking using a set of domain experts. For the first k questions and answers based on the knowledge graph, if the given query is compared, the comparison will have a sequential order, which is very vague. At this time, one can make a comparison for it, which is equivalent to a true or false question. Through such short comparisons, the uncertainty of the system can be effectively minimized.

In summary, the selection of crowdsourcing tasks generally follows the principles:

- Preference for small tasks so that workers can use the fragmented time to get paid quickly.
- Local crowdsourcing results will have an impact on the overall situation and this impact needs to be quantified and different tasks have different effects.

3.2 Who Completes Crowdsourcing Tasks

Passive crowdsourcing refers to the mode that when workers actively choose crowdsourcing tasks, and workers may participate in training before performing tasks. The principles of active crowdsourcing task allocation are as follows: randomly assigning tasks, assigning tasks according to worker quality or other criteria (for example, selecting the workers with the highest quality, selecting the nearest workers, or selecting the workers with the closest expected results, etc.). Mo et al. [49] studied a cross-task crowdsourcing problem. That is, the actual labels of data provided by different crowdsourcing workers in a crowdsourcing environment may be sparse, noisy, and unreliable. They used domain similarity and transfer learning to transfer users' domain skills in reasoning. Zheng et al. [50] introduced a field-based matching method, which decomposed all tasks into 13 fields and calculated the correlation between workers and tasks in each field. Mavridis et al. [51] adopted a skill tree-based matching method, through fine modeling of tasks and participants, and the distance on the tree to represent their correlation. Some tasks may not be able to model the task using only decision trees. At this time, tree-graph combination could be used.

3.3 How to Complete Crowdsourcing Tasks

The good completion of crowdsourcing tasks depends on various factors, mainly including how to design crowdsourcing tasks, how to motivate workers, and how to control the quality of tasks and results.

There are two ways of designing crowdsourcing tasks—explicit crowdsourcing and implicit crowdsourcing. As their names suggest, explicit crowdsourcing means that workers clearly know that they are completing crowdsourcing tasks, while implicit crowdsourcing means that workers do not know the existence of crowdsourcing tasks. An implicit crowdsourcing task is generally hidden behind some other tasks. The facial tasks are used to attract workers, and the workers unconsciously complete the crowdsourcing tasks when completing the facial ones. Compared with explicit crowdsourcing, the implicit scheme has a lower cost and better results. Two different crowdsourcing schemes have different task-designing principles. For explicit crowdsourcing, the designed tasks should be as concise as possible so that they can easily attract many workers and do not require too much completion time. Therefore, the traditional design principle tries to design small tasks. For example, binary-choice (true or false) questions are better than multiple-choice ones, and multiple-choice questions are better than fill-in-the-blank ones, which means the less interaction the better. Also, the UI design of explicit crowdsourcing should be vivid and concise. For implicit crowdsourcing, the crowdsourcing tasks need to be plunged into the facial tasks on the premise that the facial tasks are attractive enough to workers. For example, one can hide a crowdsourcing task in a game and obtains some common-sense knowledge and location information through workers' feedback. The location information can also use the worker's psychological characteristics to arouse their curiosity or distract them so that the workers can complete the crowdsourcing tasks unknowingly. Von Ahn et al. [52] introduced a game called Verbosity. The roles of the game are divided into narrator and guesser. A narrator uses a non-secret word completion template to ask a guesser to guess the secret word. Through this interesting game, users can unknowingly provide common-sense knowledge while enjoying the game (such as true statements like "snow is white"). Ni et al. [53] proposed an alternative ground truth to the eye fixation map in visual attention study called Touch Saliency, which judges the focus of a picture by the position where the user clicks on the screen when seeing the picture. The principles of implicit crowdsourcing task design include: Propose tasks unconsciously; Users can become workers; The facial task meets the needs of users, and the behind one is the crowdsourcing task; The facial task must be attractive enough to users.

Obviously, there have been several approaches to motivate workers, including money, happiness, social influence (can be divided into strong connections such as in WeChat or Facebook, and weak connections such as in Baidu Tieba), and so on. One can use a hybrid incentive mechanism such as using strong social media for publicity at the beginning of the task, using weak social media and monetary incentives after gathering certain popularity, and again using strong social media and monetary incentives to attract remaining workers at the end.

The quality control of crowdsourcing requires to consider correctness, coverage, timeliness, and consistency. Because the quality of crowdsourcing workers is uneven, there may be malicious workers such as fake qualified workers, quick deceivers (aiming to get paid by answering questions indiscriminately), etc. To deal with this tricky situation, the methods such as burying mines (that is, inserting some tasks whose answers are known to check the quality of workers) and backtracking questions (asking questions related to the previous question to prevent users from answering the questions indiscriminately) have been widely adopted. After crowdsourcing tasks are completed, the collected answers need to be verified for credibility. Some easiest method was to use gold standard data to evaluate the quality of workers' outcomes [54]. Using the data with standard answers, the quality of workers can be determined by comparing the results submitted with the standard answers. Another way that does not rely on the gold answers is to use a repeated-answering scheme, where multiple workers independently answer the same questions. The final answers are inferred from the collected multiple noisy answers, which is call the truth inference. During the past decade, a large number of true inference algorithms for crowdsourcing were proposed and achieved good performance [55].

4 Construction of Knowledge Graphs Using Crowdsourcing

In knowledge-intensive crowdsourcing, knowledge graphs can be exploited and explored. This section further focuses on the construction of knowledge graphs, where crowdsourcing provides an effective solution to gather a large amount of knowledge.

4.1 Ontology Construction

Ontology is also called entity in knowledge graphs. This concept originated from western philosophy and describes the objective existence of things. In 1993, Gruber [56] defined ontology as a conceptual and precise specification. In 1998, Studer et al. further extended the concept of ontology and defined it as a clear formal specification of a shared conceptual model [57]. In short, ontology is a data set that is used to describe a domain and the skeleton of the knowledge base. A knowledge graph model needs the support of ontology, and the concept of ontology has been widely concerned in the field of information science in recent years [58]. An ontology consists of five basic elements, including class or concept, relation, function, axiom, and instance. There are usually three approaches for ontology construction—manual construction, automatic construction, and semi-automatic construction.

Here, we introduce semi-automatic ontology construction, which is between manual construction and automatic construction. Because of the high technical requirements of fully automated ontology construction, it is difficult to achieve in most application fields. Therefore, the construction of ontology usually needs human participation, and crowdsourcing platforms just provide a good solution. DiFranzo and Hendler [59] introduced OntoPronto, which is a premeditated game. In this game, two players try to map randomly chosen Wikipedia articles to the most specific classes of the Proton ontology. If they agree on a Proton class for their articles, they will obtain points and proceed to the next specific level. Acosta et al. [60] proposed CrowdSPARQL, a new SPARQL query answer method, which combines machine-driven and human-driven capabilities. When an SPARQL query fails to respond, it will be redirected to the MTurk platform to obtain knowledge. Niepert et al. [61] proposed INPHO, a system combining statistical text processing, information extraction, human expert feedback, and logic programming, which is used to fill and expand the Dynamic Ontology in the field of Philosophy. The system uses crowdsourcing to complete the construction of the concept system.

4.2 Knowledge Mining and Filling

Knowledge is undoubtedly an indispensable part of knowledge graphs. Compared with machines, human beings have inherent advantages in knowledge acquisition and mining, which are shown in three aspects. First, humans can quickly and accurately extract triples from natural language. Second, they can accurately align triple in heterogeneous data sources. Finally, they are good at using common sense database. However, if all of the above work is completed manually, the cost of time and money will be unacceptable. Therefore, in terms of knowledge acquisition, the combination of humans and machines is the mainstream.

Crowdsourcing is widely used for knowledge acquisition, that is, extracting entities and triples from natural languages. Kondreddi et al. [62] proposed a system architecture called Higgins, which shows how to effectively integrate Information Extraction (IE) engine and Human Computing (HC) engine. The system allows players to select or fill in the subject-relation-object triples by setting game problems. Higgins system combines information extraction and human computing, which can be used to edit the relationship between characters in movies or books. First, it creates meaningful questions and answers through the IE engine, and then feeds them into the HC engine for crowdsourcing annotation, which greatly improves the accuracy and reduces the cost.

Crowdsourcing has been used to align entities from heterogeneous knowledge sources. Entity alignment includes entity disambiguation and coreference disambiguation. Zhuang et al. [63] put forward a method of human–computer combination named HIKE for entity alignment. Firstly, rough entity alignment is conducted for knowledge base through machine learning method, and then matched pairs and unmatched pairs are put into crowdsourcing platforms respectively for crowd workers to judge their correctness.

The entity collection based on crowdsourcing aims to collect a large number of open entities. It is also an important application of crowdsourcing in knowledge mining. There may be some challenges such as repetition, omission, and errors when using the method of purely manual entity collection. Crowdsourcing-based entity collection can make up for the deficiency of purely manual entity collection. Chai et al. [64] proposed an incentive-based crowdsourcing entity collection framework Crowdec, which encourages employees to use incentive strategies to provide more different projects, uses the pricing principle to encourage workers to provide non-repetitive answers, and adopts the worker elimination method to prevent the inefficient use of workers.

4.3   Refinement of Knowledge Graphs

Refinement is one of the important issues in knowledge graph research. Its main tasks include knowledge graph completion and error detection. Here, we introduce the application of crowdsourcing in the refinement stage of knowledge graphs. There are three reasons for introducing crowdsourcing to refine knowledge graphs. First, it is difficult for automatic methods to achieve both high accuracy and wide coverage. Second, documents in the network have a long tail effect, which means a large amount of knowledge is distributed sparsely. Finally, automatic processing technology usually has some defects such as high noise and difficulty in guaranteeing knowledge accuracy.

The function of crowdsourcing to fill the gaps is reflected in all encyclopedia websites, such as Wikipedia. Wikipedia is based on the principle that everyone can participate in it. It has the characteristics of open sharing, interactive collaboration, and comprehensive and accurate information. Wikipedia has also launched its own unique management and editing techniques such as page locking, when the editing level of some main pages reaches the Wikipedia standard, the page is locked to prevent other users from editing at will [65]. Singh et al. [66] proposed a knowledge acquisition system called Open Mind Common Sense, which allows participants to construct and fill natural knowledge templates to obtain facts and common-sense knowledge. In addition, there is crowdsourcing verification based on link prediction and the filling of the domain knowledge graph based on crowdsourcing.

Crowdsourcing error correction usually forms into two trains of thought. In the first scheme, we disclose all data and use crowdsourcing to find and correct errors. This scheme is suitable for large-scale websites with a huge volume of traffic, such as Google. In the second scheme, the machine first locates the possible error locations and then submits them to crowdsourcing. This scheme is suitable for small websites. In fact, as early as 2011 in China, Sogou Maps launched high-speed charging calculation and error correction functions, encouraging users to share charging data to improve the charging function. Currently, various map software also obtains user information through crowdsourcing, encouraging the users to contribute Point-Of-Interest information or correct the routes. Pavlick et al. [67] introduced the application of crowdsourcing in the problem of grammatical error correction, discarding the traditional majority voting method and using crowdsourcing to ensure quality and produce ideal results.

5   Conclusion

Crowdsourcing has provided a good venue for both creating and exploiting knowledge graphs. This paper briefly reviews the recent progress in the intersection of knowledge graphs and crowdsourcing. The paper first summarizes the characteristics of knowledge-intensive crowdsourcing and the construction procedure of knowledge graphs. Then, it discusses three key issues on knowledge-intensive crowdsourcing from the perspectives of tasks, workers, and crowdsourcing processes, which shapes the contour of current research in this field. Finally, it reviews some innovative applications and methods where crowdsourcing was utilized in the construction of knowledge graphs. We believe that this direction will continue to be a research hot spot in the future.

Acknowledgements. This work has been supported by the National Natural Science Foundation of China under grants 62076130 and 91846104, and the National Key Research and Development Program of China under grant 2018AAA0102002.

References

1. Howe, J.: The rise of crowdsourcing. Wired Mag. **14**(6), 1–4 (2006)
2. Guo, B., Liu, Y., Ouyang, Y., Zheng, V.W., Zhang, D., Yu, Z.: Harnessing the power of the general public for crowdsourced business intelligence: a survey. IEEE Access **7**, 26606–26630 (2019)
3. Kovashka, A., Russakovsky, O., Fei-Fei, L., Grauman, K.: Crowdsourcing in computer vision. Found. Trends® Comput. Graph. Vis. **10**(3), 177–243 (2016)
4. Mao, K., Capra, L., Harman, M., Jia, Y.: A survey of the use of crowdsourcing in software engineering. J. Syst. Softw. **126**, 57–84 (2017)
5. Alonso, O., Lease, M.: Crowdsourcing for information retrieval: principles, methods, and applications. In: Proceedings of the 34th International ACM SIGIR Conference on Research and Development in Information Retrieval, pp. 1299–1300 (2011)
6. Zhang, J., Wu, X., Sheng, V.S.: Learning from crowdsourced labeled data: a survey. Artif. Intell. Rev. **46**(4), 543–576 (2016). https://doi.org/10.1007/s10462-016-9491-9
7. Saez-Rodriguez, J., et al.: Crowdsourcing biomedical research: leveraging communities as innovation engines. Nat. Rev. Genet. **17**(8), 470 (2016)
8. Wazny, K.: Applications of crowdsourcing in health: an overview. J. Glob. Health **8**(1), 010502 (2018)
9. Gomez-Perez, J.M., Pan, J.Z., Vetere, G., Wu, H.: Enterprise knowledge graph: an introduction. In: Pan, J., Vetere, G., Gomez-Perez, J., Wu, H. (eds.) Exploiting linked data and knowledge graphs in large organisations, pp. 1–14. Springer, Cham (2017). https://doi.org/10.1007/978-3-319-45654-6_1
10. Lin, S.F., Lin, F.: A research on the definitions and models of crowdsourcing and their future development. Sci. Technol. Manage. Res. **35**(4), 212–217 (2015)
11. Estellés-Arolas, E., González-Ladrón-De-Guevara, F.: Towards an integrated crowdsourcing definition. J. Inf. Sci. **38**(2), 189–200 (2012)
12. Roy, S.B., Lykourentzou, I., Thirumuruganathan, S., Amer-Yahia, S., Das, G.: Task assignment optimization in knowledge-intensive crowdsourcing. VLDB J. **24**(4), 467–491 (2015). https://doi.org/10.1007/s00778-015-0385-2
13. Wan, Y.L., Xu, Q.W., Liao, P.C., Li, X.X.: Application and prospect of crowdsourcing in urban planning. J. Tsinghua Univ. (Sci. Technol.) **59**(5), 409–416 (2019)
14. Weninger, B., Poplin, A.K., Petrin, J.: Developing a typology of public participation 2.0 users: an example of Nexthamburg.de. In: Proceedings of 15th International Conference on Urban Planning and Regional Development in the Information Society, pp. 191–199 (2010)

15. Nguyen, C., Tahmasbi, N., De Vreede, T., De Vreede, G.J., Oh, O., Reiter-Palmon, R.: Participant engagement in community crowdsourcing. In: European Conference on Information Systems, vol. 41 (2015)
16. Haklay, M., Weber, P.: OpenStreetMap: user-generated street maps. IEEE Pervasive Comput. 7(4), 12–18 (2008)
17. Xiong, W., Zhou, B.: Construction and thinking of "Zhonggui Wuhan" open platform. Beijing Plann. Constr. 1, 100–102 (2016)
18. Alialy, R., et al.: A review on the applications of crowdsourcing in human pathology. J. Pathol. Inf. 9, 2 (2018)
19. Cooper, S., et al.: Predicting protein structures with a multiplayer online game. Nature 466(7307), 756–760 (2010)
20. Whitla, P.: Crowdsourcing and its application in marketing activities. Contemp. Manage. Res. 5(1), 15–28 (2009)
21. Dasgupta, N., et al.: Crowdsourcing black market prices for prescription opioids. J. Med. Internet Res. 15(8), e178 (2013)
22. Ding, Y., Che, W.X., Liu, T., Zhang, M.S.: Constructing word association network by crowdsourcing. J. Chin. Inf. Process. 27(3), 100–107 (2013)
23. Hong, L., Ran, C.J., Yu, Q.: Implementation of MOOC online question and answer system with crowdsourcing. Libr. Inf. Serv. 58(19), 118–123 (2014)
24. Qiao, L., Yang, L., Hong, D., Yao, L., Zhiguang, Q.: Knowledge graph construction techniques. J. Comput. Res. Dev. 53(3), 582–600 (2016)
25. Xu, Z.L., Sheng, Y.P., He, L.R., Wang, Y.F.: Review on knowledge graph techniques. J. Univ. Electron. Sci. Technol. China 45(4), 589–606 (2016)
26. Bollacker, K., Evans, C., Paritosh, P., Sturge, T., Taylor, J.: Freebase: a collaboratively created graph database for structuring human knowledge. In: Proceedings of the 2008 ACM SIGMOD International Conference on Management of Data, pp. 1247–1250 (2008)
27. Auer, S., Bizer, C., Kobilarov, G., Lehmann, J., Cyganiak, R., Ives, Z.: DBpedia: a nucleus for a web of open data. In: Aberer, K., et al. (eds.) The Semantic Web. ISWC 2007, ASWC 2007. Lecture Notes in Computer Science, vol. 4825, pp. 722–735. Springer, Heidelberg (2007). https://doi.org/10.1007/978-3-540-76298-0_52
28. Vrandečić, D., Krötzsch, M.: Wikidata: a free collaborative knowledgebase. Commun. ACM 57(10), 78–85 (2014)
29. Liu, H., Singh, P.: ConceptNet—a practical commonsense reasoning tool-kit. BT Technol. J. 22(4), 211–226 (2004). https://doi.org/10.1023/B:BTTJ.0000047600.45421.6d
30. Wang, Z., et al.: XLore: a large-scale English-Chinese bilingual knowledge graph. In: International Semantic Web Conference (Posters & Demos), vol. 1035, pp. 121–124 (2013)
31. Xu, B., et al.: CN-DBpedia: a never-ending Chinese knowledge extraction system. In: Benferhat, S., Tabia, K., Ali, M. (eds.) Advances in Artificial Intelligence: From Theory to Practice. IEA/AIE 2017. Lecture Notes in Computer Science, vol. 10351, pp. 428–438. Springer, Cham. https://doi.org/10.1007/978-3-319-60045-1_44
32. Lin, Y.F., et al.: A maximum entropy approach to biomedical named entity recognition. In: Proceedings of the 4th International Conference on Data Mining in Bioinformatics, pp. 56–61 (2004)
33. Zhang, Z.X., Wu, Z.X., Liu, J.H., Xu, J., Hong, N., Zhao, Q.: Analysis of state-of-the-art knowledge extraction technologies. Data Anal. Knowl. Discov. 24(8), 2–11 (2008)
34. Shen, D.Y., Sun, M.S., Huang, C.N.: Identifying Chinese Place Names in Unrestricted Text, pp. 68–74. Tsinghua University Press, Beijing (1995)
35. Zheng, J.H., Li, X.: Research on Chinese name recognition method based on corpus. J. Chin. Inf. Process. 14(1), 7–12 (2000)
36. Xu, J., Zhang, Z.X., Wu, Z.X.: Review on techniques of entity relation extraction. Data Anal. Knowl. Discov. 24(8), 18–23 (2008)

37. Yang, B., Cai, D.F., Yang, H.: Progress in open information extraction. J. Chin. Inf. Process. **20**(2), 123–151 (2014)
38. Guo, J.Y., Li, Z., Yu, Z.T.: Extraction and relation prediction of domain ontology concept instance, attribute, and attribute value. J. Nanjing Univ. **48**(4), 383–389 (2012)
39. Tan, Y.M., Yang, X.: An named entity disambiguation algorithm combining entity linking and entity clustering. J. Beijing Univ. Posts Telecommun. **37**(5), 36–40 (2014)
40. Ning, B., Zhang, F.: Named entity disambiguation based on heterogeneous knowledge base. J. Xi'an Univ. Posts Telecommun. **19**(4), 70–76 (2014)
41. Wang, Z.Q., Li, L., Wang, C.: Chinese pronominal coreference resolution based on decision tree. J. Beijing Univ. Posts and Telecommun. **29**(4), 1–5 (2006)
42. Pang, N., Yang, E.H.: The research on coreference resolution based on maximum entropy model. J. Chin. Inf. Process. **22**(2), 24–27 (2008)
43. Mendes, P.N., Mühleisen, H., Bizer, C.: Sieve: linked data quality assessment and fusion. In: Proceedings of the 2012 Joint EDBT/ICDT Workshops, pp. 116–123 (2012)
44. Fader, A., Soderland, S., Etzioni, O.: Identifying relations for open information extraction. In: Proceedings of the 2011 Conference on Empirical Methods in Natural Language Processing, pp. 1535–1545 (2011)
45. Zaveri, A., Rula, A., Maurino, A., Pietrobon, R., Lehmann, J., Auer, S.: Quality assessment for linked data: A survey. Semant. Web **7**(1), 63–93 (2016)
46. Wang, J., Li, G., Kraska, T., Franklin, M. J., Feng, J.: Leveraging transitive relations for crowdsourced joins. In: Proceedings of the 2013 ACM SIGMOD International Conference on Management of Data, pp. 229–240 (2013)
47. Zhang, C.J., Chen, L., Jagadish, H.V., Cao, C.C.: Reducing uncertainty of schema matching via crowdsourcing. Proc. VLDB Endow. **6**(9), 757–768 (2013)
48. Lin, X., Xu, J., Hu, H., Fan, Z.: Reducing uncertainty of probabilistic top-k ranking via pairwise crowdsourcing. IEEE Trans. Knowl. Data Eng. **29**(10), 2290–2303 (2017)
49. Mo, K., Zhong, E., Yang, Q.: Cross-task crowdsourcing. In: Proceedings of the 19th ACM SIGKDD International Conference on Knowledge Discovery and Data Mining, pp. 677–685 (2013)
50. Zheng, Y., Li, G., Cheng, R.: DOCS: a domain-aware crowdsourcing system using knowledge bases. Proc. VLDB Endow. **10**(4), 361–372 (2016)
51. Mavridis, P., Gross-Amblard, D., Miklós, Z.: Using hierarchical skills for optimized task assignment in knowledge-intensive crowdsourcing. In: Proceedings of the 25th International Conference on World Wide Web, pp. 843–853 (2016)
52. Von Ahn, L., Kedia, M., Blum, M.: Verbosity: a game for collecting common-sense facts. In: Proceedings of the SIGCHI Conference on Human Factors in Computing Systems, pp. 75–78 (2006)
53. Ni, B., et al.: Touch saliency: characteristics and prediction. IEEE Trans. Multimedia **16**(6), 1779–1791 (2014)
54. Zhang, Z.Q., Pang, J.S., Xie, X.Q., Zhou, Y.: Research on crowdsourcing quality control strategies and evaluation algorithm. Chin. J. Comput. **36**(8), 1636–1649 (2013)
55. Sheng, V.S., Zhang, J.: Machine learning with crowdsourcing: a brief summary of the past research and future directions. In: Proceedings of the AAAI Conference on Artificial Intelligence, pp. 9837–9843 (2019)
56. Gruber, T.R.: Toward principles for the design of ontologies used for knowledge sharing? Int. J. Hum. Comput. Stud. **43**(5–6), 907–928 (1995)
57. Studer, R., Benjamins, V.R., Fensel, D.: Knowledge engineering: principles and methods. Data Knowl. Eng. **25**(1–2), 161–197 (1998)
58. Li, S.P., Yin, Q.W., Hu, Y.J., Guo, M., Fu, X.J.: Overview of researches on the ontology. Comput. Res. Dev. **41**(7), 1041–1052 (2004)

59. DiFranzo, D., Hendler, J.: The semantic web and the next generation of human computation. In: Michelucci, P. (ed.) Handbook of Human Computation, pp. 523–530. Springer, New York (2013). https://doi.org/10.1007/978-1-4614-8806-4_39
60. Acosta, M., Simperl, E., Flöck, F., Norton, B.: A SPARQL engine for crowdsourcing query processing using microtasks–Technical report. Institute AIFB, KIT, Karlsruhe (2012)
61. Niepert, M., Buckner, C., Murdock, J., Allen, C.: InPhO: a system for collaboratively populating and extending a dynamic ontology. In: Proceedings of the 8th ACM/IEEE-CS Joint Conference on Digital Libraries, pp. 429–429 (2008)
62. Kondreddi, S.K., Triantafillou, P., Weikum, G.: Combining information extraction and human computing for crowdsourced knowledge acquisition. In: 2014 IEEE 30th International Conference on Data Engineering, pp. 988–999 (2014)
63. Zhuang, Y., Li, G., Zhong, Z., Feng, J.: Hike: a hybrid human-machine method for entity alignment in large-scale knowledge bases. In: Proceedings of the 2017 ACM on Conference on Information and Knowledge Management, pp. 1917–1926, November, 2017
64. Chai, C., Fan, J., Li, G.: Incentive-based entity collection using crowdsourcing. In: 2018 IEEE 34th International Conference on Data Engineering (ICDE), pp. 341–352 (2018)
65. Zhao, F., et al.: Research progress on Wikipedia. Doctoral dissertation. J. Univ. Electron. Sci. Technol. China **39**(3), 321–334 (2010)
66. Singh, P., Lin, T., Mueller, E.T., Lim, G., Perkins, T., Li Zhu, W.: Open mind common sense: knowledge acquisition from the general public. In: Meersman, R., Tari, Z. (eds.) On the Move to Meaningful Internet Systems 2002: CoopIS, DOA, and ODBASE. OTM 2002. Lecture Notes in Computer Science, vol. 2519, pp. 1223–1237. Springer, Heidelberg (2002). https://doi.org/10.1007/3-540-36124-3_77
67. Pavlick, E., Yan, R., Callison-Burch, C.: Crowdsourcing for grammatical error correction. In: Proceedings of the Companion Publication of the 17th ACM conference on Computer Supported Cooperative Work & Social Computing, pp. 209–212 (2014)

A Dual-Index Based Representation for Processing XPath Queries on Very Large XML Documents

Wei Hao[1,2(✉)], Kiminori Matsuzaki[2], and Shigeyuki Sato[2]

[1] Anhui University of Science and Technology, Taifeng Avenue 168,
Huanian, Anhui, China
whao@aust.edu.cn

[2] Kochi University of Technology, 185 Miyanokuchi, Tosayamada, Kami,
Kochi 782–8502, Japan
{matsuzaki.kiminori,sato.shigeyuki}@kochi-tech.ac.jp

Abstract. Although XML processing has been intensively studied in recent years, designing efficient implementations for evaluating XPath queries on XML documents remains a challenge in case XML documents are very large. In this study, we implemented a tree-shaped data structure called partial tree that is intrinsically suitable for large XML document processing with multiple computers. Our implementation uses two index sets to accelerate the evaluation of structural relationships among nodes, making it highly efficient for processing very large XML documents regarding three important classes of XPath queries: backward, order-aware and predicate-containing queries. Experiment results show that our implementation outperforms a start-of-the-art XML database BaseX in both absolute loading time and execution time for the target queries. The absolute execution time over 358 GB of XML data averagely is only seconds by using 32 EC2 instances.

Keywords: Large XML documents · XPath querying · Dual-index · Data representation · Parallel computing

1 Introduction

XML is a popular data representation, storing and exchanging language widely used in many areas, such as in database systems and web services. XPath[1] and XQuery[2] are used for navigating through elements of XML documents. The execution time of these queries come to matter in processing of very large XML documents. Even though common query processors on commodity computers suffice for evaluating queries over commonplace documents, they do not suffice

---

[1] https://www.w3.org/TR/xpath/.
[2] https://www.w3.org/TR/xquery/.

© ICST Institute for Computer Sciences, Social Informatics and Telecommunications Engineering 2021
Published by Springer Nature Switzerland AG 2021. All Rights Reserved
L. Qi et al. (Eds.): CloudComp 2020, LNICST 363, pp. 18–30, 2021.
https://doi.org/10.1007/978-3-030-69992-5_2

for doing over very large XML documents such as a DBLP[3] document dump of 1.8 GB and an UniProtKB[4] document of 358 GB. The current XML processing techniques enable us to evaluate some queries efficiently. For example, a technique [14] for extracting parent-child and ancestor-descendant relationships is efficient because it uses indices regardless of the order of results. However, due to the intrinsic nature that the elements of an XML document are ordered, order-aware queries that contain axes such as following, following-sibling, preceding, preceding-sibling axes and position function are important. Backward queries such as parent and ancestor axes used for tracking back toward the root of the XML documents are also important. Some algorithms such as structural join [1] use a join algorithm on two lists (AList for ancestors and DList for descendants) to determine child-parent and ancestor-descendant relationships. However, it takes $O((|AList| + |DList|)^2)$ time in the worst case. Thus, it will take terrible time in processing very large documents. Besides, predicates, which are an construct for filtering elements, are useful for queries, while queries efficient evaluation of predicate-containing queries also becomes an issue.

In this study, we aim at good absolute time, which is the shortest time for processing a certain amount of data, of evaluating over large XML documents, XPath queries including three classes: backward, order-aware and predicate-containing queries. We propose a novel compact representation for partial trees [11], which is a data structure dedicated to processing large XML documents on multiple computers. This representation consists of two index sets: one accelerates extracting relationships between nodes; the other enables us to avoid evaluating uninvolved nodes. With this two index sets, we can process very large XML documents efficiently. Our contributions are summarized as the follows:

– We have proposed a compact tree representation that can be used for efficiently process the three classes of XPath queries.
– Our prototype implementation have outperformed BaseX[5] and achieved good absolute evaluation time.

The experiments were conducted on Amazon Elastic Compute Cloud[6] (EC2) cloud server, which is a web service and provides flexible compute capacity in the cloud. The experiment results show that our approach outperforms a start-of-the-art XML database BaseX in better absolute time. The execution time over 358 GB of XML data is only seconds averagely.

Figure 1 shows the syntax of our target subset of XPath. Our prototype implementation accepts nested predicates, which means the location steps inside a predicate can still have predicates, making queries in this study more expressive. For the position() function, only child axis is supported.

The rest of this paper is organized in the following: Section 2 introduces our previous work: partial trees. Section 3 presents the novel compact representation.

---

[3] http://dblp.uni-trier.de/.
[4] http://www.uniprot.org/help/uniprotkb.
[5] http://basex.org/.
[6] https://aws.amazon.com/ec2/.

Section 4 shows the querying algorithms used in the experiments. Section 5 reports results and analysis. Section 6 concludes the paper and show the future work.

Query ::= '/' *LocationPath*
LocationPath ::= *Step* | *Step* '/' *LocationPath*
Step ::= *NameTest Predicate*? | *NameTest* [*integer*]
     | '/'*NameTest Predicate*? | *Axis::NameTest Predicate*?
AxisName ::= 'child' | 'parent' | 'descendant' | 'ancestor'
     | 'descendant-or-self' | 'ancestor-or-self' | 'following'
     | 'following-sibling' | 'preceding' | 'preceding-sibling'
NameTest ::= '*' | *string*
Predicate ::= '[' (*LocationPath* | *position*() = *integer*) ']'

Fig. 1. Grammar of our target subset of XPath.

2 Related Work

Existing studies [5,7,8] on evaluating XPath queries over distributed (or fragmented) XML documents dealt only with top-down path queries (also known as twig patterns), which compose a small subset of navigational XPath queries. To the best of our knowledge, navigational XPath queries over distributed documents have never been seriously investigated.

It is worth noting that applying MapReduce [9] to large-scale XML processing was well studied [5,6,8,15,16]. MapReduce enables transparent and fault-tolerant processing on clusters, while encoding XPath queries on it incurs overheads in various aspects. In order to minimize overheads and achieve high performance on clusters, dedicated in-memory processing is more appropriate than MapReduce-based processing. VXQuery [4] has been designed without MapReduce for this reason but still been under development. At least, how to process navigational XPath queries in VXQuery was not described in [4].

Apart from parallel and/or distributed processing, efficient evaluation of more expressive subsets of XPath was studied [2,3,10]. Brantner et al. [3] studied efficient compilation of XPath 1.0 with the internal algebra of an underlying XML database engine. Grust [10] accelerated evaluation of all axes with an indexing technique. SXSI [2] dealt with forward Core XPath and all text predicates in a succinct index structure. We similarly have used two indices represented with a dedicated data structure for accelerating query evaluation. We, however, do not claim that these indices and representation are technically better than existing ones. We have experimentally demonstrated that the two cheap indices in the straightforward representation based on partial trees suffice for achieving high performance processing of navigational XPath queries over large-scale documents, not only on a single computer but also clusters—this is our technical contribution.

3 Partial Tree

For high-performance data processing, a common idea is to divide a large amount of data into smaller fragments and distribute them to multiple processors for later processing. Consider an XML tree in Fig. 2 and its serialized document is divided into the following chunks ($chunk_0$ to $chunk_3$ in document order). When an XML document is divided, we could parse a chunk to construct a subgraph (a sequence of subtrees). For example, given $chunk_2$, we can construct a subgraph as shown in Fig. 3. However, because of the intrinsic tree structure of XML documents, queries cannot be directly evaluated on them after splitting. For example, we cannot select the children of b2 on the subgraph from $chunk_2$, because the path from the root of the subgraph to the root of the whole tree is missing.

$chunk_0$: `<r><b><d><c>txt1</c></d><a at="1"></a></b><b><d>`
$chunk_1$: `<c>txt2</c><d><c>txt3</c></d></d><a at="2"></a><d>`
$chunk_2$: `<c>txt4</c><c>txt5</c></d><a at="3"></a></b><b><d>`
$chunk_3$: `<c>txt6</c></d><d><d><c>txt7</c></d></d></b></r>`

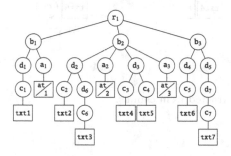

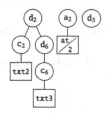

Fig. 2. An example XML tree.   **Fig. 3.** A subgraph from $chunk_2$.

To cope with the path-missing issue, we exploit a data structure called *partial tree* [11] that is suitable for representing chunked XML data of an XML documents. A partial tree can be constructed in two steps: we first parse a chunk of an XML document to generate a sequence of subtrees, and then add the path for each root of subtrees to the root of the original XML tree. For example, four partial trees are constructed from parsing $chunk_0$ to $chunk_3$ as shown in Fig. 4. A partial tree corresponding to a chunk is the minimum subgraph, that satisfies three conditions:

- a subgraph is connected, which means a subgraph is a tree.
- a subgraph contains the root of the original XML tree.
- elements(tag/attribute/text) from the same chunk are in the same subgraph.

A concrete algorithm for this computation is given in [11] (Algorithm 0). In this study, the chunks of a divided XML document begin at either a start tag or an end tag to keep the attributes and texts as closed nodes. It is useful to distinguish the four cases that a node in a partial tree has or does not have its tags in the corresponding chunk. Nodes in a partial tree are categorized into the following four types (in Fig. 5) based on the inclusion of tags in the chunk: a *closed node* with both its tags, a *left-open node* with only its end tag, a *right-open node* with only its start tag, and a *pre-node* with no tags. The left-open nodes, right-open nodes and pre-nodes are called *open nodes*.

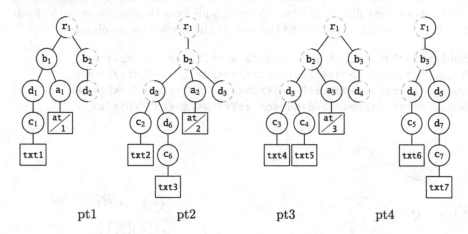

pt1   pt2   pt3   pt4

Fig. 4. Four partial trees constructed from chunks.

Fig. 5. Node types.

4   Data Representation

From the previous section, we introduced a fragmentation based on a data structured called partial trees to represent a chunked XML document, providing a good way for parallel XML processing. However, it is still a challenge to develop a high-performance implementation based this data structure, especially the concrete representation for it. For this purpose, we take two issues into consideration as the following:

Expressiveness. We use indexing (or labeling) to represent chunked XML data so that it can be efficient to store them in databases [13], exploiting its expressiveness to accelerate queries.

Compactness. The indices for the XML data are stored in memory, so that the expensive I/O cost for data exchanging are avoided.

The first design requirement relates to the efficiency of XML update. It is common that a general-purpose framework may provide supports for updates, such as ORDPATH [13]. However, such configuration tends to be expensive in case of query-intensive(or only) scenario. Therefore, we focus only on update-free case, i.e. we consider only queries with no update, making our framework much faster and easier to implement. We expect that users are able to achieve their objectives without updating, as long as appropriate programming interfaces over the framework are provided.

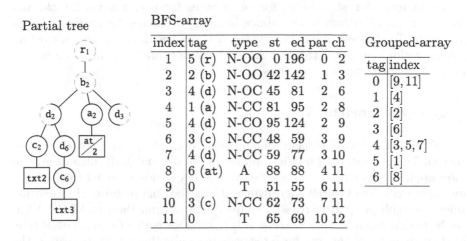

Partial tree   BFS-array   Grouped-array

index	tag	type	st	ed	par	ch
1	5 (r)	N-OO	0	196	0	2
2	2 (b)	N-OO	42	142	1	3
3	4 (d)	N-OC	45	81	2	6
4	1 (a)	N-CC	81	95	2	8
5	4 (d)	N-CO	95	124	2	9
6	3 (c)	N-CC	48	59	3	9
7	4 (d)	N-CC	59	77	3	10
8	6 (at)	A	88	88	4	11
9	0	T	51	55	6	11
10	3 (c)	N-CC	62	73	7	11
11	0	T	65	69	10	12

tag	index
0	$[9, 11]$
1	$[4]$
2	$[2]$
3	$[6]$
4	$[3, 5, 7]$
5	$[1]$
6	$[8]$

Fig. 6. A partial tree and its representation with two arrays

We consider the second requirement as the functionality our designed indices can provide. One goal of this study is to support queries with order-aware ones such as following-sibling and following. To achieve our goal, we define the following functions for processing queries on the given node x:

- Function getChildren(x) returns the children of x.
- Function getParent(x) returns the parent of x.
- Function nextSibling(x) returns the next sibling of x.
- Function prevSibling(x) returns the previous sibling of x.
- Function isDescendant(x, y) returns true if x is a descendant of the node y.
- Function isFollowing(x, y) returns true if x is strictly after the node y in terms of the document order.
- Function getNodesIn(t, x) returns nodes with the tag t in the subtree rooted at x.

For the implementation of the above functions, we designed two compact index sets, BFS-array (BFS stands for Breadth First Search, since nodes are arranged in BFS order) and Grouped-array, as shown in Fig. 6. For a single node, we design the following properties:

- *tag*: the tag name of the node, short integers that map to the strings.
- *type*: the type of the node, including four node types as shown in Fig. 5.
- *st*: the start position of the node, which is the position of the tag in the original file to avoid global counting.
- *ed*: the end position.

With BFS and these two pointers, we are able to perform high-performance functions getChildren, getParent, nextSibling, and prevSibling. With *Grouped-array*, we are allowed to evaluate the function getNodesIn efficiently.

In this implementation, the two indexes totally take 2 bytes for *tag*, 1 bytes for *type*, 8 bytes for *st*, 8 bytes for *ed*, 4 bytes for *par*, 4 bytes for *ch*, and 4 bytes for *idx*. The sum of the above is merely 31 bytes for representing an XML node. To the best of our knowledge, it is smaller than the known existing implementations of DOM trees or XML databases, and it is also the key to high-performance queries executions.

5   Query Algorithms

By dividing an XML document into chunks, multiple partial trees are constructed. The evaluation of queries applied to the original XML document, can be are applied to partial trees and the evaluation on theses partial trees can be done separately. The Overall Algorithm outlines the "big picture" of evaluating a query on multiple partial trees. The query starts from the root of the XML tree. Note that the root node corresponds to the root node of every partial tree, and they are put into the lists for intermediate results (lines 1–2). Hereafter, the loops by p over $[0, P)$ are assumed to be executed in parallel. An XPath query consists of one or more steps, and in our algorithm they are processed one by one. For each step, our algorithm calls a sub-algorithm based on its axis (given later) and updates the intermediate results (line 4). Lines 6–9 will be executed when a query has a predicate (Fig. 7).

The number of partial trees is the same as the number of the chunks. In case the number of partial trees is one, the whole original XML document is treated as a chunk, so that only one partial tree is constructed to work standalone without needing to make any change to its configuration. This is a valuable property of partial tree, making partial tree easily portable under different hardware settings.

We use the two index sets to implement the functions in Sect. 3. For child axis, getChild(x) is implemented by a set of indices as $[ch[x], ch[x + 1])$. For example, in Fig. 6, the index of •B_6• is 2 and its children are in the range getChild(2) = $[ch[2], ch[2 + 1]) = [3, 6)$. For descendant axis, isDescendant(x, y) can be implemented by $st[y] < st[x]$ *and* $ed[x] < ed[y]$. For parent axis,

---

Overall Algorithm $\text{QUERY}(steps, pt_{[P]})$

Input: *steps*: an XPath expression

      $pt_{[P]}$: an indexed set of partial trees

Output: an indexed set of results of query

1: **for** $p \in [0, P)$ **do**

2:    $ResultList_p \leftarrow \{ pt_p.root \}$

3: **for all** $step \in steps$ **do**

4:    $ResultList_{[P]} \leftarrow \text{QUERY}\langle step.axis\rangle(pt_{[P]}, ResultList_{[P]}, step.test)$

5:    **if** $step.predicate \neq \text{NULL}$ **then**

6:       $PResultList_{[P]} \leftarrow \text{PREPAREPREDICATE}(ResultList_{[P]})$

7:       **for all** $pstep \in step.predicate$ **do**

8:          $PResultList_{[P]} \leftarrow \text{PQUERY}\langle step.axis\rangle(pt_{[P]}, PResultList_{[P]}, pstep)$

9:       $ResultList_{[P]} \leftarrow \text{PROCESSPREDICATE}(PResultList_{[P]})$

10: **return** $ResultList_{[P]}$

Fig. 7. The overall algorithm for processing XPath queries over partial trees

getParent(x) is implemented by $par[x]$. For example, the index of $\bullet B_6 \bullet$'s parent is $par[2] = 1$. Since a node in the original XML tree may be split into two or more nodes on different partial trees. When such a node is selected in a partial tree (e.g., $B_6 \bullet$ on pt_1), the other corresponding nodes ($\bullet B_6 \bullet$ on pt_2 and $\bullet B_6$ on pt_3) should also be selected to be consistent. When an open node in the results is needed to share, we simply use *start* as index to notify other partial trees and let them to put the open nodes with the same *start* into the results nodes. We call this process share nodes. After processing **parent** axis, we need share nodes. For **ancestor** axis, we implement it by repeated proceeding from child to parent.

Without loss of generality, the discussion focuses on **following** and **following-sibling** axes only (**preceding** and **preceding-sibling** axes are just in opposite direction). For **following** axis, it is relatively easy that we simply compare the *end* index. We first select the node with the smallest *end* index. Then, nodes with *end* index greater than the smallest one and match the name test are selected as the results. For **following-sibling**, we need a two-phases query: the local query phase and the remote query phase. In the local query phase, we utilize the *folsib* to select siblings on the local partial tree. Then, we will ask a remote query if the parent node can have more segments on the right (i.e., right open). In the remote query phase, we select children and on the remote partial trees and merge them with their local results as final results. Note that after processing these axes, sharing nodes is needed.

We exploit the algorithms proposed in [11] (Algorithm 7 and 8) for predicate. The key idea of these two algorithms are introduced as follows: (1) create links that point to the nodes in the input lists, (2) evaluate the steps within the predicate with these links, (3) after the evaluation of all steps, we use the links to track back to the nodes in the input lists as final results.

6   Evaluation

Our evaluation have two aims: (1) to demonstrate the performance of our implementation against the state-of-the-art XML database BaseX on a single computer and (2) to explore the scalability of our implementation for processing very large XML documents on multiple computers in a parallel manner.

Datasets and XPath Queries. Table 1 shows the statistics of the XML datasets used in the experiments. For the experiments using a single EC2 instance, two XML datasets are used: DBLP and xmark100 (with factor 100^7). For the experiments using mutiple EC2 instances, xmark2000 (with factor 2000) and UniProtKB is are used. The UniProtKB dataset is well-balanced and has has a large number of children to its root, while XMark datasets are not well-balanced for they have only six children to their root. Table 2 shows the queries: XQ1 and UQ1 for long queries with nested predicates; XQ2, DQ1, DQ2, UQ2, UQ4 and UQ5 for queries with backward axes; the rest is for order-aware queries.

Table 1. Statistics of XML dataset.

Datasets	dblp	xmark100	xmark2000	uniprot
Nodes	43.13M	163.1M	3.26B	7.89B
Attributes	10.89M	42.26M	845M	9.25B
Values	39.64M	67.25M	1.34B	1.49B
Total	93.66M	272,67M	5.45B	18.64B
# of distinct tags	47	77	77	82
Depth	6	13	13	7
File size (GB)	1.78	10.95	220	358

Experiment Configuration. There were 32 m3.2xlarge instances on Amazon EC2, which were equipped with E5-2670 v2 (Ivy Bridge), 30 GB of memory and 2 X 80 GB of SSD, running Amazon Linux AMI 2016.09.0. Our prototype was implemented in Java 1.6, running on 64-Bit JVM (build 25.91-b14).

Comparison with BaseX. To compare with, we selected BaseX 8.5.3 (released on August 15, 2016) as our opponent. It was tested under two configurations: one was to put all the XML data and index sets on memory (*BXon*), and the other was to put only the index sets on memory (*BXoff*). In order to eliminate

---

[7] The factor determines the file size of an XMark generated document. It is nearly linear: $1 = 110$ MB, for example xmark100 with the factor 100 is about 11 GB, while xmark2000 with the factor 2000 sized 220 GB.

Table 2. Queries used in the experiments.

Name	Dataset	Query
XQ1	xmark	/site/closed_auctions/closed_auction[annotation/description[text/keyword]]
XQ2	xmark	/site//keyword/ancestor::mail
XQ3	xmark	/site/open_auctions/open_auction/bidder[1]/increase
XQ4	xmark	/site/people/person/name/following-sibling::emailaddress
XQ5	xmark	/site/open_auctions/open_auction[bidder/following-sibling::bidder]/reserve
DQ1	dblp	/dblp//i/parent::title
DQ2	dblp	//author/ancestor::article
DQ3	dblp	/dblp//author/following-sibling::author
DQ4	dblp	//author[following-sibling::author]
DQ5	dblp	/dblp/article/title/sub/sup/i/following::author
UQ1	uniprot	/entry[comment/text]/reference[citation/authorList[person]]//person
UQ2	uniprot	/entry//fullName/parent::recommendedName
UQ3	uniprot	/entry//fullName/following::gene
UQ4	uniprot	//begin/ancestor::entry
UQ5	uniprot	//begin/parent::location/parent::feature/parent::entry

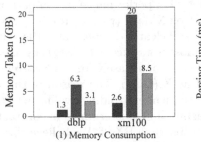
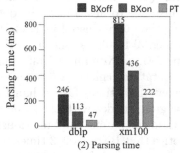

(1) Memory Consumption

(2) Parsing time

Fig. 8. Memory consumption and parsing time on dblp datasets

Table 3. Evaluation by 32 EC2 instances

Dataset	xm2000					unirpot				
Loading (s)	210					379				
Memory (GB)	173					560				
Query	QX1	XQ2	QX3	QX4	QX5	UX1	UX2	UX3	UX4	UX5
Time (ms)	5,951	819	1,710	1,168	3,349	2,573	2,408	1,324	5,909	6,220

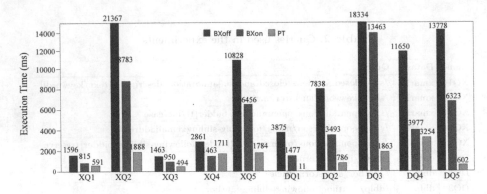

Fig. 9. Execution time of queries on XMark100) and dblp datasets

the influence of printing time for output, we simply apply count function to queries, e.g.. "count (XQ1)"; then use the time for evaluating this query as execution time. We also set the parameter INTPARSE true to use the internal XML parser that is faster, more fault tolerant and supports common HTML entities out-of-the-box.

Evaluating Queries on 1 EC2 Instance. We first conducted the experiment on 1 EC2 instance to investigate the querying performance in comparison with BaseX using the queries listed in Table 1 on XMark (with factor 100) and dblp. The experimental results as shown in Fig. 9 clearly demonstrates that our approach outperforms BXon and BXoff in most tests except for XQ4. In most case, our implementation achieves 2-6 times faster than BaseX. In some extreme case, we can achieve 100s times faster than BaseX (DQ1). The reason in this case is because we group nodes with the same tag name, avoiding evaluating unnecessary nodes and the parent-child relationship can be determined in constant time. We also notice that BXon is 2–3 times faster than BXoff. We believe this is simply because it loads all data into memory. This can be learnt from Fig. 8(1). It also shows that Bxon takes more memory than ours for all the datasets. Even we deduct the size of original XML datasets, it still exceeds our approach. As of the parsing time, we can see that in Fig. 8(2). Our approach is nearly twice faster than BXon and four times faster than BXoff in both datasets.

Evaluating Queries on 32 EC2 Instances. In this experiment, we investigated the querying performance on processing very large XML documents by using 32 EC2 instances. We used UniProtKB and XMark (with factor 2000) as experiment data. The results are shown in Table 3. With the design of 31 bytes for a node, the memory consumption should be 157 GB and 537 GB for 0.545 billion and 1.86 billion nodes respectively. The experiment results show the consumptions are 173 and 560 GB, much close to the computation. We believe the overheads result in some intermediate data generated during the parsing phase.

The parsing times in Table 3 are relatively short considering the very large data sizes. The querying is also very fast, such as XQ1 to XQ5 that took just a few seconds. The throughput of most queries is about 1 GB/s. The best throughput of One study, PP-Transducer [12], achieved the throughput of 2.5 GB/s at most with 64 cores. Although it is faster, the queries we can process are more expressive than that, which does not support order-aware queries.

7 Conclusion

In this paper, we proposed a novel dual-index (BFS and GFS) based data representation based on our previous work partial tree for high-performance XML processing, especially in terms of three classes of navigational XPath queries over very large XML documents. The basis of this approach is the chunk-based fragmentation and querying algorithms that exploit in-memory representation of chunks by dividing an XML document. We also conducted several experiments on EC2 instances. The experiment results clearly showed the efficiency of our framework outperform the state-of-the-art XML processing engine BaseX on 1 EC2 instance and achieved the throughput of about 1 GB/s using 32 EC2 instances.

The current work has a configuration that all indices are storied in memory. Therefore, our future work is to extend the ability of our implementation by developing new mechanisms to cooperate with modern distributed file systems, such as HDFS with MapReduce and related computing frameworks. In more details, we will pay our concern on data feeding, more expressive querying algorithms, error tolerance and etc.

References

1. Al-Khalifa, S., Jagadish, H., Koudas, N., Patel, J.M., Srivastava, D., Wu, Y.: Structural joins: a primitive for efficient XML query pattern matching. In: Proceedings of the 12th International Conference on Data Engineering, pp. 141–152 (2002)
2. Arroyuelo, D., et al.: Fast in-memory XPath search using compressed indexes. Softw. Pract. Exp. **45**(3), 399–434 (2015)
3. Brantner, M., Helmer, S., Kanne, C.C., Moerkotte, G.: Full-fledged algebraic XPath processing in Natix. In: Proceedings of the 21st International Conference on Data Engineering (ICDE 2005), pp. 705–716 (2005)
4. Carman, E.P., Westmann, T., Borkar, V.R., Carey, M.J., Tsotras, V.J.: A scalable parallel XQuery processor. In: Proceedings of 2015 IEEE International Conference on Big Data, pp. 164–173 (2015)
5. Choi, H., Lee, K.H., Kim, S.H., Lee, Y.J., Moon, B.: HadoopXML: a suite for parallel processing of massive XML data with multiple twig pattern queries. In: Proceedings of the 21st ACM International Conference on Information and Knowledge Management (CIKM 2012), pp. 2737–2739 (2012)
6. Choi, H., Lee, K.-H., Lee, Y.-J.: Parallel labeling of massive XML data with MapReduce. J. Supercomputing **67**(2), 408–437 (2013). https://doi.org/10.1007/s11227-013-1008-6

7. Cong, G., Fan, W., Kementsietsidis, A., Li, J., Liu, X.: Partial evaluation for distributed XPath query processing and beyond. ACM Trans. Database Syst. **37**(4), 32:1–32:43 (2012)
8. Damigos, M., Gergatsoulis, M., Plitsos, S.: Distributed processing of XPath queries using MapReduce. In: Proceedings of the 17th East European Conference on Advances in Databases and Information Systems (ADBIS 2013), Part II, pp. 69–77 (2013)
9. Dean, J., Ghemawat, S.: MapReduce: simplified data processing on large clusters. Commun. ACM **51**(1), 107–113 (2008)
10. Grust, T.: Accelerating XPath location steps. In: Proceedings of the 2002 ACM SIGMOD International Conference on Management of Data (SIGMOD 2002), pp. 109–120 (2002)
11. Hao, W., Matsuzaki, K.: A partial-tree-based approach for XPath query on large XML trees. J. Inf. Process. **24**(2), 425–438 (2016)
12. Ogden, P., Thomas, D., Pietzuch, P.: Scalable XML query processing using parallel pushdown transducers. Proc. VLDB Endow. **6**(14), 1738–1749 (2013)
13. O'Neil, P., O'Neil, E., Pal, S., Cseri, I., Schaller, G., Westbury, N.: ORDPATHs: insert-friendly XML node labels. In: Proceedings of the 2004 ACM SIGMOD International Conference on Management of Data (SIGMOD 2004), pp. 903–908 (2004)
14. Qin, L., Yu, J.X., Ding, B.: TwigList: make twig pattern matching fast. In: the 12th International Conference on Database Systems for Advanced Applications, pp. 850–862 (2007)
15. Sauer, C., Bächle, S., Härder, T.: Versatile XQuery processing in MapReduce. In: Catania, B., Guerrini, G., Pokorný, J. (eds.) ADBIS 2013. LNCS, vol. 8133, pp. 204–217. Springer, Heidelberg (2013). https://doi.org/10.1007/978-3-642-40683-6_16
16. Wu, H.: Parallelizing structural joins to process queries over big XML data using MapReduce. In: Decker, H., Lhotská, L., Link, S., Spies, M., Wagner, R.R. (eds.) DEXA 2014. LNCS, vol. 8645, pp. 183–190. Springer, Cham (2014). https://doi.org/10.1007/978-3-319-10085-2_16

IAS-BERT: An Information Gain Association Vector Semi-supervised BERT Model for Sentiment Analysis

Linkun Zhang$^{(\boxtimes)}$ (ID), Yuxia Lei (ID), and Zhengyan Wang (ID)

Qufu Normal University, Rizhao 276800, Shandong, China
ilinkzhang@gmail.com

Abstract. With the popularity of large-scale corpora, statistics-based models have become mainstream model in Natural Language Processing (NLP). The Bidirectional Encoder Representations from Transformers (BERT), as one of those models, has achieved excellent results in various tasks of NLP since its emergence. But it still has shortcomings, such as poor capability of extracting local features and exploding of training gradients. After analyzing the shortcomings of BERT, this paper proposed an Information-gain Association Vector Semi-supervised Bidirectional Encoder Representations from Transformers (IAS-BERT) model, which improves the capability of capturing local features. Considering the influence of feature's polarity to overall sentiment and association between two word-embeddings, we use information gain on the training corpus. And then, the information gain results are used as an annotation of training corpus to generate a new word embedding. At the same time, we use forward-matching to optimize the computational overhead of IAS-BERT. We experiment the model on dataset of sentiment analysis, and it have achieved good results.

Keywords: Information gain · Semi-supervised · Local feature

1 Introduction

Sentiment analysis is one of the important components in Natural Language Processing (NLP), and is the main branch of text classification. It helps us to understand human emotional behavior, and be used in many places, such as movie evaluation [1], opinion mining [2], behavior prediction [3], social network [4], etc. There are many sentiment analysis models with excellent effects, like Neural Network Language (NNL) [5], Support Vector Machines (SVM) [6], Word2vec [7], Embedding from Language Models (ELMo) [8], Generative Pre-Training (GPT) [9] and the Bidirectional Encoder Representation from Transformers (BERT) [10]. The task of sentiment analysis can be understood as reflecting specific corpus to different sentiment categories [11].

In 2003, Yoshua Bengio proposed Neural Network Language (NNL) [5]. And then, NLP methods based on neural networks was impacted by what based on Support Vector

L. Qi et al. (Eds.): CloudComp 2020, LNICST 363, pp. 31–42, 2021.
https://doi.org/10.1007/978-3-030-69992-5_3

Machines (SVM) [6]. SVM achieves good results with less samples. However, its robustness of missing data is poor, and interpretation of high-dimensional kernel functions is not strong.

In 2013, the Google team led by Tomas Mikolov proposed Word2vec method [7]. They proposed two important models: Continuous Bag-Of-Words Model (CBOW) and Continuous Skip-gram Model (Skip-gram) [12]. Word2vec transforms word embeddings from high-dimensional and sparse representation to low-dimensional and dense representation. At the same time, it considers the context information, and makes semantic information more accurate [13].

In 2018, Matthew E. Peter proposed Embedding from Language Models (ELMo) [8]. ELMo solves ambiguity problem by saving multiple word embeddings of a word [14]. OpenAI proposed the Generative Pre-Training (GPT) [9]. GPT has made great progress in feature extraction [15]. In October, Google proposed the Bidirectional Encoder Representation from Transformers (BERT) [10]. BERT is a general model for natural language processing. Compared with the previous model, this model has achieved good results on most tasks.

Although the existed models, especially BERT, are very helpful for sentiment analysis, their structure without RNN and CNN makes their capability of capturing local features reduced [16, 17]. Due to the structure of Transformer, BERT performs poorly of capturing sequential sequences [18]. In later study, constructing auxiliary sentences [19] and window slicing [20] were also proposed, but their improvement is not obvious.

The contributions of this paper are as follows:

1. In order to improve model's capability of capturing local features and get better training gradient, we propose a new model called IAS-BERT. In this model, we simulate RNN structure to improve the model's understanding capability of sentence deeper implication. In terms of processing sequence information, RNN-like structure performs better than single sequence rearrangement structure of Transformer.
2. Considering the effect of feature polarity frequency in corpus during model learning, we balance feature polarity for word embedding. By annotating the corpus with information gain and association vector results, it learns the knowledge about different features frequency on model training. It improves accuracy by balancing features polarity frequency.
3. IAS-BERT is scientifically tested on English public datasets CoLA, SST-2 and Chinese public datasets waimai_10k, weibo_senti_100k to prove the valid of it.

In what follows, the framework of IAS-BERT will be introduced in Sect. 2. The results of IAS-BERT on experimental dataset will be introduced in Sect. 3. Finally, the paper is concluded in Sect. 4.

2   Model and Method

2.1   Framework of IAS-BERT

IAS-BERT is improved on $BERT_{BASE}$. The description of $BERT_{BASE}$ is as follows [10]:

$$P(\omega_t = ''BERT''|\omega_1, \omega_2, ..., \omega_{(t-1)}; \theta) \tag{1}$$

$$L = \sum_{\omega \in C} \log^{P(\omega | context(\omega))} \tag{2}$$

This model is a stack of multilayer bidirectional Transformer encoders and decoders. In IAS-BERT, its presentation layers, hidden layers, self-attention heads and feedforward size are 12, 768, 12 and 3072 respectively.

The input is word embeddings. In general, word embedding is constituted by token embedding, segment embedding and position embedding. However, the input of IAS-BERT consists by token embedding, segment embedding, position embedding and annotation embedding. We use information gain as corpus annotation to generate new word embeddings. It will be outputted after multi-layer encoding and decoding (see Fig. 1).

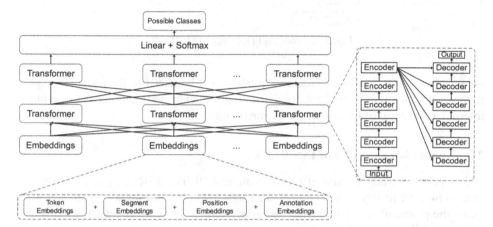

Fig. 1. Framework of IAS-BERT

2.2 Encoder and Decoder of IAS-BERT

In the Transformer, encoder is composed with two layers: Self-attention and Feed Forward. Decoder is composed with three layers: Self-attention, Encode-Decode Attention, and Feed Forward [15].

IAS-BERT's Encoder and Decoder are add annotation classifier layer before Self-attention layer to balance the weight of features polarity. Self-attention layer focuses on predicted words of current word embedding. Encode-decode attention layer focuses on unpredicted words of current word embedding. IAS-BERT can eliminate the impact on polarity weights between high-frequency words and low-frequency words by this design, and it would enhance the understanding of training corpus (see Fig. 2).

In LSTM-models, some researchers have proposed methods for sparse self-attention to solve sentence implication, and those methods have achieved better results [21]. Therefore, we add annotation embeddings by information gain and association vector to improve the understanding of local features on sentences. It will balance the weight of features polarity by annotation classifier. After this process, the optimized weight and

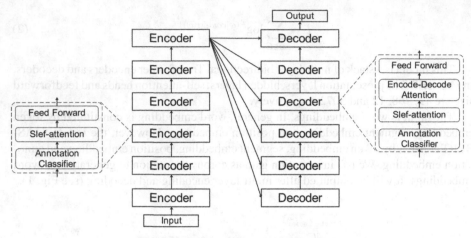

Fig. 2. Encode and Decode of IAS-BERT

association vector based on residual calculation will be added to the residual weight. It solves the problem of unilaterally reordering sequence and ignoring the weight of internal association of feature words during training.

2.3 Annotation Classifier of IAS-BERT

Different polarity has different effects on features [22]. The $\text{BERT}_{\text{BASE}}$ pay more attention to high-frequency features rather than low-frequency. Information gain can well solve the problem of low-frequency features' weight. The calculation of information gain is as follows:

$$IG(E) = H(C) - H(C|E) \tag{3}$$

where $H(C)$ represents information entropy and $H(C|E)$ represents conditional entropy.

$$H(C) = -\sum_{i=1}^{n} p(C_i) \log_2^{p(C_i)} \tag{4}$$

$$H(C|E) = \sum_{i=1}^{n} p(e_i) H(C|E = e_i) \tag{5}$$

In sentiment analysis, $T = t$ usually indicates existing feature word, and $T = \bar{t}$ usually indicates opposite situation. The conditional entropy is calculated by this definition.

$$H(C|E) = p(t)H(C|t) + p(\bar{t})H(C|\bar{t}) = -p(t) \sum_{i=1}^{n} p(C_i|t) \log^{p(C_i|t)} - p(\bar{t}) \sum_{i=1}^{n} p(C_i|\bar{t}) \log^{p(C_i|\bar{t})} \tag{6}$$

Id	Negative	Positive	Sentiment
1	Y	Y	Negative
2	N	N	Negative
3	Y	N	Positive
4	N	Y	Negative
5	Y	Y	Negative
6	Y	N	Negative
7	Y	N	Positive
8	N	N	Negative
9	N	N	Positive
10	N	N	Negative
11	N	Y	Negative
12	Y	N	Positive
13	N	N	Positive
14	Y	Y	Negative
15	Y	Y	Negative

	Negative		Positive		Total
	Y	N	Y	N	
Positive	3	2	0	5	5
Negative	5	5	6	4	10
Sum	8	7	6	9	15

Fig. 3. Annotation training corpus (The Negative column represents the feature of negative polarity in the corpus, and the Positive column represents the feature of positive polarity in the corpus. The Y means appear, and the N means not appear. The Sentiment column represents the sentiment tendency of the corpus.)

IAS-BERT gets the information gain of training corpus by following steps. Firstly, we annotation the training corpus (see Fig. 3).

After calculation, results are as follows:

$$H(C) \approx 0.9182$$

$$H_{Negative=Y}(C|E) \approx 0.9543$$

$$H_{Negative=N}(C|E) \approx 0.8631$$

$$H_{Positive=Y}(C|E) = 0$$

$$H_{Positive=N}(C|E) \approx 0.2983$$

$$IG_{Negative}(E) \approx 0.0065$$

$$IG_{Positive}(E) \approx 0.7392$$

According to results, in example corpus, the information gain of Positive is bigger than that of Negative. In other words, Positive is more important than Negative. However, Negative's word frequency is higher than Positive. In summary, the information gain of IAS-BERT can solve the problem about imbalance corpus polarity caused by word frequency.

Association vectors focus on the internal features of successively entered words. In this way, the relevance between two word-embeddings is improved, and the model learns associative memory.

$$A(E_1, E_2) = \sum_{i=1}^{n} \delta(E_{1i}, E_1)(E_{2i}, E_2) = \frac{\sum_{i=1}^{n} E_{1i} \times E_{2i}}{\sqrt{\sum_{i=1}^{n} E_{1i}^2 \sum_{i=1}^{n} E_{2i}^2}} \tag{7}$$

where E_{1i} represents i th of the first input, and E_{2i} represents i th of the follow word. The inputted word embedding is represented as $E = E_1 E_2 ... E_i ... E_n$.

The weight function is set in annotation classifier layer as follows:

$$w_j = \frac{IG(D, a_j)}{\sum_{j=1}^{K} IG(D, a_j)} + \frac{\sum_{i=1}^{n} E_{1i} \times E_{2i}}{\sqrt{\sum_{i=1}^{n} E_{1i}^2 \sum_{i=1}^{n} E_{2i}^2}} \tag{8}$$

where, a_j represents the information gain of j th feature in the corpus D. In addition, the ReLU activation function is usually added to two linear transformations in feedforward network layer [15].

$$FFN(Z) = max(0, ZW_1 + b_1)W_2 + b_2 \tag{9}$$

After normalized by w_j and $FFN(Z)$, it will pass to the next encoder (see Fig. 4).

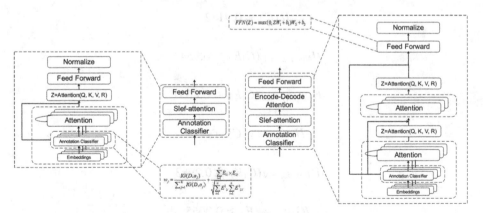

Fig. 4. Annotation classifier of IAS-BERT

2.4 Computational Overhead of IAS-BERT

IAS-BERT uses forward-matching regular expression form, and combines with following loss function:

$$L = \sum_{r \in R} l(\{e_i, P(e_i|E, PV; \hat{\theta})|i \in S_r\}) \tag{10}$$

$$L = \sum_{r \in R} \sum_{i \in S_r} e_i \log^{P(e_i|E,PV;\hat{\theta})} \tag{11}$$

In this way, the gradients in training is optimized. Using a forward-matching regular expression can reduce the computational overhead for deep networks. The forward-matching regular expression is as follows:

$$\frac{\partial \varepsilon}{\partial E_l} = \frac{\partial \varepsilon}{\partial E_L} \times (1 + \sum_{k=1}^{L-1} \frac{\partial \xi(LN(E_k), \theta_k)}{\partial E_L}) \tag{12}$$

Under the optimization of forward-matching regular expression, the state of $L + 1$ layer as follows: $x_{l+1} = Y(y_0, y_1, ..., y_l) = \sum_{k=0}^{l} W_k^{l+1} LN(e_k)$.

Some studies have pointed out that pre-processing corpus can achieve better results [23, 24]. IAS-BERT mainly improves capturing local features of $\text{BERT}_{\text{BASE}}$ by information gain and association vector.

3 Experiment

3.1 Datasets

In this paper, we use CoLA, SST-2, waimai_10k and weibo_senti_100k to verify the validity of IAS-BERT [25]. Where CoLA is a classification corpus, and its classification labels are unbalanced. The purpose of adding this database is to verify the scalability of IAS-BERT in other problems in NLP. Table 1 summarizes the details of each dataset.

Table 1. Information of datasets

Dataset	Metric	Train			Dev	Test
		Total	Positive	Negative		
CoLA	MCC	8551	6023	2528	527	516
SST-2	ACC	6119	3195	2924	3984	2391
waimai_10k	ACC	10798	3599	7199	3258	4102
weibo_senti_100k	ACC	110289	54410	55879	5648	30635

Note: Table 1 includes metrics for model, training/dev/test sizes (in number of sentences), and positive/negative samples.

These datasets contain sentiment and labels. We randomly shuffle the datasets firstly to make experiment repeatable. And then, we cut out 60% from entire datasets as the training, 20% as the dev, and the remaining 20% as the test. Finally, due to the requirements of model, we add the start tag [CLS] at the beginning of each sentence and the end tag [SEP] at the end of each sentence.

3.2 Parameter Setting

In training, we set learning function as follows:

$$l = d_{model}^{-0.5} \cdot \min(step\_num^{-0.5}, step\_num \cdot warmup\_steps^{-1.5}) \tag{13}$$

After setting learning function, we use the optimal one. Considering the impact of training epoch times, we experiment 20 epochs (see Fig. 5).

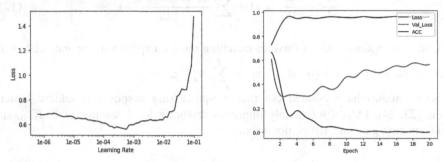

Fig. 5. Parameter of IAS-BERT

From Fig. 5, we get the maximum learning rate before the loss increasing sharply. The maximum learning rate is $e^{-6} + e^{-5}$. Thus, we set the learning rate as $2(e^{-6} + e^{-5})$. When the epoch is less than 3, Val_loss and Loss decrease together. It shows that model has achieved good results. When the epoch is more than 3, Loss is still decrease, but Val_loss has begun to increase. It shows that model works well on the training, but not well on the dev and test. This situation indicates that training has overfitted. In general, when setting epochs is 3, the training achieves best results.

3.3 Iteration and Loss

In this section, we use BiLSTM and BERT$_{BASE}$ comparing with our new model (see Fig. 6).

From Fig. 6, at the beginning of iteration, IAS-BERT has the best gradient among three models, and it is the fastest optimized model. As the iteration goes on, the loss of three models being consistency gradually. At the end of the iteration, IAS-BERT finds the optimum loss firstly. At the same time, the loss of IAS-BERT and BERT$_{BASE}$ still fluctuate within a larger range, while BiLSTM fluctuates within a smaller range. It is caused by different framework between Transformer and LSTM.

3.4 Experimental Results

Evaluation Metrics

In order to rigorous analyze IAS-BERT, we adopted multiple measures, including precision (P), recall (R), F1-score (F1), Matthews Correlation Coefficient (MCC), accuracy (ACC) and area under curve (AUC).

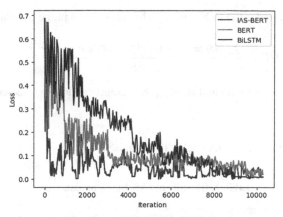

Fig. 6. Iteration VS loss for IAS-BERT, BERT$_{BASE}$ and BiLSTM

Accuracy, recall, and F1-score are a set of metrics widely used in model evaluation. TP indicates that the sample is positive, and the model predicts it as a positive sample. TN indicates that the sample is negative, and the model predicts it as a negative sample. FP indicates that the sample is negative, and the model predicts it as a positive sample. FN indicates that the sample is positive, and the model predicts it as a negative sample.

The precision is the ratio of positive samples classified correctly to samples classified as positive.

$$P = \frac{TP}{TP + FP} \tag{14}$$

The recall is the ratio of positive samples correctly classified to actual positive samples.

$$R = \frac{TP}{TP + FN} \tag{15}$$

F1-score is the weighted average of precision and recall.

$$F_1 = 2 \cdot \frac{precision \cdot recall}{precision + recall} \tag{16}$$

MCC is the Matthews Correlation Coefficient. This indicator comprehensively considers TP, TN, FP and FN. It has a good effect on different quantity between positive and negative samples.

$$MCC = \frac{TP \times TN - FP \times FN}{\sqrt{(TP + FP)(TP + FN)(TN + FP)(TN + FN)}} \tag{17}$$

ACC is the ratio of correctly classified test samples to the total number of test samples. It is used to measure the capability of a model to correctly predict classification of new data.

$$ACC = \frac{TP + TN}{TP + TN + FP + FN} \tag{18}$$

AUC is an area under the ROC curve, which is used to judge the validity of models.

$$AUC = \frac{\sum ins_i \in positiveclass Rank_{ins_i} - \frac{M \times (M+1)}{2}}{M \times N} \tag{19}$$

where, $\sum ins_i \in positiveclass$ and $Rank_{ins_i}$ represents randomly selected samples in the area.

Results

Table 2 records the results of IAS-BERT on datasets.

Table 2. Results of IAS-BERT on datasets

Dataset	ACC	F1	AUC	MCC	Precision	Recall
CoLA	74.2	82.6	65.5	42.9	77.0	89.0
SST-2	96.5	96.6	96.5	93.0	96.7	96.6
waimai_10k	95.2	92.7	94.3	89.1	93.7	91.8
weibo_senti_100k	98.1	98.1	98.1	96.2	99.6	96.6

From Table 2, both English datasets and Chinese datasets are achieved good results. And with the increasing scale of data in training, the score of IAS-BERRT is improved.

Table 3. Score comparison of models on CoLA, SST-2, waimai_10k and weibo_senti_100k

Model	CoLA	SST-2	waimai_10k	weibo_senti_100k
	MCC	ACC	ACC	ACC
CBOW	–	80.0	–	–
LSTM	–	84.9	93.1	95.2
BiLSTM	11.6	82.2	94.3	96.0
DCNN	–	86.8	–	–
DSCNN	–	89.1	–	–
Pre-OpenAI SOTA	35.0	93.2	–	–
BiLSTM + ELMo	32.1	89.3	–	–
BiLSTM + ELMo + Attn	36.0	90.4	–	–
OpenAI GPT	45.4	91.3	–	–
BERT$_{BASE}$	52.1	93.5	90.1	97.9
BERT$_{LARGE}$	60.5	94.9	–	–
Mobile BERT	51.1	92.6	–	–
IAS-BERT	42.9	96.5	95.2	98.1

We compare the results with CBOW, LSTM, BiLSTM, DCNN, DSCNN, Pre-OpenAI SOTA, BiLSTM + ELMo, BiLSTM + ELMo + Attn, OpenAI GPT, BERT$_{BASE}$, BERT$_{LARGE}$ and Mobile BERT [7, 10, 12, 16, 26]. Table 3 records the comparison results.

According to Table 3, we can draw the following conclusions:

Although IAS-BERT achieved higher-than-benchmark scores in CoLA, it was still lower than OpenAI GPT, BERT$_{BASE}$, BERT$_{LARGE}$ and Mobile BERT. It shows that the adaptability of IAS-BERT is poor when the proportion of positive samples and negative samples in the corpus huge different. However, in SST-2, waimai_10k and weibo_senti_100k, it has achieved higher scores than existed models. It shows that our model is valid on emotion equipartition characteristics datasets.

4 Conclusions

In this paper, we proposed a model called IAS-BERT for sentiment analysis in NLP. Comparing with existed models, it improves the capability of extracting local features by association vector. And it balances the polarity of training corpus features by information gain annotation. Our new model achieves good results in both English datasets and Chinese datasets. However, due to the framework of Transformer, IAS-BERT lacks the capability of capturing sequence order and processing long sequence.

For future work, we will focus on improving the adaptability of long sequence.

Funding. This work is partly supported by the Undergraduate Education Reform Project in Shandong Province (no. Z2018S022).

References

1. Palkar, R.K., Gala, K.D., Shah, M.M., Shah, J.N.: Comparative evaluation of supervised learning algorithms for sentiment analysis of movie reviews. Int. J. Comput. Appl. **142**(1), 20–26 (2016)
2. Pak, A., Paroubek, P.: Twitter as a corpus for sentiment analysis and opinion mining. In: LREc, vol. 10, no. 2010, pp. 1320–1326, May 2010
3. Sisk, J.: U.S. Patent Application No. 13/308,496 (2013)
4. Deitrick, W., Hu, W.: Mutually enhancing community detection and sentiment analysis on twitter networks (2013)
5. Bengio, Y., Ducharme, R., Vincent, P., Jauvin, C.: A neural probabilistic language model. J. Mach. Learn. Res. **3**(Feb), 1137–1155 (2003)
6. Chang, Y.W., Hsieh, C.J., Chang, K.W., Ringgaard, M., Lin, C.J.: Training and testing low-degree polynomial data mappings via linear SVM. J. Mach. Learn. Res. **11**(4), 1471–1490 (2010)
7. Le, Q., Mikolov, T.: Distributed representations of sentences and documents. In International Conference on Machine Learning, pp. 1188–1196, January 2014
8. Peters, M.E., et al.: Deep contextualized word representations. arXiv preprint arXiv:1802. 05365 (2018)
9. Radford, A., Narasimhan, K., Salimans, T., Sutskever, I.: Improving language understanding by generative pre-training (2018)
10. Devlin, J., Chang, M.W., Lee, K., Toutanova, K.: Bert: pre-training of deep bidirectional transformers for language understanding. arXiv preprint arXiv:1810.04805 (2018)

11. Soh, C., Yu, S., Narayanan, A., Duraisamy, S., Chen, L.: Employee profiling via aspect-based sentiment and network for insider threats detection. Expert Syst. Appl. **135**, 351–361 (2019)
12. Mikolov, T., Chen, K., Corrado, G., Dean, J.: Efficient estimation of word representations in vector space. arXiv preprint arXiv:1301.3781 (2013)
13. Rong, X.: word2vec parameter learning explained. arXiv preprint arXiv:1411.2738 (2014)
14. Cheng, J., Dong, L., Lapata, M.: Long short-term memory-networks for machine reading. arXiv preprint arXiv:1601.06733 (2016)
15. Vaswani, A., et al.: Attention is all you need. In: Advances in Neural Information Processing Systems, pp. 5998–6008 (2017)
16. Santos, I., Nedjah, N., de Macedo Mourelle, L.: Sentiment analysis using convolutional neural network with fastText embeddings. In: 2017 IEEE Latin American Conference on Computational Intelligence (LA-CCI), pp. 1–5. IEEE, November, 2017
17. Lee, J., et al.: BioBERT: a pre-trained biomedical language representation model for biomedical text mining. Bioinformatics **36**(4), 1234–1240 (2020)
18. Alsentzer, E., et al.: Publicly available clinical BERT embeddings. arXiv preprint arXiv:1904.03323 (2019)
19. Sun, C., Huang, L., Qiu, X.: Utilizing BERT for aspect-based sentiment analysis via constructing auxiliary sentence. arXiv preprint arXiv:1903.09588 (2019)
20. Lei, Y., Wu, Z.: Time series classification based on statistical features. EURASIP J. Wireless Commun. Netw. **2020**(1), 1–13 (2020). https://doi.org/10.1186/s13638-020-1661-4
21. Deng, D., Jing, L., Yu, J., Sun, S.: Sparse self-attention LSTM for sentiment lexicon construction. IEEE/ACM Trans. Audio Speech Lang. Process. **27**(11), 1777–1790 (2019)
22. Tang, J., et al.: Progressive self-supervised attention learning for aspect-level sentiment analysis. arXiv preprint arXiv:1906.01213 (2019)
23. Chen, T., Xu, R., He, Y., Wang, X.: Improving sentiment analysis via sentence type classification using BiLSTM-CRF and CNN. Expert Syst. Appl. **72**, 221–230 (2017)
24. Tien, N.H., Le, N.M., Tomohiro, Y., Tatsuya, I.: Sentence modeling via multiple word embeddings and multi-level comparison for semantic textual similarity. Inf. Process. Manage. **56**(6), 102090 (2019)
25. Warstadt, A., Singh, A., Bowman, S.R.: Neural network acceptability judgments. Trans. Assoc. Comput. Linguist. **7**, 625–641 (2019)
26. Kim, Y.: Convolutional neural networks for sentence classification. arXiv preprint arXiv: 1408.5882 (2014)

A Concept Lattice Method for Eliminating Redundant Features

Zhengyan Wang$^{(\boxtimes)}$, Yuxia Lei , and Linkun Zhang

Qufu Normal University, Rizhao 276800, Shandong, China
zhengywanggm@gmail.com

Abstract. Microarray gene technology solves the problem of obtaining gene expression data. It is a significant part for current research to obtain effective information from omics genes quickly. Feature selection is an important step of data preprocessing, and it is one of the key factors affecting the capability of algorithm information extraction. Since single feature selection method causes the deviation of feature subsets, we introduce ensemble learning to solve the problem of clusters redundancy. We propose a new method called Multi-Cluster minimum Redundancy (MCmR). Firstly, features are clustered by L1-normth. And then, redundant features among clusters are removed according to the mRMR algorithm. Finally, it can be sorted by the calculation results of each feature MCFS_score in the features subset. By this process, the feature with higher score can be used as the output result. The concept lattice constructed by MCmR reduces redundant concepts while maintaining its structure and improve the efficiency of data analysis. We verify the valid of MCmR on multiple disease gene datasets, and its ACC in Prostate_Tumor, Lung_cancer, Breast_cancer and Leukemia datasets reached 95.4, 94.9, 96.0 and 95.8 respectively.

Keywords: Concept lattice · Gene expression data · Integrated feature selection

1 Introduction

The development of microarray gene technology has enabled researchers to obtain a large amount of gene expression data. These samples have the characteristics of small-scale samples at high dimension [1]. At the same time, there are a number of unrelated genes in the obtained data. Therefore, when mining deep information, it is the key that selecting a valid method to obtain accurate sets of pathogenic genes for analyzing gene expression data.

Formal Concept Analysis (FCA), proposed by R. Wille in 1980s, is an effective tool for data analysis. It essentially reflects the association between objects and attributes (samples and features), and embodies relationship between instantiation and generalization by Hasse. FCA is applied to gene expression data to mine deep information. The existed methods have extended and applied concept lattices in many ways.

In 2009, Mehdi proposed two algorithms based on inter-ordinal scaling and pattern structures, and the pattern-structures algorithm calculates interval algebra by adjusting

© ICST Institute for Computer Sciences, Social Informatics and Telecommunications Engineering 2021
Published by Springer Nature Switzerland AG 2021. All Rights Reserved
L. Qi et al. (Eds.): CloudComp 2020, LNICST 363, pp. 43–53, 2021.
https://doi.org/10.1007/978-3-030-69992-5_4

standard algorithm [2]. In 2010, Dexing Wang introduced association rules to reduce concept lattice on biological information data [3]. In 2011, Benjamin J found gene sets that reflected the strong relationship among multiple diseases in the gene expression data of similar diseases by constructing concept lattice [4]. In 2018, Hongxiang Tang used the data structural dependence to construct concept lattice and mined interesting information in genetic data [5]. At present, there are many methods can get better results. However, in the constructed concept lattice, interesting concepts containing important information and redundant concepts caused by redundant genes are difficult to select.

Feature selection, as an important data preprocessing process, can select important feature genes in biological data to alleviate high-dimensional problems while removing irrelevant feature genes [6]. In genetic data, a sample often contains tens of thousands gene expression values, most of which cannot account for the disease. Therefore, feature selection selects the smallest number of features from the original data to contain as much information as possible [7]. The concept lattice constructed in this way achieves the purpose of reducing redundant concepts and improving the valid and accuracy of data expression. There are many feature selection methods. Single feature selection methods may make bias of classification and ignore interesting genes.

Chong Du proposed an integrated feature selection method. This model improves the accuracy of single selection method in gene expression. Maghsoudloo established a hybrid feature selection framework for extracting crucial genes of asthma and other lung diseases as biomarkers [8]. Gang Fang used feature selection of ensemble learning methods to find genes related to stroke patients and predict acute stroke in the dataset [9, 10].

The contributions of this paper are listed as follows:

1. This paper proposed an integrated feature selection method called Multi-Cluster minimum Redundancy (MCmR). It improves redundant features of multiple clusters and reduces the interference of redundant genes on feature selection. This method can obtain excellent feature subsets in multiple clusters.
2. This paper uses Prostate_Tumor, Lung_cancer, Breast_cancer and Leukemia to verify the valid of MCmR. The experimental results show that it obtains an excellent subset of features in all datasets. Compared with other methods, our method gets better results on feature selection set.

In what follows, Sect. 2 introduces the definition and concepts of related methods. Section 3 shows the experiment and results on datasets. Section 4 summarizes this paper.

2 Related Work

2.1 Formal Concept Analysis

FCA takes concepts as basic elements, and each node represents a concept. As the core of data analysis, the concept lattice constructs the conceptual hierarchy structure in the formal context out of the partial order relationship among concepts [1, 2]. As a visualization method of concept lattice, Hasse intuitively describes the information of data.

Definition 1: Let a triple $K = (G, A, I)$ composed of object set G, attribute set A and binary relation set I between objects and attributes constitute a formal context collection, where $G = (g_1, g_2, ..., g_n)$, $A = \{a_1, a_2, ..., a_m\}$, $I \subseteq G \times M$ [4]. In I, for any g in G and any a in A satisfy "$(g, a) \in K$" or "gIa", it means that the object g has attribute a, which is represented by 1 (otherwise, it is represented by 0).

Definition 2: Set a tuple (X, M) extracted from the formal context $K = (G, A, I)$ satisfies $X' = M$ and $M' = X$, and can be called a formal concept (abbreviated as concept, C). Where, $X \in G$, $M \in A$. X is called the extension of the concept, which is a set of objects shared by all attributes of the concept, and M, as the set of the attributes shared by all objects of the concept, is called the intension of the concept [11]. Where, X' and M' satisfy the following equation:

$$X' = \{a | a \in A, \forall x \in X, xIa\}, X \subseteq G$$
$$M' = \{x | x \in G, \forall a \in M, xIa\}, M \subseteq A \tag{1}$$

Definition 3: Suppose two concepts (X_1, M_1) and (X_2, M_2) in the formal context, named C_1 and C_2. If the relationship conform to $X_1 \subseteq X_2$ (equivalent to $M_2 \subseteq M_1$), (X_1, M_1) is called a sub-concept of (X_2, M_2), and (X_2, M_2) is called a super-concept of (X_1, M_1), denoted as $C_1 \leq C_2$ [5, 12]. This relationship between concepts construct complete concept lattice, which called partial order. Formulated as follows (see Fig. 1) (Table 1):

$$(X_1, M_1) \subseteq (X_2, M_2) \Leftrightarrow A_1 \subseteq A_2$$
$$(X_1, M_1) \subseteq (X_2, M_2) \Leftrightarrow B_2 \subseteq B_1 \tag{2}$$

Table 1. Formal context

G\A	a1	a2	a3	a4	a5	a6
g1	1	1		1		1
g2			1		1	
g3		1		1	1	
g4	1			1		1
g5		1				1

2.2 Feature Selection Method

It achieves the purpose of removing redundant features by selecting feature subsets with strong resolution capacity from the high-dimensional raw data. The selected features retain information of raw data as much as possible [7]. Applying the feature selection method to gene data can obtain a subset of disease feature genes, and remove redundant

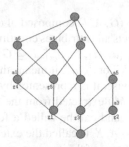

Fig. 1. The concept lattice.

genes. Feature selection are divided into supervised and unsupervised algorithms [13]. Unsupervised method become popular since it does not need to obtain labels in advance.

MCFS

Multi-Cluster Features Selection (MCFS) method spectral embedding for cluster analysis achieves the purpose of reducing dimensionality by constructing graph, defining the weight matrix (such as heat kernel weighting) and mapping feature. Eigenvalues and eigenvectors of the Laplacian matrix L will be calculated by the following formula [10]:

$$Ly = \lambda Dy \tag{3}$$

D is diagonal matrix, and $D_{ii} = \sum_j W_{ij}$. Thus, Laplacian $L = D - W$. $Y = [y_1, y_2, ..., y_k]$ and y_k is the eigenvector corresponding to the smallest k non-zero eigenvalues [14].

Sparse coefficient vectors $\{a_k\}_{k=1}^K \in \mathbb{R}^M$ measure the significance of each dimension and the capability of each feature to distinguish different clusters, which can be calculated by LARs algorithm to optimize L1-normth [15]. We obtain k sparse coefficient vectors by solving the L1-normth of every y_k in Y.

$$\min_{a_k} ||y_k - X^T a_k||^2$$
$$s.t. a_k| \leq \gamma \tag{4}$$

Definition 4: For each feature j, $MCFS(j) = \max_k |a_{k,j}|$. It calculates the MCFS_score, and selects the top d features according to descending order [10].

mRMR

The maximum correlation minimum redundancy (mRMR) method uses mutual information for feature selection [16]. The correlation between features and target categories is represented by mutual information $I(f_i; c)$. Redundancy between features is represented by mutual information $I(f_i; f_j)$ [6]. The feature subset selected by mRMR has maximum correlation and minimum redundancy.

$$mRMR = \max_S [D(S) - R(S)] \tag{5}$$

where $R(S) = \frac{1}{|S|^2} \sum\limits_{f_i, f_j \in S} I(f_i; f_j)$ represents the redundancy of all features in set S,

and $D(S, c) = \frac{1}{|S|} \sum\limits_{f_i \in S} I(f_i; c)$ represents the correlation between all features in S and category c.

Assuming that n features are already in the subset S_n, selecting the next feature from set $\{S - S_n\}$ according to the following formula [17]:

$$\max_{f_i \in S - S_t} [I(f_i; C) - \frac{1}{t} \sum_{f_i \in S_t} I(f_j; f_i)] \tag{6}$$

2.3 Multi-cluster Minimum Redundancy

MCFS uses correlation within the cluster to select features, calculates MCFS_score for the selected features, and gets the first d features. This method only performs better when the clusters is less than 50, and it is not detected whether there is redundancy between features of clusters before calculating the score. The mRMR performs feature redundancy detection between clusters and eliminates features with higher redundancy. Thus, it can be used for further screening of feature selection to achieve its purpose. Therefore, we propose an integrated feature selection method named MCmR, which maintains its advantages in large scale clusters [17]. MCmR makes full use of effective information (see Fig. 2). This proposed feature selection algorithm effectively reduces the formal context and concept lattice [18].

The MCmR is described as follows:

1. The inputting data will be performed by spectral cluster. It will get diagram matrix D from weights matrix W, and gain set $Y = [y_1, y_2, ..., y_k]$ by $Ly = \lambda Dy$.
2. Get k sparse coefficient vectors by solving the L1-regularized regression of each y_k in Y.
3. Set threshold of mRMR to filter the features with higher redundancy by $mRMR = \max\limits_{S}[D(S) - R(S)]$.
4. The MCFS_scores of selected features will be calculated and sorted in descending order. Thus, the top d features will be selected.
5. Output Feature subset S.

MCmR can not only gets more information feature genes cluster with less number, but also maintain accuracy when cluster is increases. MCmR makes up the shortcoming of single feature selection method in large number cluster, and improves the accuracy of feature selection by multiple selection with feature sets [19].

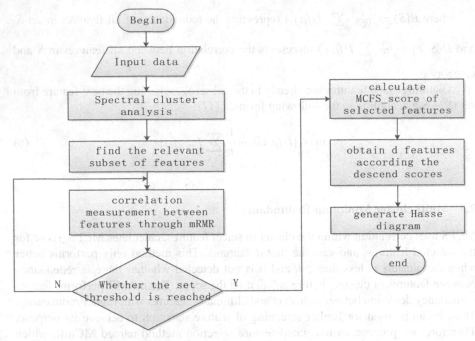

Fig. 2. The process of feature selection by MCmR.

3   Experiment and Results

3.1   Datasets

This paper verified the valid of MCmR on Prostate_Tumor, Lung_Cancer, Breast Cancer and Leukemia. The detail informations of datasets are shown in Table 2.

Table 2. Detail information of datasets

Tag	Dataset	Sample	Features	Positive	Negative
1	Prostate_Tumor	124	10510	62	62
2	Lung_cancer	203	12600	42	161
3	Breast_cancer	147	1213	98	49
4	Leukemia	72	5328	47	25

3.2 Experiment

Evaluation Metrics
During the experiment, we take the Normalized Mutual Information (NMI) metric and Accuracy as evaluation metrics [14]. Comparing the cluster label calculated by algorithm and raw set can measure the cluster performance. Assuming two cluster labels set L and L', which respectively include the label provided by data and algorithm. The normalized mutual information metric $MI(L, L')$ is defined as follows:

$$MI(L, L') = \sum_{i=1}^{|L|} \sum_{j=1}^{|L'|} P(i, j) \log\left(\frac{P(i, j)}{P(i)P'(j)}\right) \tag{7}$$

where, $P(i)$ is the probability that a feature picked at random falls into class L_i. $P(i, j)$ is the probability that a feature picked at random falls into both class L_i and L'_j.
The NMI is as follows:

$$NMI(L, L') = \frac{MI(L, L')}{\sqrt{H(L)H(L')}} \tag{8}$$

where, $H(L)$ and $H(L')$ represent the entropies of L and L' respectively. The evaluation criterion ranges from 0 to 1. It is similar between A and B when the value is bigger. NMI $= 1$ if the two sets of clusters are identical, and NMI $= 0$ if the two sets are independent [10].

Results
In this part, we compare performance of MCmR with MCFS, mRMR and Relief for various cluster number on Prostate_Tumor (see Fig. 3).

In Fig. 3, it shows that the performance of different algorithms on 30, 50, 70 and 90 clusters. Picture (a) shown that MCmR performs as well as MCFS when the features are less than 50. Picture (b) and (c) show that the performance of MCmR is improving gradually, and always higher than MCFS when cluster is 50 and 70. MCFS gets best results when cluster is 70. When cluster is more than 90, the experiment performance become worse. Picture (d) shows that MCmR gets the best performance when cluster is 90. Too many clusters lead to more redundant genes. On country, it results in filtering out disease-related genes. Comparing with 70 and 110 clusters, MCmR gets better results on Prostate_Tumor when cluster is 90. The quantity of features also affects experimental results. It is shown from picture (a–d), MCmR gets the best performance when feature is 130. The quantity of feature d is half of the features set satisfied threshold of mRMR. Then, we compare the experimental effects in different features numbers, and verify the best d.

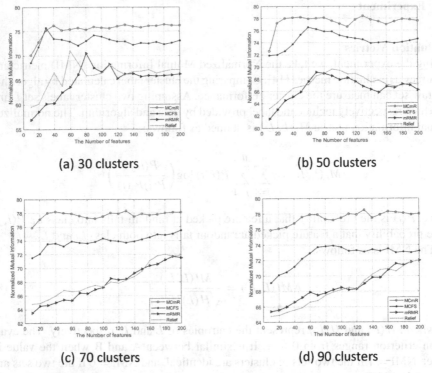

Fig. 3. The performance of MCmR, MCFS, mRMR and relief for various cluster number on Prostate_Tumor.

Table 3. Cluster performance (%) by using 130 features on Prostate_Tumor

	30 clusters	50 clusters	70 clusters	90 clusters	Average
MCmR	**75.0 ±1.1**	**75.9 ±2.5**	**77.3 ±4.1**	**79.6 ±6.8**	**76.9**
MCFS	74.9 ± 2.9	74.2 ± 2.3	72.9 ± 1.4	69.1 ± 0.8	72.8
mRMR	64.2 ± 7.3	65.3 ± 3.8	65.6 ± 2.1	64.8 ± 1.3	64.9
Relief	65.8 ± 6.2	66.4 ± 3.2	66.7 ± 1.9	65.4 ± 1.0	66.1

In Table 3, it shows that MCmR gets the best results on Prostate_Tumor. This prove our new method is valid. Compared with MCFS, mRMR and Relief, MCmR is improved by 4.1, 12 and 10.8 respectively.

In Table 4, it is easy to know that the ACC of Relief and mRMR are close which reaches 82.0 and 82.4 on average. The effect of MCFS is better than those two, which reaches 89.8 on average. The highest ACC belongs to MCmR that it is 95.5 on average. It shows the valid and superiority of MCmR in feature selection.

Table 4. The ACC of methods on various datasets.

	Prostate_Tumor ACC	Lung_cancer ACC	Breast_cancer ACC	Leukemia ACC	Average ACC
Relief	81.4	82.6	82.5	81.6	82.0
mRMR	85.1	80.9	81.4	82.3	82.4
MCFS	90.1	89.8	89.2	90.1	89.8
MCmR	**95.4**	**94.9**	**96.0**	**95.8**	**95.5**

Table 5. The number of concept in different datasets.

Datasets	Feature	mRMR	Relief	MCFS	MCmR	C	Reduce
Prostate_Tumor	10510	79	58	28	12	72	9.8%
Lung_cancer	12600	210	93	32	16	94	10.1%
Breast_cancer	1213	48	32	19	9	35	2.5%
Leukemia	5328	56	39	21	12	42	7%

In Table 5, we use MCmR to construct a concept lattice in each dataset. Compared with MCFS, MCmR has less concept in concept lattice. It can be seen from the table that MCmR performs differently in different datasets. Among them, it performed best in Lung_cancer, with a concept reduction of 10.1%. Using feature selection to remove redundant genes from high-dimensional gene expression data and obtain feature genes. It can reduce the formal context and concepts in concept lattice (see Fig. 4).

The experimental results show that MCmR improves the accuracy of related gene selection and reduces redundant genes compared with other methods.

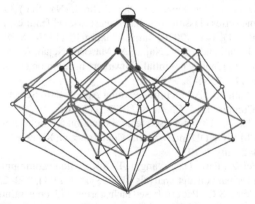

Fig. 4. MCmR Reduce Breast_cancer concept lattice

4 Conclusion

Aiming at the problem of poor feature selection effect in case of a large number of clusters, this paper proposes an integrated feature selection method MCmR to improve the capability of feature selection on genetic data. We focus on the extraction of feature genes by clustering to reduce attribute genes concept. Our experiments show that MCmR improved the accuracy of data classification. And it also reduces concept of concept lattices at the same time. However, this method has high computational overhead. Thus, we try to reduce it through improve framework of MCmR. For future work, we will pay attention to find a way to reduce computational overhead.

Funding. This work is partly supported by the Undergraduate Education Reform Project in Shandong Province (no. Z2018S022).

References

1. Kaytoue-Uberall, M., Duplessis, S., Napoli, A.: Using formal concept analysis for the extraction of groups of co-expressed genes. In: Le Thi, H.A., Bouvry, P., Pham Dinh, T. (eds.) Modelling, Computation and Optimization in Information Systems and Management Sciences. MCO 2008. Communications in Computer and Information Science, vol. 14, pp. 439–449. Springer, Heidelberg (2008). https://doi.org/10.1007/978-3-540-87477-5_47
2. Kaytoue M., Duplessis S., Kuznetsov S.O., Napoli A. (2009) Two FCA-based methods for mining gene expression data. In: Ferré, S., Rudolph, S. (eds.) Formal Concept Analysis. ICFCA 2009. Lecture Notes in Computer Science, vol. 5548, pp. 251–266. Springer, Heidelberg. https://doi.org/10.1007/978-3-642-01815-2_19
3. Wang, D., Cui, L., Wang, Y., Yuan, H., Zhang, J.: Association Rule mining based on concept lattice in bioinformatics research. In: 2010 International Conference on Biomedical Engineering and Computer Science, pp. 1–4. IEEE, April 2010
4. Keller, B.J., Eichinger, F., Kretzler, M.: Formal concept analysis of disease similarity. AMIA Summits Transl. Sci. Proc. **2012**, 42 (2012)
5. Tang, H., Xia, F., Wang, S.: Information structures in a lattice-valued information system. Soft. Comput. **22**(24), 8059–8075 (2018). https://doi.org/10.1007/s00500-018-3097-x
6. Chong, D.U., Chang Yin, Z.H.O.U., Yue, L.I., et al.: Application of ensemble feature selection in gene expression data. J. Shandong Univ. Sci. Technol. (Nat. Sci.) **38**(1), 85–90 (2019)
7. Lei, Y., Wu, Z.: Time series classification based on statistical features. EURASIP J. Wireless Commun. Netw. **2020**(1), 1–13 (2020). https://doi.org/10.1186/s13638-020-1661-4
8. Maghsoudloo, M., Jamalkandi, S.A., Najafi, A., Masoudi-Nejad, A.: An efficient hybrid feature selection method to identify potential biomarkers in common chronic lung inflammatory diseases. Genomics **112**, 3284–3293 (2020)
9. Fang, G., Liu, W., Wang, L.: A Machine Learning Approach to Select Features Important to Stroke Prognosis. Comput. Biol. Chem. **88**, 107316 (2020)
10. Cai, D., Zhang, C., He, X.: Unsupervised feature selection for multi-cluster data. In: Proceedings of the 16th ACM SIGKDD International Conference on Knowledge Discovery and Data Mining, pp. 333–342. July 2010
11. Hao, F., Min, G., Pei, Z., Park, D.S., Yang, L.T.: $ K $-clique community detection in social networks based on formal concept analysis. IEEE Syst. J. **11**(1), 250–259 (2015)
12. Henriques, R., Madeira, S.C.: Pattern-based biclustering with constraints for gene expression data analysis. In: Pereira, F., Machado, P., Costa, E., Cardoso, A. (eds.) Progress in Artificial Intelligence. EPIA 2015. Lecture Notes in Computer Science, vol 9273. Springer, Cham (2015). https://doi.org/10.1007/978-3-319-23485-4_34

13. Xie, J.Y., Ding, L.J., Wang, M.Z.: Spectral clustering based unsupervised feature selection algorithm. Ruan Jian Xue Bao/J. Softw. **31**(4), 1009–1024 (2020)
14. He, X., Cai, D., Niyogi, P.: Laplacian score for feature selection. In: Advances in Neural Information Processing Systems, pp. 507–514 (2006)
15. Efron, B., Hastie, T., Johnstone, I., Tibshirani, R.: Least angle regression. Ann. Stat. **32**(2), 407–499 (2004)
16. Zhang, Y., Ding, C., Li, T.: Gene selection algorithm by combining reliefF and mRMR. BMC Genomics **9**(S2), S27 (2008). https://doi.org/10.1186/1471-2164-9-S2-S27
17. Shao, M., Liu, M., Guo, L.: Vector-based attribute reduction method for formal contexts. Fundamenta Informaticae **126**(4), 397–414 (2013)
18. Mundra, P.A., Rajapakse, J.C.: SVM-RFE with MRMR filter for gene selection. IEEE Trans. Nanobiosci. **9**(1), 31–37 (2009)
19. Liu, D., Hua, G., Viola, P., Chen, T.: Integrated feature selection and higher-order spatial feature extraction for object categorization. In: 2008 IEEE Conference on Computer Vision and Pattern Recognition, pp. 1–8. IEEE, June 2008

Secure Cloud Systems and Cloud-Based Privacy

Exploring Self-attention Mechanism of Deep Learning in Cloud Intrusion Detection

Chenmao Lu[1], Hong-Ning Dai[1(✉)], Junhao Zhou[1], and Hao Wang[2]

[1] Macau University of Science and Technology, Taipa, Macau SAR
cmlu.sec@gmail.com, hndai@ieee.org, junhao_zhou@qq.com
[2] Norwegian University of Science and Technology, Gjøvik, Norway
hawa@ntnu.no

Abstract. Cloud computing offers elastic and ubiquitous computing services, thereby receiving extensive attention recently. However, cloud servers have also become the targets of malicious attacks or hackers due to the centralization of data storage and computing facilities. Most intrusion attacks to cloud servers are often originated from inner or external networks. Intrusion detection is a prerequisite to designing anti-intrusion countermeasures of cloud systems. In this paper, we explore deep learning algorithms to design intrusion detection methods. In particular, we present a deep learning-based method with the integration of conventional neural networks, self-attention mechanism, and Long short-term memory (LSTM), namely CNN-A-LSTM to detect intrusion. CNN-A-LSTM leverages the merits of CNN in processing local correlation data and extracting features, the time feature extracting capability of LSTM, and the self-attention mechanism to better exact features. We conduct extensive experiments on the KDDcup99 dataset to evaluate the performance of our CNN-A-LSTM model. Compared with other machine learning and deep learning models, our CNN-A-LSTM has superior performance.

Keywords: Deep learning · Convolution neural network · Self-attention · Long short-term memory · Network intrusion detection

1 Introduction

Cloud computing can greatly complement to computing insufficiency of mobile devices or personal computers and the Internet of Things (IoT) nodes. Moreover, the recent advances in artificial intelligence, such as deep learning also put forth more stringent requirements on the computing capability of end devices. Moreover, the massive volumes of various data also drive the high storage capacity of end devices. However, either mobile devices and IoT nodes cannot cater to the rising demands on computing and storage capacity due to the built-in limitations while cloud computing facilities can fulfill the stringent computing requirements and provide users with elastic and ubiquitous computing services.

L. Qi et al. (Eds.): CloudComp 2020, LNICST 363, pp. 57–73, 2021.
https://doi.org/10.1007/978-3-030-69992-5_5

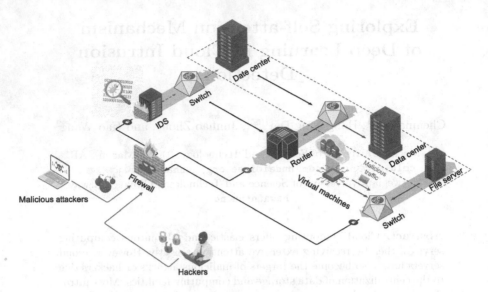

Fig. 1. An overview of cloud intrusion detection

However, cloud computing is also faced with more and more security concerns [14,15,27]. For example, malicious cloud users (or tenants) may install malicious software (or malware) to a virtual machine (VM), which may infect other VMs. Meanwhile, malicious VMs may launch malicious attacks, such as distributed denial of services (DDoS) attack to affect other VMs or even paralyze the entire cloud. It is worth mentioning that those malicious attacks mainly happen inside the cloud network (i.e., internal network traffic) or outside the cloud network (i.e., external network traffic) as shown in Fig. 1.

There are a diversity of solutions to malicious attacks in cloud computing systems. Among them, intrusion detection for cloud network is the most crucial method since it is often the prerequisite for other countermeasures. The idea of intrusion detection for cloud networks is to analyze cloud network traffic and identify abnormal traffic. Thus, intrusion detection is essentially equivalent to a classification problem in machine learning. As a result, many recent studies attempt to apply machine learning methods to solve this classification problem.

Although conventional machine learning classifiers such as naive Bayes, logistic regression, decision tree, random forest have been adopted in intrusion detection systems (IDS), most of them suffer from poor performance in terms of classification accuracy. The root cause of the poor performance of these machine learning methods can mainly owe to the fact that they are incapable of properly processing and analyzing network intrusion detection data, which has the characteristics of high dimension and feature redundancy. Thus, sophisticated feature engineering is often required to process the network intrusion detection data. Different from conventional machine learning classifiers, the recent advances in deep learning methods can handle high-dimensional and redundant data without extract efforts on feature engineering.

Although deep learning methods have been used in intrusion detection and demonstrate the performance improvement over conventional machine learning methods [3, 8, 22, 29], most of them adopt a singular structure, which may be beneficial to several dimensions of intrusion data while is struggling to handle other dimensions properly. Therefore, we present a composite deep learning model in this paper for cloud intrusion detection.

The key contributions of this paper are listed as follows.

- We propose a novel framework combining conventional neural networks, self-attention mechanism, and Long short-term memory, namely CNN-A-LSTM, for network intrusion detection.
- CNN-A-LSTM can well conduct network intrusion detection task. In particular, the CNN structure can process network intrusion data with spatial correlation while the self-attention mechanism can improve the learned parameters. The LSTM module can extract key time features from intrusion data. In this way, the characteristics of the network intrusion dataset can be better extracted.
- We evaluate our proposed CNN-A-LSTM model by conducting extensive experiments. Experimental results compare our model with other state-of-the-art methods and show that our CNN-A-LSTM achieves superior performance than other methods.

Following the introduction, Sect. 2 reviews related work. We then conduct a problem analysis in Sect. 3. Section 4 next briefs the main framework of CNN-A-LSTM and Sect. 5 presents the implementation details of CNN-A-LSTM. Section 6 gives the experiments results. Finally, Sect. 7 summarizes the paper.

2   Related Work

This section presents a literature survey on cloud security and challenges as well as traditional methods and deep learning models for detecting related security events.

2.1   Cloud Security and Challenges

Although cloud computing can provide users with elastic and ubiquitous computing servers, the centralization of cloud architecture also results in security vulnerabilities. Many research scholars have done relevant studies. Khalil et al. [7] conducted a comprehensive study of cloud security and privacy issues, categorizing known security threats and attacks, identifying 28 cloud security threats, and dividing them into five categories. Meanwhile, Singh et al. [19] introduced cloud computing challenges in eight categories. The main security challenges in cloud computing mainly include illegal access, data security, etc. [19, 21, 23, 24]. In particular, the authors make a comparative analysis of existing data security and privacy protection technologies in cloud computing in [23]. From another dimension, the work of [20] provides an overview of security issues that affect cloud computing and some security issues related to public and private cloud management. As in [5], the authors attempt to address human and technology-related threats and find security solutions.

2.2   Network Intrusion Detection

There is no denying that quickly identifying the security vulnerabilities of the network is critical to secure cloud computing. Network intrusion detection system (NIDS) has great potential to help detect threats and address security concerns. NIDS can detect abnormal behaviors that compromise the security of computer systems. We roughly divide the recent research on NIDS into two types: conventional methods and deep learning methods.

Conventional Methods. Behl et al. [2] delved into several ways to secure cloud infrastructure and also compare their weaknesses. A scalable architecture for the deployment of IDS in the cloud for new application scenarios is proposed in [16]. Some traditional detection methods have been adopted in cloud computing, such as rule-based [1,11,12] for monitoring network traffic. They [10,12,18] have the limitations as follows: i) An unknown attack in the dataset cannot be detected. ii) The model needs to be regularly training to maintain a high detection rate. iii) Getting tag data is extremely difficult. iv) False positives are still high.

Deep Learning Methods. Encouraged by the advent of machine learning and deep learning methods in computer vision and natural language processing fields, some related deep learning methods [3,8,13,17,22,28,29,31] have been applied to intrusion detection. The work [29] proposed the CNN-based NIDS model to extract intrusion identification information through supervised learning. An RNN IDS based on computational efficiency is proposed in [3]. Kim et al. [8] presented a host IDS based on exceptions, which adopts the LSTM model and system call language modeling method. Furthermore, Wang et al. [28] combine CNN and LSTM to learn the spatial and temporal respectively among multiple network packets.

Despite the progress of deep learning methods in intrusion detection, most of them adopt a singular structure, which cannot properly handle the high-dimensional data.

3   Problem Analysis

In related research experiments, the KDDcup99 network intrusion dataset [25] is one of widely used training sets. In previous studies such as [13], the KDD-cup99 dataset was adopted to test the semi-supervised machine learning model using a trapezoidal network. We also choose the KDDcup99 dataset to conduct the intrusion detection analysis. The KDDcup99 dataset contains 41 attributes,

Category R (1~9)					Category G (10~22)					Category Y (23~31)			Category B (32~41)		label
duration	...	service	...	urgent	hot	...	num_shells	...	...	serror_rate	...	...	dhsc	...	label
0		ecr_i		0	0		0			0.00			147		attack
1		smtp		0	0		0			0.00			246		attack
75		telnet		0	2		2			0.00			101		attack
198		telnet		0	3		2			0.00			1		attack
137		login		2	0		0			0.00			1		attack
98		telnet		1	1		0			0.00			4		attack
804		telnet		3	7		0			0.00			4		attack
36438		private		0	0		0			0.00			1		attack
8		pop_3		0	0		0			0.00			59		attack
0		smtp		0	0		0			0.99			77		normal
2399		telnet		3	0		0			0.00			1		normal
38		telnet		0	0		0			0.00			20		normal

Fig. 2. The example records of KDDcup99 dataset

including both discrete and continuous attributes. As shown in Fig. 2, these attributes can be divided into four categories: i) network connection basic characteristics in Category R, ii) network connection content characteristics in Category G, iii) network traffic time-based statistical characteristics in Category Y, iv) network traffic host-based statistical characteristic in Category B. In these categories, we also show the representative attributes (e.g., 'duration', 'service' and 'hot'). Moreover, we add a new attribute (namely 'label') to represent the state of each network connection, marking as 'normal' or 'attack'.

3.1 Preliminary Analysis

We conduct a preliminary analysis by classifying and analyzing all the attributes of KDDcup99. Since the dataset contains 41 attribute features, it has more complex spatial features.

- Category R contains attribute 1 to 9 in KDDcup99 dataset, representing the basic characteristics of a transmission control protocol (TCP) connection. In particular, the 'duration' attribute corresponds to continuous data and the 'service' attribute corresponds to discrete data.
- Next, the following 13 attributes in Category G represent TCP connection content characteristics. For example, 'hot' attribute represents the times of access system-sensitive files and directories, and 'num_shells' attribute represents the number of shell terminals opened. In addition, all the data in Category G is continuous data.
- Category Y contains 9 attributes, i.e., 23 to 31, which are mainly applied to depict time-based network traffic statistical characteristics. In this category,

the data of every attribute is continuous data (e.g., 'serror_rate': the percentage of connections with synchronized sequence numbers (SYN) errors in the past two seconds).

- The remaining 10 attributes fall into Category B, being mainly used to describe host-based network traffic statistical characteristics. For example, 'dst_host_srv_count (dhsc)' is the number of connections with the same target host and service as the current connection in the previous 100 connections.

Since the dataset consists of the continuous data and discrete data with heterogeneous types of attributes and the attributes contain the complex temporal and spatial features, it is difficult to properly select and fully extract the attribute features via the traditional methods.

3.2   Challenges

Preliminary analysis in Sect. 3.1 implies the following characteristics of network intrusion detection datasets.

1. *The dataset contains heterogeneous types of attributes, resulting in the complex spatial relationship between them.* Traditional methods are difficult to extract the spatial content characteristics and to reflect the intrusion behavior effectively.
2. *There are a lot of attributes based on time characteristics in the dataset.* However, the statistical time of the network intrusion is too short (only 2 s). Therefore, it is difficult to learn the features and get an effective relationship between these attributes.
3. *The dataset has a strong temporal correlation.* In general, it is difficult to identify whether the state of a connection is 'attack' or 'normal', by only making statistics of connections between the current and the previous connection record in a period of time.

Therefore, the above characteristics pose challenges in conducting network intrusion detection with existing methods. To this end, we propose a CNN-A-LSTM model to address the above challenges. In particular, we adopt our approach to solve the problems of complex spatial and time relationships, obtaining the interdependent features of content over long distances.

4   Overview of Architecture

We propose CNN-A-LSTM model to detect network intrusion in this paper. The proposed model is composed of the following components, and its overview architecture is shown in Fig. 3.

1. **Data Preprocessing.** At this stage, we conduct preliminary analysis and preprocessing on network intrusion traffic in the KDDcup99 dataset.

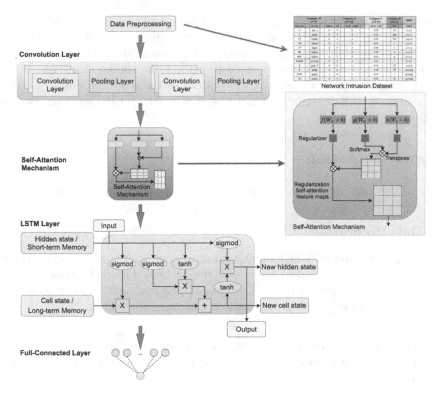

Fig. 3. An architecture of our CNN-A-LSTM model

2. **Convolution Layer.** The Convolution layer can effectively extract features from the dataset through a neural network. Motivated by [28], we exploit the CNN structure since the components of CNN can extract the spatial dependent characteristics of network intrusion traffic.
3. **Self-attention Mechanism.** For the sake of better filter out the features to get the network flow volume from the CNN layer, which is helpful to realize more accurate network traffic classification, we leverage the self-attention mechanism. The attention mechanism is used to analyze the importance of the packet vector and to obtain more prominent fine-grained features for malicious traffic detection.
4. **LSTM Layer.** Fundamentally, LSTM is an improved version of RNN proposed by [6] and further improved by [9]. As shown in Fig. 3, the LSTM layer in our model consists of three LSTM units (input gate, output gate and forget gate) with end-to-end training.
5. **Fully-connected Layer.** After the above several layers of training, at the bottom layer, we use a fully-connected layer composed of multiple neurons to extract key features.

Our target is to design a stable model for network intrusion detection. To achieve this goal, we employ 1 CNN layer to capture the features for the network intrusion traffic. The importance of packet vectors is analyzed by using the attention mechanism to obtain more prominent fine-grained features for malicious traffic detection. Moreover, based on the timing dependence of network intrusion data, the LSTM layer is used to extract the timing characteristics of network intrusion data. Finally, at the bottom of the model, a fully-connected layer is utilized. It can reduce the dimension of spatial representations used for detection.

5   Implementation

In this section, we present the details on the implementation of CNN-A-LSTM.

5.1   Data Preprocessing

In this paper, we choose KDDcup99 dataset to conduct the intrusion detection experiments. First, we need to preprocess the dataset, due to the symbolic data attributes of KDDcup99 dataset. The dataset pretreatment has two processes, namely: numerical standardization and numerical normalization.

Numerical Standardization. First, the average value and average absolute error of each attribute can be calculated by the following Eq. (1) and Eq. (2), respectively:

$$\overline{a_k} = \frac{1}{n} \sum_{p=1}^{n} a_{pk}, \tag{1}$$

$$T_j = \sqrt{\frac{1}{n} \sum_{p=1}^{n} (a_{pj} - \overline{a_j})^2}, \tag{2}$$

where a_j represents the mean value of the j-th attribute, T_j represents the average absolute error of the j-th attribute, and a_{pj} represents the j-th attribute recorded in p-th records.

A standardized measurement is then performed for each data record, as shown in Eq. (3):

$$Y_{pj} = \frac{a_{pj} - \overline{a_j}}{T_j}, \tag{3}$$

where Y_{pj} represents the j-th attribute value of the normalized p data record.

Numerical Normalization. As shown in Eq. (4), each value is normalized to the interval $[0, 1]$:

$$a^* = \frac{a - d_{\min}}{d_{\max} - d_{\min}}, \tag{4}$$

where $d_{\max}$ is the maximum and $d_{\min}$ is the minimum value of the sample data, and a is the standardized data.

5.2   CNN

In general, network traffic (e.g., KDDcup99 dataset) consists of several different types of packets. Since the features in different types of packets are quite discrepant, we need to extract the features of them separately. In our CNN-A-LSTM model as shown in Fig. 3, we use a convolution layer to obtain the spatial features of each network traffic. The convolution layer can effectively maintain the spatial continuity and facilitate the extraction of local characteristics of network traffic. In order to reduce the dimension of the hidden layer and the computation of the subsequent layer, the pooling layer uses the max-pooling or mean-pooling, in addition to providing rotation invariance.

In particular, we also employ a one-dimensional CNN layer to process time series analysis and analyze signal data with a fixed length period, since the internal features in our model can be easily extracted and mapped from one-dimensional sequence data via the one-dimensional CNN layer. Therefore, due to the simplicity of the one-dimensional CNN layer, our model can further reduce the computational complexity.

5.3   Self-attention Mechanism

Then, in order to obtain the interdependent features of content over long distances, we use the self-attention mechanism. Using the self-attention mechanism, our model can pay more attention to the significant features of network intrusion in KDDcup99 dataset. This mechanism can act on the internal elements of the source or the target [30]. Therefore, it can improve the effectiveness of the learning features in the training phase via self-attention mechanism calculation.

Furthermore, self-attention is capable of linking the connection directly between any two parts of the relevant content through a calculation step in the calculation process. The distance between the long-distance dependence features is greatly shortened, which is conducive to the effective use of these features.

The equation for calculating the output result of self-attention is as follows,

$$u_t = \tanh\left(W \cdot h_t\right), \tag{5}$$

$$\alpha_{t,i} = \frac{\exp\left(\text{score}\left(u_t, u\right)\right)}{\sum_{t=1}^{T} \exp\left(\text{score}\left(u_t, u\right)\right)}, \tag{6}$$

$$s = \sum_{t=1}^{T} \alpha_t \cdot h_t. \tag{7}$$

In Eq. (5), h_t gets the output u_t. The allocation coefficient is obtained by comparing u_t in Eq. (6) with a trainable parameter matrix u (random initialization) used to represent context information. The softmax normalization is then carried out. Finally, as shown in Eq. (7), the focused vector s is obtained.

5.4   LSTM

In order to better extract and learn the characteristics of traffic bytes in each packet data, we add an LSTM layer after the self-attention mechanism. Using LSTM can greatly improve the efficiency of our experimental training. Since the dataset we used in the experiment has 41 attributes, the LSTM forget gate can discard the attributes with less correlation. In our model, the LSTM layer can make use of the previous information of the data for effective feature learning and can learn the sequential features within the traffic bytes. The traffic bytes of each packet are input into the LSTM layer sequentially. Therefore, we can get a vector for the packet data finally.

The key implementation of the LSTM layer in our model is to control the long-term state d. In particular, the LSTM layer controls the information transfer by comparing the internal storage unit d through the design of three gates (input gate, forget gate, and output gate). The first gate is the input gate to control the continuation of the long-term state d. The second gate is the forget gate to control the information preserving or discarding. For example, when the input information is satisfied the requirements of our model, the learning features will be retained. Otherwise, the feature will be forgotten by the forget gate. Moreover, the third gate is the output gate to control the long-term state d as the output of the current LSTM layer.

Equations for calculating the output result of the LSTM layer are as follows,

$$p_i = \sigma \left(X_p \cdot [q_{i-1}, n_i] + g_p \right), \tag{8}$$

$$a_i = \sigma \left(X_a \cdot [q_{i-1}, n_i] + g_a \right), \tag{9}$$

$$\tilde{d_i} = \tanh \left(X_d \cdot [q_{i-1}, n_i] + g_d \right), \tag{10}$$

$$d_i = p_i \cdot d_{i-1} + a_i \cdot \tilde{d_i}, \tag{11}$$

$$m_i = \sigma \left(X_m [q_{i-1}, n_i] + g_m \right), \tag{12}$$

$$q_i = m_i \cdot \tanh \left(d_i \right). \tag{13}$$

In the above equations, Eq. (8) is the formula for the forget gate, where the weight matrix of forget gate is X_p. The term $[q_{i-1}, n_i]$ represents a valid way to connect two vectors into a longer vector. Besides, the Eq. (9) refers to the calculation formula of the output gate. Meanwhile, we employ Eq. (10) to calculate the current input $\tilde{d_i}$. Furthermore, we use Eq. (11) to calculate the current unit state d_i. Moreover, the impact of long-term memory on the current output is controlled by Eq. (12). Lastly, Eq. (13) refers to the final output of LSTM depends on both the output gate and the unit state.

6 Performance Evaluation

We conduct the experiments to evaluate the performance of the proposed CNN-A-LSTM model in this section. Most importantly, in Sect. 6.1, we present the detailed experimental setup and performance metrics. The comparison results of our proposed CNN-A-LSTM method with other baseline models are also presented. Finally, we conduct the parameter study in Sect. 6.2.

6.1 Preliminary Results

Experiment Settings. *a) Dataset description:* We use the network intrusion data from KDDcup99 dataset to conduct the experiments. The attack types are divided into four categories, including Probe, Dos, U2R, R2L. Moreover, they can also be subdivided into 39 subcategories. In our experiment, we employ 22 types of attack data as a training set and the remaining data as a testing set [32].

b) Model setting: In our experiment, we conduct experiments by configuring 1 CNN layer, then add the self-attention mechanism and LSTM component. We vary different dropout values as well as the different number of epochs. In every model, we set dropout equal to 0.01, 0.1, 0.5, and epoch equal to 50, 100, and 1000.

c) Performance metrics: In these experiments, we adopt four metrics, namely Accuracy, Precision, Recall, and F1-score (F1) to compare the proposed model with other baseline models. In particular, we calculate these metrics via four parameters, including True positives (TP), False positives (FP), False negatives (FN), True negatives (TN).

- **Accuracy:** It is one of the most common metrics. The number of the correct samples is divided by the number of total samples. In general, the higher accuracy results represent better performance.

$$accuracy = \frac{TP + TN}{TP + FP + TN + FN}, \tag{14}$$

- **Precision:** It is a measure of the accuracy of the algorithm. The rate of the number of the exact positive samples is divided into the number of actually positive samples.

$$precision = \frac{TP}{TP + FP}, \tag{15}$$

- **Recall:** It is a measure of coverage. Obviously, the calculation method and result of recall rate are identical with the sensitivity.

$$recall = \frac{TP}{TP + FN}, \tag{16}$$

- **F1:** It is an index used to evaluate the accuracy of the binary classification model, considering both precision and recall rate. It can be regarded as a harmonic average of precision rate and recall rate.

$$F1 = \left(1 + \beta^2\right) * \frac{precision * recall}{\beta^2 \left(precision + recall\right)}, \tag{17}$$

Table 1. Summary of test result for KDDcup99

Algorithm	Accuracy	Precision	Recall	F1
Naive Bayes	0.4533	0.93	0.07	0.61
Logistic Regression	0.7114	0.87	0.58	0.69
Decision Tree	0.8080	0.97	0.69	0.80
Random Forest	0.7759	0.97	0.63	0.76
KNN	0.924037	0.984880	0.908875	0.945352
DNN	0.930129	0.997936	0.915116	0.954733
CNN	0.929582	0.998391	0.914018	0.954343
LSTM	0.922038	0.943180	0.965217	0.954071
CNN-LSTM	0.934726	0.998423	0.920387	0.957818
CNN-A-LSTM	**0.945126**	0.997432	0.925494	**0.960117**

where $\beta = 1$ (means that Precision is as important as Recall).

Performance Comparison. *Baseline models:* After performing these experiments, we select the following representative baseline models for comparisons with the proposed model.

- **KNN:** The main idea of KNN algorithm is to infer your category by your neighbors [26]. We use KNN to conduct the network intrusion detection experiments.
- **DNN:** DNN is a feedforward neural network with at least one hidden neural layer. For the comparison experiments, we use both ReLU and Sigmoid as the activation function and the threshold function, respectively. We set the dropout to be 0.01 and set 100 epochs.
- **CNN:** CNN is a feedforward neural network, which is usually composed of a convolution layer, a pooling layer, and a full connection layer. It can effectively utilize the two-dimensional structure of input data. In this paper, we use a CNN layer model to carry out the experiment of network intrusion detection.
- **LSTM:** LSTM is a time recursive neural network, which plays a very good role in processing and predicting data based on time series. We use the 1-layer LSTM model to conduct network intrusion detection experiments.
- **CNN-LSTM:** In CNN-LSTM and CNN-A-LSTM, we set dropout = 0.1 and also epoch = 100 to conduct the network intrusion detection experiment.

We consider Keras as a wrapper on top of TensorFlow as the software framework [4]. The experiment is performed on a personal laptop MSI GL63 8RE, which has a configuration of an Intel Core i7-8750H CPU @ 2.20 GHz, 24 GB memory and using GPU acceleration. In the binary classification experiments, we have compared the performance with a Naive Bayes, Logistic Regression,

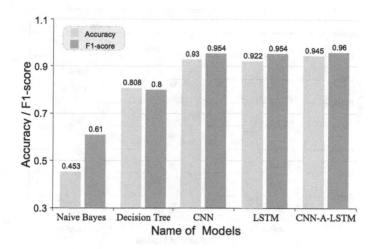

Fig. 4. Accuracy and F1-score of different models

Decision Tree, Random Forest, KNN, DNN, CNN, LSTM, CNN-LSTM, and CNN-A-LSTM. The results are as shown in Table 1.

From these experiments, we find that the CNN-A-LSTM model has the highest accuracy, compared with other algorithms. It is worth noting that although the DNN framework is very simple, it still shows its ability in dichotomy.

Moreover, we select Naive Bayes, Decision Tree, CNN, and LSTM and compare them with our CNN-A-LSTM model. Figure 4 plots accuracy and F1-score and made the comparison. We can observe that our CNN-A-LSTM model achieves the highest scores in both accuracy and F1-score, implying the superior performance of our model.

6.2 Parameter Study

We next evaluate the impacts of parameters on the performance of our CNN-A-LSTM model. We use 1 CNN layer to do the experiment. Then, we add the LSTM layer and self-attention mechanism. In 1 CNN layer, we vary different dropouts (0.01, 0.1 and 0.5) and different epochs (50, 100 and 1000). As shown in Fig. 5, when dropout is 0.01 or 0.1, the accuracy of the training set is very high. In order to reduce the number of dropouts and improve the accuracy, dropout is selected as 0.1. Figure 6 shows that when the dropout is equal to 0.1 and the dense is equal to 128, the accuracy of each model will be very high. So, we set dropout = 0.1, dense = 128 and epoch = 100 in CNN, CNN-LSTM as well as CNN-A-LSTM. Figure 7 shows the accuracy of testing, and our model is the most stable and accurate one, and it demonstrates the best performance.

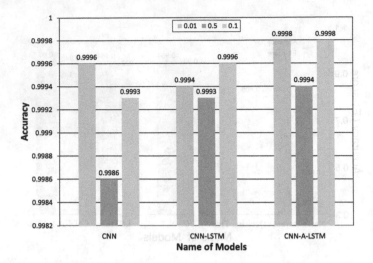

Fig. 5. Accuracy of different dropout of different models

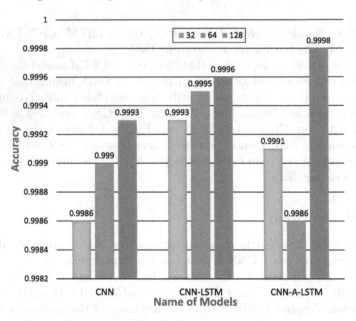

Fig. 6. Accuracy of different dense of different models

We also compare the CNN-A-LSTM model along with different models in every epoch in terms of Accuracy and Loss values. Figure 8 shows the results. The accuracy of the CNN-A-LSTM model is always higher than those of the other two models. It shows stable performance with the lowest loss. Therefore, its performance is the best among those models.

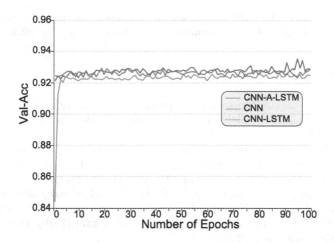

Fig. 7. Testing Val-Acc of different models

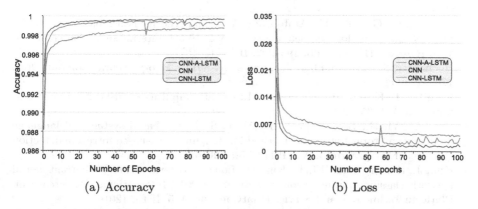

(a) Accuracy   (b) Loss

Fig. 8. Accuracy (a) and Loss (b) of different models

7   Conclusion

Cloud computing can provide users with elastic and ubiquitous computing and data storage services. However, cloud servers have also become targets for malicious attacks. The network intrusion detection is the prerequisite for taking countermeasures against malicious attacks. The recent advances in deep learning bring the chances to network intrusion detection. In this paper, we propose a new intrusion detection model namely CNN-A-LSTM by integrating CNN, LSTM, and the attention mechanism together. Experimental results show that our CNN-A-LSTM model achieves superior performance compared with other existing methods. In the future, we will explore the usage of our CNN-A-LSTM model for more complex network intrusion detection tasks, such as multinomial classification.

Acknowledgement. The work described in this paper was partially supported by Macao Science and Technology Development Fund under Grant No. 0026/2018/A1.

References

1. Alfaro, J.G., Boulahia-Cuppens, N., Cuppens, F.: Complete analysis of configuration rules to guarantee reliable network security policies. Int. J. Inf. Secur. **7**(2), 103–122 (2008)
2. Behl, A.: Emerging security challenges in cloud computing: an insight to cloud security challenges and their mitigation. In: 2011 World Congress on Information and Communication Technologies, pp. 217–222. IEEE (2011)
3. Chawla, A., Lee, B., Fallon, S., Jacob, P.: Host based intrusion detection system with combined CNN/RNN model. In: Alzate, C., et al. (eds.) ECML PKDD 2018. LNCS (LNAI), vol. 11329, pp. 149–158. Springer, Cham (2019). https://doi.org/10.1007/978-3-030-13453-2_12
4. Géron, A.: Hands-On Machine Learning with Scikit-Learn, Keras, and TensorFlow: Concepts, Tools, and Techniques to Build Intelligent Systems. O'Reilly Media (2019)
5. Ghaffari, F., Gharaee, H., Arabsorkhi, A.: Cloud security issues based on people, process and technology model: a survey. In: 2019 5th International Conference on Web Research (ICWR), pp. 196–202. IEEE (2019)
6. Hochreiter, S., Schmidhuber, J.: Long short-term memory. Neural Comput. **9**(8), 1735–1780 (1997)
7. Khalil, I.M., Khreishah, A., Azeem, M.: Cloud computing security: a survey. Computers **3**(1), 1–35 (2014)
8. Kim, G., Yi, H., Lee, J., Paek, Y., Yoon, S.: LSTM-based system-call language modeling and robust ensemble method for designing host-based intrusion detection systems. arXiv preprint arXiv:1611.01726 (2016)
9. Kim, J., Kim, J., Thu, H.L.T., Kim, H.: Long short term memory recurrent neural network classifier for intrusion detection. In: 2016 International Conference on Platform Technology and Service (PlatCon), pp. 1–5. IEEE (2016)
10. Kimani, K., Oduol, V., Langat, K.: Cyber security challenges for IOT-based smart grid networks. Int. J. Crit. Infrastruct. Prot. **25**, 36–49 (2019)
11. Kumar, V., Sangwan, O.P.: Signature based intrusion detection system using snort. Int. J. Comput. Appl. Technol. Inf. Technol. **1**(3), 35–41 (2012)
12. Modi, C.N., Patel, D.R., Patel, A., Rajarajan, M.: Integrating signature apriori based network intrusion detection system (NIDS) in cloud computing. Procedia Technol. **6**, 905–912 (2012)
13. Nadeem, M., Marshall, O., Singh, S., Fang, X., Yuan, X.: Semi-supervised deep neural network for network intrusion detection (2016)
14. Peng, K., Leung, V., Zheng, L., Wang, S., Huang, C., Lin, T.: Intrusion detection system based on decision tree over big data in fog environment. Wireless Commun. Mobile Comput. **2018**, Article ID 4680867, 10 (2018)
15. Rafique, W., Qi, L., Yaqoob, I., Imran, M., Rasool, R.U., Dou, W.: Complementing IoT services through software defined networking and edge computing: a comprehensive survey. IEEE Commun. Surv. Tutorials **22**, 1761–1804 (2020)
16. Roschke, S., Cheng, F., Meinel, C.: Intrusion detection in the cloud. In: 2009 Eighth IEEE International Conference on Dependable, Autonomic and Secure Computing, pp. 729–734. IEEE (2009)

17. Roy, S.S., Mallik, A., Gulati, R., Obaidat, M.S., Krishna, P.V.: A deep learning based artificial neural network approach for intrusion detection. In: Giri, D., Mohapatra, R.N., Begehr, H., Obaidat, M.S. (eds.) ICMC 2017. CCIS, vol. 655, pp. 44–53. Springer, Singapore (2017). https://doi.org/10.1007/978-981-10-4642-1_5

18. Saenko, I., Kotenko, I.: Administrating role-based access control by genetic algorithms. In: Proceedings of the Genetic and Evolutionary Computation Conference Companion, pp. 1463–1470. Association for Computing Machinery (2017). https://doi.org/10.1145/3067695.3082509

19. Singh, A., Chatterjee, K.: Cloud security issues and challenges: a survey. J. Network Comput. Appl. **79**, 88–115 (2017)

20. Singh, S., Jeong, Y.S., Park, J.H.: A survey on cloud computing security: issues, threats, and solutions. J. Network Comput. Appl. **75**, 200–222 (2016)

21. Sood, A.K., Enbody, R.J.: Targeted cyberattacks: a superset of advanced persistent threats. IEEE Secur. Priv. **11**(1), 54–61 (2012)

22. Staudemeyer, R.C.: Applying long short-term memory recurrent neural networks to intrusion detection. South Afr. Comput. J. **56**(1), 136–154 (2015)

23. Sun, Y., Zhang, J., Xiong, Y., Zhu, G.: Data security and privacy in cloud computing. Int. J. Distrib. Sens. Netw **10**(7), 190903 (2014)

24. Takabi, H., Joshi, J.B., Ahn, G.J.: Security and privacy challenges in cloud computing environments. IEEE Secur. Priv. **8**(6), 24–31 (2010)

25. Tavallaee, M., Bagheri, E., Lu, W., Ghorbani, A.A.: A detailed analysis of the KDD cup 99 data set. In: 2009 IEEE Symposium on Computational Intelligence for Security and Defense Applications, pp. 1–6. IEEE (2009)

26. Vinayakumar, R., Soman, K., Poornachandran, P.: Applying convolutional neural network for network intrusion detection. In: 2017 International Conference on Advances in Computing, Communications and Informatics (ICACCI), pp. 1222–1228. IEEE (2017)

27. Wang, W., Du, X., Shan, D., Qin, R., Wang, N.: Cloud intrusion detection method based on stacked contractive auto-encoder and support vector machine. IEEE Trans. Cloud Comput. 1–1 (2020). https://doi.org/10.1109/TCC.2020.3001017

28. Wang, W., et al.: HAST-IDS: learning hierarchical spatial-temporal features using deep neural networks to improve intrusion detection. IEEE Access **6**, 1792–1806 (2017)

29. Xiao, Y., Xing, C., Zhang, T., Zhao, Z.: An intrusion detection model based on feature reduction and convolutional neural networks. IEEE Access **7**, 42210–42219 (2019)

30. Yang, R., Qu, D., Gao, Y., Qian, Y., Tang, Y.: nLSALog: an anomaly detection framework for log sequence in security management. IEEE Access **7**, 181152–181164 (2019). https://doi.org/10.1109/ACCESS.2019.2953981

31. Yin, C., Zhu, Y., Fei, J., He, X.: A deep learning approach for intrusion detection using recurrent neural networks. IEEE Access **5**, 21954–21961 (2017)

32. Zheng, W.F.: Intrusion detection based on convolutional neural network. In: 2020 International Conference on Computer Engineering and Application (ICCEA), pp. 273–277. IEEE (2020)

A Fraud Detection Approach Based on Combined Feature Weighting

Xiaoqian Liu[1,3,4(✉)], Chenfei Yu[1], Bin Xia[2], Haiyan Gu[1], and Zhenli Wang[1]

[1] Department of Computer Information and Cyber Security, Jiangsu Police Institute, Nanjing 210031, China
liuxiaoqian@jspi.edu.cn, 1578898262@qq.com, {guhaiyan,wangzhenli}@jspi.cn
[2] Jiangsu Key Laboratory of Big Data Security and Intelligent Processing, Nanjing University of Posts and Telecommunications, Nanjing 210023, China
bxia@njupt.edu.cn
[3] Jiangsu Electronic Data Forensics and Analysis Engineering Research Center, Nanjing, China
[4] Jiangsu Provincial Public Security Department Key Laboratory of Digital Forensics, Nanjing, China

Abstract. Data mining technology has yielded fruitful results in the area of crime discovery and intelligent decision making. Credit card is one of the most popular payment methods, providing great convenience and efficiency. However, due to the vulnerabilities of credit card transactions, criminals are able to commit fraud to infringe on the interests of the state and citizens. How to discover potential fraudsters while guaranteeing high efficiency becomes an extremely valuable problem to solve. In this work, we talk about the advantages and disadvantages of different models to detect credit card fraud. We first introduce the data preprocessing measures for handling imbalanced fraud detection dataset. Then we compare related models to implement fraudster recognition. We also propose a feature selection approach based on combined feature weights. Some future research interests are also envisioned.

Keywords: Fraud detection · Imbalanced dataset · Fisher score · Feature weighting

1 Introduction

With the prosperity of the Internet technology, the number of netizens is rapidly increasing. According to the 45th statistical report on Internet development in China issued by China Internet Network Information Center, by March 2020, the number of Internet users in China has reached 904 million. In the meantime, the online life is significantly facilitated by credit card payment or other third party payment methods. According to the statistical data in the blue book on the development of China's bank card industry (2019), the number of credit card issuers has increased from 186 million to 970 million, and the total amount of credit card transactions has increased from 3.5 trillion yuan to 38.2 trillion yuan,

L. Qi et al. (Eds.): CloudComp 2020, LNICST 363, pp. 74–82, 2021.
https://doi.org/10.1007/978-3-030-69992-5_6

nearly 10 times more. Credit card payment has become one of the most popular payment methods.

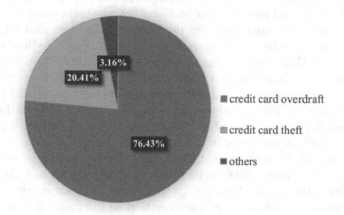

Fig. 1. The detailed proportion of credit card fraud cases

However, credit card fraud frequently happens and brings severe challenges to credit card management and seriously damages the interests of banks [1]. According to the Special report (2016 to 2018) on judicial big data of financial fraud issued by China judicial big data research institute, the number of credit card fraud is over 6 thousand. In these cases, credit card overdraft accounts for the largest proportion. Credit theft is also a major financial fraud type. More details are illustrated in Fig. 1. In comparison, according to the statistics from

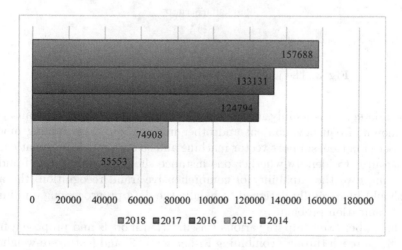

Fig. 2. The credit card fraud reports in the US from 2014 to 2018

the Shift Credit Card Processing company[1], the number of credit card fraud reported has increased from 55 thousand to more than 157 thousand as shown in Fig. 2. The US leads as the most credit fraud prone country with over 9.36 billion dollar losses in 2018. Most cases happen in the way of "card-not-present". Point-of-sale fraud and identity theft are another two main causes.

Clearly, there is a game between professional fraudsters and financial risk management party. The risk management department of Credit Card Center has summarized three main characteristics of current credit card frauds, i.e., concealment, professionalism and large-scale. Fraudsters often use professional Internet knowledge to steal card information of normal users and counterfeit individual identities. Besides, through packaging personal information, forging Internet behavior and other ways to improve personal qualifications, malicious users cheat to obtain credit cards and implement theft.

As demonstrated above, it is difficult but valuable to design accurate and efficient fraud detection methods, therefore to effectively protect the profits of card users and the banks. Intelligent credit card fraud detection is the joint area of financial risk management, information security and data mining etc., as illustrated in Fig. 3. Situations such as improper credit review and individual information breaches usually cause financial fraud crimes. To counter these conditions, data mining models are often applied to implement automatic fraud pattern discovery.

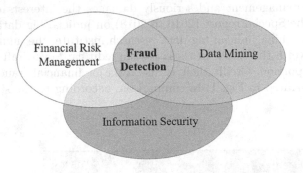

Fig. 3. The joint area of intelligent fraud detection

Fraud detection is mainly implemented based on the analysis of transaction time, amount, frequency, content and other information. Data mining models, such as decision tree, support vector machine and so on, provide automatic modeling measures to identify whether one instance should be labeled as fraud. In order to improve the capability of comprehensive fraud recognition, the algorithm should be carefully designed to handle the data preprocessing and imbalanced classification problems.

In this paper, we compare various classification models and propose a fraud detection approach through combining Fisher score [2] and feature re-weighting,

---

[1] https://shiftprocessing.com/credit-card-fraud-statistics/.

which improves the performance of the above mentioned classification models. Based on the experimental results, we demonstrate that the proposed feature handling approach provides satisfying accuracy and efficiency.

2   Fraud Detection Architecture and Implementing Approaches

Existing fraud discovery approaches take advantage of the advanced data mining models to solve imbalanced classification problems. In fraud detection, the target population is often very small. Misclassifying a target instance costs a lot. Therefore, the imbalanced data should be carefully preprocessed before being fed to the models. In Sect. 2.1 and Sect. 2.2, we discuss the architecture of the fraud detection models and compare the merits and demerits of each implementing approach.

2.1   Architecture

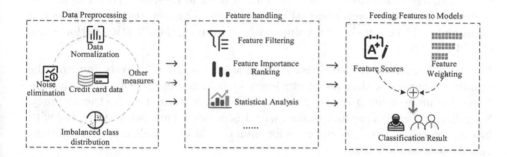

Fig. 4. The architecture of fraud detection models

Figure 4 illustrates an overview of the fraud detection architecture. In the following, we introduce each part of the architecture in detail.

Data Preprocessing. Data normalization and noise elimination are frequently applied for data preprocessing. While data imbalance is the most distinctive feature in financial fraud detection. It also widely exists in the fields of medical treatment, industry and advertising services [3]. In these areas, the true target label, such as true fraud record, severely underrepresents the other. Sampling methods, such as random oversampling and undersampling et al., attempt to balance the representative proportions of labels in the datasets [4]. In contrast, cost-sensitive learning methods consider the costs associated with misclassifying instances, therefore to improve the importance of the minority label [5,6].

Besides the sampling methods, Guo and Viktor propose the DataBoost-IM approach to adaptively generate synthetic instances to enrich the original dataset

[7]. Deep models are also talked about to learn more discriminative deep feature embeddings to maintain both inter-cluster and inter-class margins in imbalanced classification [8].

Feature Handling. In the classification task, high dimension usually infringes on both accuracy and efficiency. Dimension reduction methods are often applied to filter out the unimportant features and select the representative ones. Chandrashekar and Sahin give a comprehensive survey on feature selection focusing on Filter, Wrapper and Embedded methods [9]. Common dimension reduction methods include principal component analysis, multidimensional scaling, linear discriminant analysis, etc. [10]. In heuristic models such as decision tree, the importance of each feature is evaluated with a score, such as information gain, gini index etc. Jiang et al., propose a deep feature weighting (DFW) approach through deeply computing feature weighted frequencies from training data for the Naïve Bayes classifier [11]. In contrast, Zhang et al., propose two adaptive feature weighting approaches for Naïve Bayes text classifiers to improve model simplicity and reduce execution time [12].

In the feature handling step, crucial features are highly scored and selected. While under the premise of data privacy and security being paid more and more attention, researchers also have done a lot of work to preserve privacy in feature selection. To guarantee individual privacy, carefully generated randomness can be introduced to cover the true values without injuring classification performance [13,14].

Feeding Features to Models. Feature selection can effectively improve the training accuracy with a bit of efficiency loss. In our approach, we use a combined feature weighting strategy to prioritize features and improve the accuracy. Specifically, features are first ranked with Fisher score and then re-weighted with evaluation criteria such as information gain etc. More details about the process can be seen in Sect. 2.2.

2.2   Implementing Approaches

We compare the advantages and disadvantages of different classification models to solve the fraud detection problem in Table 1, where variables n, d, k denote the number of instances, the number of features and the number of single-trees, respectively. Both single and ensemble tree models are listed, including traditional decision tree, random forest, GBDT and XGBoost. Logistic regression and support vector machine are also compared for their simplicity and robustness, respectively.

The process of fraud detection is listed in four steps as below.

1. **Data imbalance handling**
   Perform data normalization and handle the imbalance problem through adaptively randomly sampling (cost-sensitive factor can also be introduced).
2. **Primary competitor training**
   Feed the processed data to each classification competitor derived in Step 1. and train. Calculate the AUC values and training time.

Table 1. The comparison of classification algorithms to implement fraud detection

Algorithms	Advantages	Disadvantages	Time complexity	Applicable scenarios
Decision Tree	Strong interpretability	Easy to over-fit and low accuracy	$O(n*\log(n)*d)$	Large datasets
Random Forest	Balance errors with ensemble	Sensitive to noise	$O(n*\log(n)*d*k)$	Large datasets
GBDT	Higher accuracy	Difficult to parallel for dependent learners	$O(n*\log(n)*d*k)$	Large low-dimensional datasets
Logistic Regression	Small computation and low storage occupancy	Poor performance for non-linear problems	$O(n*d)$	Large low-dimensional datasets
Support Vector Machine	Better robustness	Difficult to handle multi-classification	$O(n*n*d)$	Small datasets
XGBoost	Simple model	Difficult to tune parameters	$O(n*\log(n)*d*k)$	Large low-dimensional datasets

3. **Fisher competitor training**
   Select features based on Fisher score or other criteria. Train each classification competitor with the features selected and calculate the AUC values and record training time.
4. **Re-weighted competitor training**
   Weight features with a combined metric with both Fisher score and information gain etc., and train each classification competitor. Calculate the AUC values and record training time.

3 Combined Feature Weighting Approach and Evaluation Results

As mentioned above, features are evaluated with a combined metric with both Fisher score and information gain in the proposed strategy. Notice that the combined feature weighting step trades a little bit of efficiency for classification accuracy. In Sect. 3.1, we give the formal description of the combined feature weighting approach. We also give the accuracy and efficiency evaluation in Sect. 3.2.

3.1 A Feature Weighting Approach

Fisher score selects the optimal feature by calculating the inter class and intra class dispersion, which is simple and effective. The calculation of the Fisher score of feature j is shown in Eq. (1). Class labels are chosen from the set $\{0, 1, \ldots, c\}$. n_l denotes the number of instances taken label l. Specifically, let μ_l^j and σ_l^j be the mean and standard deviation of label l, corresponding to the j-th feature.

Let μ^j and σ^j denote the mean and standard deviation of the whole data set corresponding to the j-th feature [2].

$$F\left(\mathbf{x}^j\right) = \frac{\sum_{l=0}^{c} n_l \left(\mu_l^j - \mu^j\right)^2}{\left(\sigma^j\right)^2} \quad where$$

$$\left(\sigma^j\right)^2 = \sum_{l=1}^{c} n_l \left(\sigma_l^j\right)^2 \tag{1}$$

Information gain quantifies the effectiveness of each feature for contributing the decrease of class distribution chaos [15]. The larger the information gain is, the more important the feature is. It is calculated with entropy and conditional entropy. Given the j-th feature with i possible values, the calculation of entropy, conditional entropy and information gain with the j-th feature are shown in Eq. (2), (3) and (4) respectively.

$$H_C(D) = -\sum_{l=0}^{c} \frac{n_l}{n} \log \frac{n_l}{n} \tag{2}$$

$$H_{C|j}(D) = \sum \frac{n_i}{n} H_C\left(D_i\right) \tag{3}$$

$$InfoGain(j, D) = H_C(D) - H_{C|j}(D) \tag{4}$$

Combining Fisher score feature selection and information gain, we have the combined ranking score of the j-th feature shown in Eq. (5).

$$score_j = F\left(\mathbf{x}^j\right) * InfoGain(j, D) \tag{5}$$

3.2 Accuracy and Efficiency Evaluation

In the imbalanced classification problem of fraud detection, AUC is more suitable than classification accuracy [4]. In this paper, we use the open credit card fraud detection dataset provided by the Kaggle platform[2]. There are 284807 instances with 29 features in the dataset and the percentage of fraudulent users and normal users was 0.17% and 99.83% respectively. Obviously, the dataset is highly imbalanced. The dataset has been collected and analyzed during a research collaboration of Worldline and the Machine Learning Group (http://mlg.ulb.ac.be) of ULB (Université Libre de Bruxelles) on big data mining and fraud detection.

In the experiments, we compare the impacts of the combined feature weighting strategy with the classification accuracy (AUC used) and training time. Each experiment has been repeated for 200 times to record the means. The experimental results with and without combined feature weighting are shown in Table 2 and Table 3. Notice that the competitor without combined feature weighting has

---

[2] http://www.kaggle.com/mlg-ulb/creditcardfraud.

just applied feature selection with Fisher score, as proposed by Dong et al., in [16]. In the experiments, information gain is used to further weight the features.

Table 2. AUC comparison with (without) feature weighting

Algorithms	Mean of AUC without feature weighting	Mean of AUC with feature weighting
Decision Tree	0.9038	0.9056
Random Forest	0.9717	0.9724
GBDT	0.9699	0.9701
Logistic Regression	0.9736	0.975
Support Vector Machine	0.9786	0.9796
XGBoost	0.968	0.9687

Table 3. Training time comparison with (without) feature weighting

Algorithms	Mean of training time without feature weighting(s)	Mean of training time with feature weighting(s)
Decision Tree	0.005	0.0059
Random Forest	0.1545	0.1564
GBDT	0.14	0.1474
Logistic Regression	0.0064	0.0078
Support Vector Machine	0.0038	0.004
XGBoost	0.0612	0.0663

Based on the experimental results shown in the above tables, combining Fisher score and other feature weighting metrics, such as information gain, has improved the classification performance of most compared models with a small efficiency cost.

4   Conclusions

Fraud detection is an important classification task. Fisher score can effectively shorten the training time of the classifier. To further improve the classification performance, we introduce the combined feature weighting strategy. The feature weighting approach performs especially well in logistic regression and support vector machine. In our future work, we will consider the privacy preservation of the feature selection process while balancing privacy and accuracy.

Acknowledgement. This work is supported in part by the Natural Science Foundation of the Jiangsu Higher Education Institutions of China under Grant No. 19KJB510022, the Research Start-up Funds for the Introduction of High-level Talents at Jiangsu Police Institute under Grant No. JSPIGKZ, the National Natural Science Foundation of China under Grant No. 61802205, the Research Project of Higher Education Reform in Jiangsu Province under Grant No. 2019JSJG595, the 13th Five-Year Plan for Jiangsu Education Science under grant No. D/2020/01/22. We also express our thanks to the Jiangsu Electronic Data Forensics and Analysis Engineering Research Center and Jiangsu Provincial Public Security Department Key Laboratory of Digital Forensics.

References

1. Caneppele, S., Aebi, M.F.: Crime drop or police recording flop? On the relationship between the decrease of offline crime and the increase of online and hybrid crimes. Policing J. Policy Pract. **13**(1), 6–79 (2019)
2. Gu, Q., Li, Z., Han, J.: Generalized fisher score for feature selection. arXiv preprint arXiv:1202.3725 (2012)
3. Haixiang, G., Yijing, L., Shang, J., Mingyun, G., Yuanyue, H., Bing, G.: Learning from class-imbalanced data: review of methods and applications. Expert Syst. Appl. **73**, 220–239 (2017)
4. He, H., Garcia, E.A.: Learning from imbalanced data. IEEE Trans. Knowl. Data Eng. **21**(9), 1263–1284 (2009)
5. Khan, S.H., Hayat, M., Bennamoun, M., Sohel, F.A., Togneri, R.: Cost-sensitive learning of deep feature representations from imbalanced data. IEEE Trans. Neural Netw. Learn. Syst. **29**(8), 3573–3587 (2017)
6. Sun, Y., Kamel, M.S., Wong, A.K., Wang, Y.: Cost-sensitive boosting for classification of imbalanced data. Pattern Recogn. **40**(12), 3358–3378 (2007)
7. Guo, H., Viktor, H.L.: Learning from imbalanced data sets with boosting and data generation: the DataBoost-IM approach. ACM SIGKDD Explor. Newslett. **6**(1), 30–39 (2004)
8. Huang, C., Li, Y., Loy, C.C., Tang, X.: Learning deep representation for imbalanced classification. In: Proceedings of the IEEE Conference on Computer Vision and Pattern Recognition, pp. 5375–5384 (2016)
9. Chandrashekar, G., Sahin, F.: A survey on feature selection methods. Comput. Electr. Eng. **40**(1), 16–28 (2014)
10. Zhang, T., Yang, B.: Big data dimension reduction using PCA. In: 2016 IEEE International Conference on Smart Cloud (SmartCloud), pp. 152–157. IEEE (2016)
11. Jiang, L., Li, C., Wang, S., Zhang, L.: Deep feature weighting for naive Bayes and its application to text classification. Eng. Appl. Artif. Intell. **52**, 26–39 (2016)
12. Zhang, L., Jiang, L., Li, C., Kong, G.: Two feature weighting approaches for naive Bayes text classifiers. Knowl.-Based Syst. **100**, 137–144 (2016)
13. Anandan, B., Clifton, C.: Differentially private feature selection for data mining. In: Proceedings of the Fourth ACM International Workshop on Security and Privacy Analytics, pp. 43–53 (2018)
14. Yang, J., Li, Y.: Differentially private feature selection. In: 2014 International Joint Conference on Neural Networks (IJCNN), pp. 4182–4189. IEEE (2014)
15. Quinlan, J.R.: Induction of decision trees. Mach. Learn. **1**(1), 81–106 (1986)
16. Dong, Y., Liu, X., Li, B.: Click fraud detection method based on user behavior feature selection. Comput. Sci. (10), 27 (2016)

Data Privacy Protection of Industrial Blockchain

Huaqiu Long[1(✉)] iD, Jun Hou[2], Qianmu Li[3], Na Ma[3], Jian Jiang[4], Lianyong Qi[5],
Xiaolong Xu[6], and Xuyun Zhang[7]

[1] Intelligent Manufacturing Department, Wuyi University, Jiangmen 529020, China
502080285@qq.com
[2] Nanjing Institute of Industry Technology, Nanjing 210023, China
[3] School of Cyber Science and Engineering, Nanjing University of Science and Technology,
Nanjing 210094, China
[4] Jiangsu Zhongtian Internet Technology Co., Ltd., Nantong 226009, China
[5] School of Information Science and Engineering, Qufu Normal University,
Jining 272000, China
[6] Nanjing University of Information Science and Technology, Nanjing 210023, China
[7] Department of Computing, Macquarie University, Sydney, Australia

Abstract. This paper studies the data privacy protection of industrial block chain. Aiming at the privacy leakage problem of industrial blockchain, combining symmetric encryption and homomorphic encryption, The data privacy protection method is proposed to ensure the confidentiality and privacy of industrial block chain and improve the privacy security of industrial enterprises. This paper designs common basic chain code, security service chain code and privacy protection chain code in the chain code layer, USES AES algorithm to encrypt sensitive information of industrial enterprises, and USES Paillier algorithm to encrypt maintenance cost. The chain code of privacy protection can be used for security access and fault event audit to guarantee the privacy security of industrial enterprises. In addition, in order to achieve the unity of call chain code, the call chain code is encapsulated to provide support for fast and highly concurrent upload data and access data. Finally, the existing sensitive and private data storage methods of industrial block chain are analyzed, and the experimental comparison with the method in this paper proves the effectiveness of this method.

Keywords: Blockchain · Data privacy protection · Fault diagnosis

1 Introduction

Blockchain technology is a distributed, non-tamper-proof sharing technology that can realize the common storage of data and achieve decentralization in a distributed environment without mutual trust [1]. It is an emerging solution to improve the traditional centralized architecture. In the blockchain platform of remote industrial fault diagnosis, users' fault logs and diagnostic data are stored in clear text in LevelDB or CouchDB nodes [2–6]. Users can directly obtain all the information of fault events, which lacks privacy and confidentiality guarantee and is easy to leak the privacy of enterprise users.

L. Qi et al. (Eds.): CloudComp 2020, LNICST 363, pp. 83–99, 2021.
https://doi.org/10.1007/978-3-030-69992-5_7

In order to avoid the leakage of industrial enterprise privacy caused by the public storage of data, this paper adopts the fusion protection mode of AES algorithm and Paillier algorithm to design a data privacy protection scheme. The schema is shown in Fig. 1.

(1) **Client-side privacy protection middleware** [7–9]. The user calls the specified chain code function by executing the command on the client side, and interacts with the ledger for data. Each call requires the operation-related parameters to be written into the complex command. Therefore, in order to reduce the performance degradation caused by complex chain code invocation and satisfy fast and highly concurrent client requests, the process of chain code invocation is encapsulated in the client privacy protection middleware based on Node.js to provide a unified interface for the connection between client applications and chain code. The client-side privacy protection middleware is divided into fault event submission SDK and fault event query SDK. The fault event submission SDK is responsible for submitting the data of the client, uploading the request, and executing the key-value uploading operation. The FAULT event query SDK is responsible for submitting the data query request of the client and performing the fault event history query or fault event status query operation.

(2) **Chain code** [10–12]. In order to satisfy the security storage of different types of fault logs and diagnostic data, this paper combines symmetric encryption algorithm and homomorphic encryption algorithm, designs common security service chain code and privacy protection chain code based on Golang language, and provides confidentiality guarantee for uploading, querying and auditing of fault logs and diagnostic data. Among them, the security service chain code provides symmetric encryption interface and homomorphic encryption interface, which is designed based on AES algorithm, and homomorphic encryption interface is designed based on Paillier cipher system, supporting key generation, data encryption and decryption, data homomorphic operation and other functions. The chain code of privacy protection needs to invoke the interface in the chain code of security service to carry out different levels of privacy protection on the data request submitted by the client, so as to protect the writing, reading and auditing of data privacy protection and improve the privacy security of industrial enterprises in the distributed storage environment. In order to reduce the performance degradation caused by chain code execution, the basic chain code is designed to provide common data storage and query, as well as the common data processing function of the chain code layer.

(3) **Books** [13]. In this scheme, CouchDB is used as the data repository to store the fault log and diagnosis data submitted by the user and the mixed key information of the user.

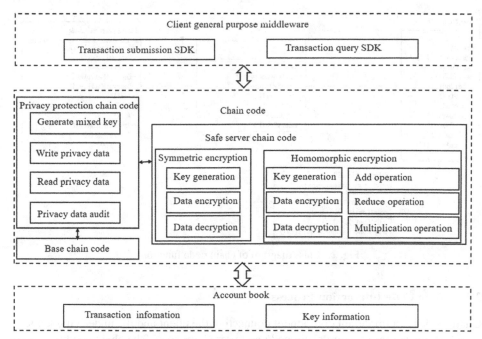

Fig. 1. The architecture of block chain data privacy protection scheme based on fusion protection

2 Design of Chain Code with Privacy Protection Function

The chain code function class diagram of block chain data privacy protection scheme is shown in Fig. 2. BaseChaincode relies on the shim API at the bottom of the blockchain, providing basic data read-write chain code functions, such as read(), Write(), and general data processing interfaces, such as getJSON(), getCurrnentUser(), etc. The security service chain code relies on the Golang native API, which supports AES symmetric encryption and Paillier homomorphic encryption, provides key generation, data encryption and decrypting, and specific mathematical operation interfaces, such as GeneratePaillierKey(), EncryptPaillier(), EncryptAES(), Add(), etc. The privacy protection chain code inherits the basic chain code and extends the chain code function to meet the specific data processing requirements. In addition, the privacy chain code relies on the security service chain code to invoke the corresponding interface for specific data encryption, decryption, and auditing functions, including genHK(), writeByEncrypt(), readByDecrypt(), writePvt(), readPvt(), Compute(), and auditPvt().

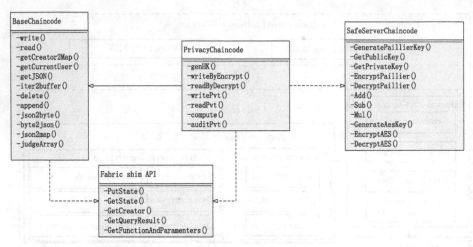

Fig. 2. Class diagram of chain code function.

2.1 Chain Code Interaction Process

Chain code is an important component connecting the client and the underlying ledger, which is divided into system chain code and user chain code. The chain code involved in this paper is user chain code. System chain code is responsible for logical processing of fault events, system configuration, etc., and is solidified in the system; The user chain code is written by the user, responsible for executing the custom processing logic, running in the Docker container, connecting with Peer nodes through gRPC, and communicating with each other through sending ChaincodeMessage messages. The interactive process is shown in Fig. 3, and the specific steps are as follows:

(1) After the gRPC connection is created, the user chain code calls the shim.Start() method, sends a ChaincodeMessage_REGISTER to the Peer node for registration, and waits to receive the response from the Peer node, at which time the state is created;

(2) After the Peer node receives the ChaincodeMessage_REGISTER, it is registered in the local Handler structure and returns the ChaincodeMessage_REGISTERED to the chain code. At this time, the state of the Peer node is ESTABLISHED. After the chain code receives the ChaincodeMessage_REGISTERED, the update state is established and the chain code registration is completed.

(3) Peer node sends ChaincodeMessage_READY to the chain code, and the update status is Ready. The chain code is also updated to Ready after receiving ChaincodeMessage_READY.

(4) Peer node sends ChaincodeMessage_INIT message to chain code and initializes the chain code.

(5) After receiving the ChaincodeMessage_INIT message, the chain code container calls Init() method to initialize, and returns the ChaincodeMessage_COMPLETED message to the Peer node after success. The chain code initialization is complete, and the chain code state is callable at this time.

(6)   Peer node sends ChaincodeMessage_TRANSACTION message to chain code and executes chain code call.

(7)   After receiving the ChaincodeMessage_TRANSACTION message, the chain code calls the Invoke() method, executes the specific chain code function logic, and sends the database operation message to the Peer node.

(8)   After receiving the database operation message, the Peer node executes the corresponding data operation and returns the ChaincodeMessage_RESPONSE message to the chain code.

(9)   Send ChaincodeMessage_COMPLETE to Peer node after the chain code call is completed.

(10) During the above message interaction, Peer nodes and chain codes regularly send ChaincodeMessage_KEEPALIVE messages to each other to ensure that they are online.

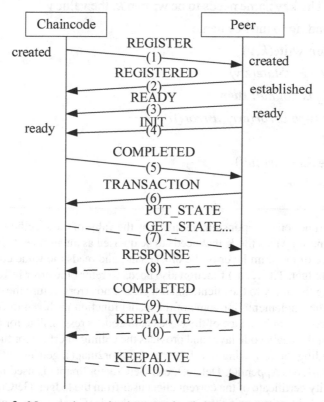

Fig. 3. Message interaction between the chain code and the Peer node.

The middle layer of chain code and Peer node interaction is called Shim layer. The Shim layer provides a series of Shim apis to interact with the underlying ledger for developers to write user chain codes. In this paper, the Shim API on the basis of the relevant chain code design.

2.2 Basic Chain Code

The write() function is responsible for storing individual key-value data in the ledger. This function takes the key name K and the corresponding value V as arguments, calls the PutState() interface of the Shim layer, adds a pair of key values to the ledger, or updates the value of the specified key name. The written key is appended to Writes first, and as soon as the billing node validates, the key is written to the ledger. In the process of writing data, errors may occur, resulting in the failure of data writing, so the resulting errors need to be handled (all chain code functions in this article need to be monitored when performing write/read data operations, this step is omitted in the related chain code function algorithm later, but it is essential in the actual operation). The implementation logic of the write() function is shown in Algorithm 1.

Algorithm 1 write() function

Input: The key name needs to be written k, the value v corresponding to the key name

1: **function** write(k, v)

2: err_{PS} ← *PutState(k,v)*

3: **if** err_{PS} *is not null* **then**

4:      **reture** *Error(err_{PS}.Error())*

5: **end if**

6: **reture** *Success(null)*

7: **end funtion**

The read() function is responsible for querying the value of the specified key from the ledger. This function takes the K that needs to be queried as an argument, calls the GetState() interface of the shim layer of the blockchain, and reads the value corresponding to K from the ledger. The read() function also needs to return the error information that occurred during the query to the client, and if there are no errors, return the query results to the client. The implementation logic of the read() function is shown in Algorithm 2.

The data processing interface of the basic chain code is responsible for the data processing logic of the chain code layer and provides the calling interface for the chain code function, including the following interfaces: getCreator2map(), getCurrentUser(), getJSON(), Iter2Buffer(), Append(), Delete(), etc. GetCreator2map() is used to obtain and parse the identity certificate of the current client user from the ledger. GetCreator2map() extracts the user's identity certificate from signatureheader.Creator from signedProposal by calling the fault event submitter interface at the bottom of the blockchain GetCreator(), parses the properties of the certificate, and returns. CurrentUser() is used to obtain the current client user ID from the ledger identity certificate (in this case, the user ID is the unique ID that the user registers in the blockchain, which is the user name). Other data processing interface functions in the basic chain code are shown in Table 1.

Algorithm2 read() function

Input: The key name needs to be read k

Output: look up the read value $kBytes$

1: **function** read(k)

2: $kBytes, err_{GS} \leftarrow GetState(k)$

3: **if** err_{GS} *is not null* **then**

4:      **reture** $Error(err_{GS}.Error())$

5: **end if**

6: **reture** $Success(kBytes)$

7: **end funtion**

Table 1. Partial data processing interface in basic chain code.

Interface	Functional description
getJSON	The JSON string data is read from the account book, converted into a JSON object, and called by the chain code function
iter2buffer	Cache the iterator data in the buffer
append()	Append elements to an array
delete()	Deletes elements from an array
json2byte()	JSON objects are converted into bytes
byte2json()	The byte is converted to a JSON object
json2map()	JSON objects are converted to maps
judgeArray()	Determine whether the elements in the array exist

(1) Safe Server Chain Code

SafeServerChaincode supports AES symmetric encryption algorithm and Paillier cryptography system, combined with Golang native interface, provides key generation, data encryption, data decryption, data homomorphism operation and other interfaces. Among them, symmetric encryption provides key generation, data encryption, data decryption and other interfaces, and the functional description of each interface is shown in Table 2. Homomorphic encryption provides functions such as key generation, key acquisition, data encryption, data decryption, data addition operation, subtraction operation and multiplication operation. The functional description of each interface is shown in Table 3.

(2) Privacy Chain Code

PrivacyChaincode inherits the basic chain code, relies on Shim API and security service chain code, and provides the storage and query functions of data using different encryption types and fusion protection.

Table 2. Symmetric encryption interface

Interface	Functional description
GenerateAESKey()	Generation of AES session key by salting mechanism
EncryptAES()	Use AES to encrypt the plaintext
DecryptAES()	Use AES to decrypt the ciphertext

Table 3. Homomorphic encryption interface

Interface	Functional description
GeneratePaillierKey()	Generate the Paillier key
GetPublicKey()	Get public key
GetPrivateKey()	Get private key
EncryptPaillier()	Data encryption
DecryptPaillier()	Data decryption
Add()	Ciphertext addition
Sub()	Ciphertext subtraction
Mul()	Ciphertext multiplication

In order to ensure the privacy security in the fault log and diagnosis data submitted by industrial enterprises, each registered user in the scheme in this paper holds mixed key information and encrypts the fault log and diagnosis data submitted by users. Hybrid key includes three parts: PubKey Paillier the public key and secret key PriKey Paillier, AES initial key AesKey PubKey responsible for encrypt plaintext data, based on Paillier encryption logic PriKey responsible for unlock data, based on Paillier decryption logic AesKey is responsible for providing initial key value of AES encryption algorithm, when the initial key when the need for AES encryption salt processing, can guarantee the real key to encrypt and decrypt every time different. The structure of mixed key data based on Golang is as follows:

```
type HybridKey struct {

    PriKey      string  `json:"prikey"`

    PubKey      string  `json:"pubkey"`

    AesKey      string  `json:"aeskey"` }
```

The writePvt() function is responsible for writing fault logs and diagnostic data to the ledger based on fusion protection. This function inherits the data storage logic of the write() function and can protect the privacy of data with industrial enterprise privacy.

First, the parameters received are converted into the specified data privacy protection structure (such as the structure of the privacy order data in Sect. 5 of this article). The data privacy protection structure contains four types of attributes: privacy attribute priAttr, non-privacy attribute pubAttr, maintenance cost money, and failure event type TXType. Privacy attribute refers to the sensitive data in the failure event, such as mobile phone number; Non-private attributes refer to data that can be exposed to others, such as time of failure events; Maintenance cost refers to the expenditure or income of completing a failure event; Failure event types are used to count a certain type of failure event. The writePvt() function supports different encryption methods for different attributes: AES encryption privacy attributes, Paillier encryption maintenance costs. The implementation logic of writePvt() function is shown in Algorithm 3, and the general process is as follows:

Algorithm 3 writePvt() function

Input : The key name needs to be written *key*, the relevant parameters needs to be written *args*

1 : **function** writePvt(*key, args*)

2 : *ret* ← *PrivateData(args)*

3 : *uid* ← *getCurrentUser()*

4 : *hk* ← *getJSON("HK" + uid)*

5 : **if** *ret['priAttr']* is not null **then**

6 :   *s* ← *DecryptPaillier(hk.PriKey, hk.AesKey)*

7 :   *aeskey* ← *GenerateAESKey(s)*

8 :   **for** *k, v in range(ret['priAttr'])* **do**

9 :   *ret['priAttr'][k]* ← *EncryptAES(v, aeskey)*

10 :   **end for**

11 : **end if**

12 : **if** *ret['money']* is not null **then**

13 :   *ret['money']* ← *EncryptPaillier(hk.PubKey, ret['money'])*

14 : **end if**

15 : *retByte* ← *json2byte(ret)*

16 : *PutState(key, retByte)*

17 : **end function**

---

(1) Convert the input fault log and diagnostic data into the specified data privacy protection PrivateData structure;

(2) Get the user ID of the current client through getCurrentUser() function, and get the user's mixed key according to the user ID;

(3) If the fault event has privacy attributes, salt the decrypted AES initial key and encrypt all privacy attributes via the EncryptAES() function;

(4) EncryptPaillier() encryption using Paillier public key if there is maintenance fee for the failure event;

(5) PutState(), a data storage interface based on the Shim layer of block chain, stores encrypted fault logs and diagnosis data into the ledger.

The readPvt() function is responsible for reading the fault log and diagnostic data of a given user from the account book in a fusion protection-based manner, returning plaintext data.This function inherits the data query logic of the read() function, invokes the security service chain code interface to decrypt the obtained fault event ciphertext, and returns the decrypted data to the client.The logic of the readPvt() function is similar to that of the writePvt() function. The implementation logic is shown in Algorithm 4, and the general process is as follows:

Algorithm 4 readPvt() function

Input: User ID uid, specified key name k

1: **function** readPvt(uid, k)

2: $res \leftarrow getJSON(k)$

3: $ret \leftarrow json2map(res)$

4: $hk \leftarrow getJSON('HK' + uid)$

5: **if** $ret['priAttr']$ *is not null* **then**

6:     $s \leftarrow DecryptPaillier(hk.PriKey, hk.AesKey)$

7:     $aeskey \leftarrow GenerateAESKey(s)$

8:     **for** k, v *in range*($ret['priAttr']$) **do**

9:         $ret['priAttr'][k] \leftarrow DecryptAES(v, aeskey)$

10:     **end for**

11: **end if**

12: **if** $ret['money']$ *is not null* **then**

13:     $ret['money'] \leftarrow DecryptPaillier(hk.PriKey, ret['money'])$

14: **end if**

15: $retBytes \leftarrow json2byte(ret)$

16: **reture** $Success(retBytes)$

17: **end function**

---

(1) Query the fault log and diagnostic data of the specified key name from the account book;

(2) Query the mixed key of the designated user from the account book;

(3) If the fault log and diagnostic data contain the privacy attribute(priAttr), DecryptAES() decrypts all the privacy attribute with the salted AES initial key;

(4) If there is a repair cost for the failure event, the repair cost is encrypted with Paillier public key through EncryptPaillier();

(5) Returns the decrypted fault log and diagnostic data to the client.

3 Design of Fault Detection Middleware for Client Privacy Protection

The fault detection middleware for client privacy protection is written based on Node.js. On the block chain Node SDK, it encapsulates common chain code functions for client users, including fault event submission SDK and fault event query SDK. Before performing the failover detection middleware, the user must ensure that the client is connected to the blockchain. In the scheme of this paper, users connect to the block chain by setting the network configuration file, in which the network configuration file information includes CA server address, database address, channel path, chain code name, Peer node server address, Orderer node server address and other configuration parameters. After the successful connection, the chain code can be called to conduct data interaction with the blockchain ledger.

3.1 Failure Event Submission SDK

The implementation interface of the FAULT event submission SDK is the invokeTx() method, which provides the function of uploading or updating the fault log and diagnosing data for users on the client side, and invokes the chain code function of the fault event category in the chain code layer.

The invokeTx() method implementation logic is shown in Algorithm 5. After the client executes the invokeTx() method, it will write or update the key value to the ledger, and new fault event or block will be generated during the execution process. Therefore, it is necessary to specify the endorsement node, add the node endorsement and fault event to the block, and then update the local ledger through the node. Before the invokeTx() method is executed, the connection configuration file must be specified to connect the block chain. In the connection configuration file, CA server, database, server, database, channel, chain code, Peer node, Orderer node and other network configuration parameters of the block chain need to be set. After the successful connection, the module interface in the Blockchain Node SDK is called with the chain function name and chain function as the input parameters of the invokeTx() method to obtain the relevant information of the current blockchain network, and the channel module interface sendTransactionProposal sends the fault event to the Node and returns the submission result of the fault event. The results include txID (fault event ID), blockNum (block number of fault event), isDelay, and so on, which can be used by the client user to analyze the execution of the fault event.

Algorithm 5 invokeTx() method

Input : Specified chain code function name *ccf*, required parameters of
chain code function *args*

Output : transaction submission results *invokeResult*

1 : **function** invokeTx *(ccf ,.., args)*

2 : **if** *ccf is null* **then**

3 :   **reture** "Missing chain code function name"

4 : **end if**

5 : *tgs* ← [] // endorsement node

6 : **if** *len(this.targets)* < *1* **then** // *this* refers to the current fabric network

7 :   *tgs.push(this.peer)*

8 : **else**

9 :   *tgs* ← *this.targets*

10 : **end if**

11 : *tid* ← *this.client.newTransactionID()*

12 : *this.txids.set(tid.getTransactionID(),null)*

13 : *req* ← {*targets:tgs,*

14 :   *chaincodeId : this.chaincode_id,*

15 :   *fcn : ccf,*

16 :   *args : args,*

17 :   *chainId : this.channel_id,*

18 :   *txId : tid*}

19 : *invokeResult* ← *this.channel.sendTransactionProposal(req)*

20 : **reture** *invokeResult*

21 : **end funtion**

3.2 Failure Event Query SDK

The implementation interface of the FAULT event query SDK is queryTx() method,
which provides the client with the unified fault log and diagnostic data query function
for users, invokes the chain code function of non-indorsed fault event category in the
chain code layer, and returns the chain code invocation result to the client.

The queryTx() method reads key-value data from the ledger, and execution does not
result in a new failure event or block, so there is no need to endorse a failure event.

Before execution queryTx() method, the client should also with block chain network connection, with chain code function name as an input parameter, call blocks in the chain of module interface to get information about the current industrial chain network fault detection blocks, queryByChaincode interface module using channels to submit failure event query request, after the query returns the query results, the results content depends on the chain code function returns the result. The queryTx() method implementation logic is shown in Algorithm 6.

Algorithm 6 queryTx() method

Input： Specified chain code function name *ccf*, required parameters of chain code
       function *args*

Output : transaction query results *queryResult*

1 : **function** queryTx*(ccf ,.., args)*

2 : **if** *ccf is null* **then**

3 :   **reture** "Missing chain code function name"

4 : **end if**

5 : *tgs* ← []

6 : *tgs.push(this.peer)*

7 : *tid* ← *this.client.newTransactionID()*

8 : *req* ← *{targets:tgs,*

9 :   *chaincodeId : this.chaincode_id,*

10 :   *fcn : ccf ,*

11 :   *args : args,*

12 :   *chainId : this.channel_id,*

13 :   *txId : tid}*

14 : *queryResult* ← *this.channel.queryByChaincode(req)*

15 : **reture** *queryResult*

16 : **end funtion**

---

4   Blockchain Sensitive Privacy Data Storage Method

Block chain, introduced the concept of sensitive private data collection. Based on SideDB (lateral database) mechanism to save the failure events of sensitive private data, allow specific organization node access to sensitive private data, other members without permission is only know the sensitive private data exist, don't know the real content of sensitive private data.

Sensitive privacy data set includes data in two parts: sensitive privacy data entity and hash value of sensitive privacy data. Sensitive private data entities are accessible only to nodes with specific permissions, stored in the node's private state database (PrivateDB), and transmitted between nodes with permissions via the Gossip protocol, with no sorting services involved. The hash value of sensitive private data is written into the public State database (PublicDB) of each node in the channel after endorsement and sorting as the proof of the existence of failure events.

To execute sensitive private data storage, complex chain code commands are required to define sensitive private data set configuration files, which include the following information: Collection name (Name), signature policy, minimum recognized node (required-PeerCount), maximum number of Peer nodes (maxPeerCount), and blockToLive (duration of sensitive private data retention). The collection name indicates where the data is stored in the ledger. The signature policy defines an organization member that persists the collection data, such as "OR('org1msp.member', 'org2mSP.member')"; The minimum number of approved nodes means the minimum number of Peer nodes that need to distribute sensitive private data before the endorsement signature is returned to the client. The maximum number of Peer nodes refers to the number of Peer nodes that endorse nodes to distribute sensitive private data to save data redundancy. BlockToLive should be set to 0 if it is necessary to keep sensitive private data indefinitely. BlockToLive should be set to 0 if it is necessary to keep sensitive private data indefinitely. After the configuration is complete, the sensitive private data storage interfaces PutPrivateData() and the sensitive private data query interface GetPrivateData() interact with the ledger.

When the data needs to be kept secret among members in the channel and propagated among all organizations, certain members are required to have access to part of the data of the failure event, and the Orderer node needs to be kept secret, then the block chain USES sensitive private data storage method to improve the security of the fault log and diagnostic data.

Although the blockchain sensitive and private data storage method can guarantee sensitive data privacy in fault events, it still has shortcomings, which are mainly reflected in two aspects: (1) fault log and diagnostic data are still stored in the ledger of the node in clear text, and attackers can easily obtain fault event information directly from the ledger; (2) Node access authorization needs to provide complex operations. Fault logs and diagnostic data are stored in two state libraries, which can easily reduce the performance of the block chain itself.

5   Experiment and Analysis

The block chain data privacy protection scheme proposed in this paper is mainly aimed at industrial fault detection block chain users to protect privacy among users. Based on high concurrent request and high load, this experiment USES three methods, namely, the proposed scheme, the blockchain sensitive private data storage method and the original industrial fault detection blockchain (without privacy protection), to process client requests, obtain performance test results, and verify the feasibility of the proposed scheme by evaluating the test results. The test measures are Transactions Per Second (TPS) and average Time Per Transaction (TPT) Per Transaction. TPS is used to evaluate the number of data requests that can be processed Per unit Time, and TPT is used to evaluate the Time required to process a data request under a specified amount of concurrency.

This experiment mainly tests the upload data request and access data request submitted by the client, executes the client-side middleware invokeTx() method and queryTx() method in batches, and invokes different chain code functions. Among them, the chain code functions called when uploading and accessing data are: writePvt() and readPvt(); the chain code functions called when uploading and accessing data by native industrial fault detection block chain are write() and read(); the chain code interfaces called when uploading and accessing data by sensitive private data storage method of industrial fault detection block chain are PutPrivateData() and GetPrivateData() respectively. In the experimental environment, the host computer with CPU Intel(R)Core(TM) i7–6700@3.40 GHz and four Core eight threads was used to simulate data requests for 10 rounds with different concurrency values, calculate the average TPS and average TPT under each concurrency value, and finally analyze the results.

(1) Upload data to request test results

The experimental results are shown in Fig. 4. The horizontal axis represents the concurrency of the upload data request, while the vertical axis represents the average TPS under each concurrent amount. The concurrency value ranges from 0 to 2000 with intervals of 100. Can be seen from the Fig. 4, under the same concurrency, this scheme can handle the upload data request number per unit time is basic block chain, close to the native industrial fault detection when the concurrency value is less than 700, this scheme can handle the upload data request number per unit time is far more than the industrial chain of fault detection block sensitive private data storage methods. Therefore, the blockchain data privacy protection scheme proposed in this paper does not reduce the performance of industrial fault detection blockchain when executing the upload data request.

(2) Access data request test results

The experimental results are shown in Fig. 5. The horizontal axis represents the amount of concurrency of access data request, while the vertical axis represents the average TPS under each amount of concurrency, with the range of concurrency increasing successively from 0 to 4000, with the interval of 100. As can be seen from Fig. 5, with the same amount of concurrency, compared with the number of requests that can be processed per unit time in the original industrial fault detection block chain, the scheme in this paper has been reduced, slightly higher than the sensitive private data storage method of the industrial fault detection block chain. Therefore, the data privacy protection scheme of industrial fault detection blockchain based on fusion protection proposed in this paper slightly reduces the performance of industrial fault detection blockchain when executing access data request, and is superior to the sensitive privacy data storage method of industrial fault detection blockchain.

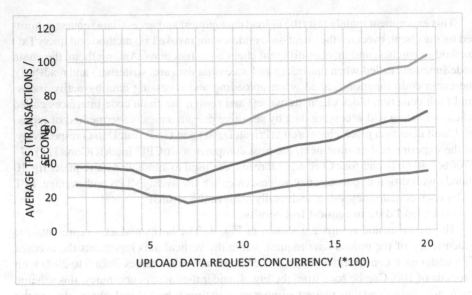

Fig. 4. Average TPS test results for upload data requests.

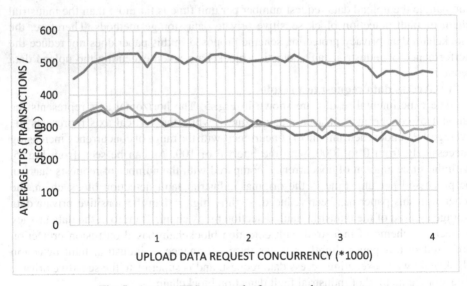

Fig. 5. Average TPS test results for access data requests.

6 Conclusion

This paper studies the data privacy protection storage of block chain, proposes a data privacy protection scheme based on fusion protection, introduces encryption method to partially encrypt the data uploaded to block chain, and realizes the data confidentiality storage and audit in distributed ledger. The usability of the proposed scheme is verified by experimental comparison with the blockchain sensitive private data storage method and the native blockchain.

Funding. This work was supported in part by the Key Research Base of Philosophy and Social Sciences in Jiangsu Universities "Huang Yan-Pei Vocational Education Thought Research Society Academic Center", 2019 Industrial Internet Innovation and Development Project from Ministry of Industry and Information Technology of China, 2018 Jiangsu Province Major Technical Research Project "Information Security Simulation System", Fundamental Research Funds for the Central Universities (30918012204), 2019 Jiangmen Basic and Theoretical Scientific Research Projects "Research on Feature Selection and Data Fusion of Industrial Big Data for Intelligent Manufacturing".

References

1. Li, Q., Song, Y., Zhang, J., Sheng, V.S.: Multiclass imbalanced learning with one-versus-one decomposition and spectral clustering. Expert Syst. Appl. **147**, 113152 (2020). https://doi.org/10.1016/j.eswa.2019.113152
2. Li, Q., Yin, X., Meng, S., Liu, Y., Ying, Z.: A security event description of intelligent applications in edge-cloud environment. J. Cloud Comput. **9**(1), 1–13 (2020). https://doi.org/10.1186/s13677-020-00171-0
3. Hou, J., Li, Q., Tan, R., Meng, S., Zhang, H., Zhang, S.: An Intrusion tracking watermarking scheme. IEEE Access **7**, 141438–141455 (2019). https://doi.org/10.1109/ACCESS.2019.2943493
4. Hou, J., Li, Q., Cui, S., Meng, S., Zhang, S., Ni, Z., Tian, Y.: Low-cohesion differential privacy protection for industrial Internet. J. Supercomput. **76**(11), 8450–8472 (2020). https://doi.org/10.1007/s11227-019-03122-y
5. Li, Q., Tian, Y., Wu, Q., Cao, Q., Shen, H., Long, H.: A cloud-fog-edge closed-loop feedback security risk prediction method. IEEE Access **8**(1), 29004–29020 (2020)
6. Li, Q., et al.: Safety risk monitoring of cyber-physical power systems based on ensemble learning algorithm. IEEE Access **7**, 24788–24805 (2019)
7. Li, Q., Meng, S., Wang, S., Zhang, J., Hou, J.: CAD: command-level anomaly detection for vehicle-road collaborative charging network. IEEE Access **7**, 34910–34924 (2019)
8. Li, Q., Meng, S., Zhang, S., Hou, J., Qi, L.: Complex attack linkage decision-making in edge computing networks. IEEE Access **7**, 12058–12072 (2019)
9. Li, Q., Wang, Y., Ziyuan, P., Wang, S., Zhang, W.: A time series association state analysis method in smart internet of electric vehicle charging network attack. Transp. Res. Rec. **2673**, 217–228 (2019)
10. Cui, S., Li, T., Chen, S.C., Shyu, M.-L., Li, Q., Zhang, H.: DISL: deep isomorphic substructure learning for network representations. Knowl.-Based Syst. **189** (2020). https://doi.org/10.1016/j.knosys.2019.105086
11. Meng, S., Li, Q., Zhang, J., Lin, W., Dou, W.: Temporal-aware and sparsity-tolerant hybrid collaborative recommendation method with privacy preservation. Concurrency Comput.-Pract. Exp. **32**(2) (2020). https://doi.org/10.1002/cpe.5447
12. Li, Q., Hou, J., Meng, S., Long, H.: GLIDE: a game theory and data-driven mimicking linkage intrusion detection for edge computing networks. Complexity **2020** (2020). https://doi.org/10.1155/2020/7136160. Article no. 7136160, 18 pages
13. Hou, J., Li, Q., Meng, S., Ni, Z., Chen, Y., Liu, Y.: DPRF: a differential privacy protection random forest. IEEE Access **7**, 130707–130720 (2019). https://doi.org/10.1109/ACCESS.2019.2939891

Cloud-Based IoT Architecture

Lightweight Anonymous Communication Model Based on Anonymous IBE

Yanli Wang, Xinying Yu, and Fengyin Li[✉]

School of Computer Science, Qufu Normal University, Rizhao 276826, China
Lfyin318@126.com

Abstract. With increasing application of big data technology, a large amount of personal information is stored and processed on the Internet, which makes people have a greater demand for privacy. In addition, the development of mobile Internet and cloud computing requires the communication model to be as efficient and low-bandwidth as possible on the basis of security. In order to achieve the goal of protecting users' data privacy, this paper firstly presents a new anonymous Identify-Based Encryption (IBE) scheme, and designs a new lightweight anonymous communication model by introducing the proposed anonymous IBE scheme into an anonymous communication model. This model effectively guarantees the anonymity of system users and the security of messages in the communication process. Performance analysis shows that our communication model can effectively resists node eavesdropping, traffic analysis attacks, and finally achieve communication security and anonymity. Compared with other anonymous communication systems, our scheme has significant advantages in efficiency and relatively low cost. In the future, it has good application prospects.

Keywords: Anonymous communication model · Privacy protection · Identify-based encryption · Bilinear map

1 Introduction

In the era of big data, as more personal information and organizational information are involved, data privacy becomes more and more important. As we all known, our protection of data privacy requires not only the protection of the content of the message, but also the protection of the identity, communication time and communication path of both parties to the communication. However, the existing encryption technologies [2] find it difficult to protect the communication participants' private information such as identity, behavior, and network address. Hackers use traffic-analysis attacks [1] to obtain identity information and communication relationships in the communication process, which leads to the privacy leakage of the users. Therefore, it is extremely important to construct an anonymous communication model and take certain measures to conceal the communication relationship in the communication streams, making it difficult for eavesdroppers to obtain contents and derive the relationship of the parties in the communication.

© ICST Institute for Computer Sciences, Social Informatics and Telecommunications Engineering 2021
Published by Springer Nature Switzerland AG 2021. All Rights Reserved
L. Qi et al. (Eds.): CloudComp 2020, LNICST 363, pp. 103–110, 2021.
https://doi.org/10.1007/978-3-030-69992-5_8

After the first paper on anonymous communication model was published in 1981 [13], many research efforts have been made in the field of anonymous communication. The existing research on anonymous communication can be divided into three categories. Firstly, Reed [9] proposed an onion routing. People encrypt message and transmit it through a series of network nodes called "onion routers", each node "stripping" a single layer to reveal the next destination of the data. When the final layer is decrypted, the message arrives at its destination, so each node cannot know the original and final message at the same time. By this way, onion routing achieves the anonymity of the sender [16], but it cannot resist traffic attacks [12,17], exiting node vulnerability attacks [15] and other security problems. In order to undertake traffic analysis, Chaum et al. [7] proposed an anonymous communication model based on DC-net. The model defines an N-number group, and only one member is allowed to send messages in a given round. Messages are sent via broadcasting without the need for a trust center. However, due to the cooperation of all members, it is vulnerable to internal dishonest members, and it is easy to break the security of the model. The last anonymous communication model based on a flooding algorithm, which uses flooding, epidemic and other algorithms for flooding [8,14]. When the sender initiates an anonymous transmission, the path of the anonymous transmission is unclear. Therefore, the adversary cannot distinguish where the next hop of the node will be. But the main challenge for anonymous communication models based on the flooding algorithm is that the model will generate a large amount of network transmission traffic during the communication process, and has a great demand for network bandwidth. At the same time, the stability and reliability of system algorithms are not satisfactory.

Based on the above analysis, we find that the existing anonymous communication systems have demanding requirements for network bandwidth and memory, and cannot guarantee stability and reliability. In this case, anonymous communication systems are used in small groups, which are not only inefficient and expensive, but also insecure. Therefore, the demand for lightweight anonymous communication systems for small groups is very immanent. For example, bidders need to hide their identities and whistleblowers need to protect their privacy. In the future, the lightweight anonymous communication system can be applied to information transmission between sensors and servers in the Internet of Things [11], as well as proprietary security protection in cloud services [4]. Nevertheless, there are few existing research studies on lightweight anonymous communication systems. For this purpose, the following are the main contributions of this paper.

(1) An anonymous IBE algorithm is proposed to encrypt messages in the communication model, taking advantage of that the anonymous IBE algorithm has a high degree of ciphertext expansion and does not require certificates management. It can meet the conditions of anonymous communication on the basis of ensuring message security.

(2) A lightweight anonymous communication model based on the proposed IBE scheme is proposed, the new model simultaneously implements anonymity, efficiency and security.

The roadmap of this paper is as follows. Section 2 introduces the preliminary work of this project, such as bilinear groups, complexity assumptions, IBE and security model, etc. Section 3 describes our proposed anonymous IBE scheme and in Sect. 4, a lightweight anonymous communication model based on anonymous IBE is proposed. Before summarising this paper in Sect. 6, Sect. 5 analyses the performance of the proposed model in this paper.

2   Preliminary

2.1   Bilinear Map

Let G_1 and G_2 be multiplicative cyclic groups of prime order p, g is a generator of G_1. The bilinear map $e : G_1 \times G_1 \to G_2$ has the following properties [6]:

(1) Bilinearity: For all $P, Q \in G_1$ and for all $a, b \in Z_p$, we have $e(P^a, Q^b) = e(P, Q)^{ab}$.

(2) Non-degeneracy: $e(g, g) \neq 1$.

(3) Computability: For all $P, Q \in G_1$, there is an algorithm that can compute $e(P, Q)$ efficiently.

2.2   Bilinear Diffie-Hellman Assumption

The BDH problem [3,6] in G_1 is as follows: Input a tuple $g, g^\alpha, g^b, g^c \in G_1$, output $e(g, g)^{abc} \in G_2$. An algorithm $\mathcal{A}$ has advantage ε in solving BDH in G_1 if

$$\Pr\left[\mathcal{A}\left(g, g^\alpha, g^b, g^c\right) = e(g, g)^{abc}\right] \geq \varepsilon \qquad (1)$$

where the probability is over the random choice of α, b, c in Z_p^* and the random bits used by $\mathcal{A}$. Similarly, an algorithm $\mathcal{B}$ that outputs $b \in \{0, 1\}$ has advantage ε in solving the decision BDH problem in G_1 if

$$\left|\Pr\left[\mathcal{B}\left(g, g^\alpha, g^b, g^c, e(g, g)^{abc}\right) = 0\right] - \Pr\left[\mathcal{B}\left(g, g^\alpha, g^b, g^c, T\right) = 0\right]\right| \geq \varepsilon \qquad (2)$$

where the probability is over the random choice of α, b, c in Z_p^*, the random choice of $T \in G_2^*$, and the random bits of $\mathcal{B}$.

Definition 1. The (Decision) (t, ε)-BDH assumption holds in G_1 if no t-time algorithm has advantage ε at least in solving the (Decision) BDH problem in G_1.

Occasionally we drop t and ε and refer to the BDH and Decision BDH assumptions in G_1.

2.3   IBE Scheme

In the IBE scheme, participants generally include private key generators (PKG) and users. PKG as a trusted third party, uses the system master key and user ID to generate a private key. Subsequently, the private key is distributed to the corresponding users by PKG. Furthermore, the identity of the user makes IBE different from the public key of the traditional public key crypto-system. Therefore, IBE scheme is widely used in the field of information security protection. An Identity Based Encryption (IBE) scheme is a tuple of PPT algorithms, it is defined in a message space $\mathcal{M}$, an identity space $\mathcal{I}$ and a ciphertext space $\mathcal{C}$ as follows:

Setup: On input (in unary) a security parameter k, generate public parameters *params* and a master secret key MSK. And $\mathcal{M}, \mathcal{C}, params$ is public. MSK is kept by PKG.

Key generation: On input a master secret key MSK and an identity $ID \in \mathcal{I}$, derive and output a secret key d_{ID} for identity ID.

Encryption: On input public parameters *params*, an identity $ID \in \mathcal{I}$, and a message $m \in \mathcal{M}$, output a ciphertext $C \in \mathcal{C}$ that encrypts m under identity ID.

Decryption: On input a secret key d_{ID} for identity $ID \in \mathcal{I}$ and a ciphertext $C \in \mathcal{C}$, output m' if C is a valid encryption under identity ID, output a failure symbol $\perp$ otherwise.

2.4   Security Model

Boneh and Franklin defined the chosen ciphertext security for IBE systems under a chosen identity attack in paper [5]. In the model, the adversary is allowed to adaptively choose the public key it wants to attack (the public key on which it will be challenged). Informally, if the adversary cannot obtain the public key ID in the ciphertext and has the characteristics of indistinguishability under the chosen ciphertext attack, we believe that the scheme has ANON-IND-ID-CCA (anonymous, indistinguishable and based on ID's chosen ciphertext attack) security. More precisely, the security of anonymous IBE scheme is defined using the following game [10].

We define $\mathcal{A}$ as an adversary and $\mathcal{B}$ as a challenger.

Setup: $\mathcal{B}$ runs setup, and forwards parameters to $\mathcal{A}$.

Phase 1: Proceeding adaptively, $\mathcal{A}$ issues queries $q_1, \cdots, q_m$ where q_i is one of the following:

Key generation query $\langle ID_i \rangle$: $\mathcal{B}$ runs *Key generation* on ID_i and forwards the resulting private key to $\mathcal{A}$.

Decryption query $\langle ID_i, C_i \rangle$: $\mathcal{B}$ runs *Key generation* on ID_i, decrypts C_i with the resulting private key, and sends the result to $\mathcal{A}$.

Challenge: $\mathcal{A}$ submits two plaintexts m_0, m_1, two identities ID_0, ID_1. ID_0, ID_1 or their prefix cannot appear in any key generation query in Phase 1. $\mathcal{B}$ chooses a random bit $k, l \in \{0, 1\}$, sets $C^* = Encrypt(params, ID_k, m_l)$, and sends C^* to $\mathcal{A}$ as its challenge ciphertext.

Phase 2: This is identical to Phase 1, except that $\mathcal{A}$ may not request the private key for ID_0, ID_1 or the decryption of $\langle ID_0, C^* \rangle, \langle ID_1, C^* \rangle$.

Guess: $\mathcal{A}$ submits a guess $k', l' \in \{0, 1\}$. $\mathcal{A}$ wins if $k' = k, l' = l$. We call an adversary $\mathcal{A}$ in the above game as an ANON-IND-ID-CCA adversary. The advantage ε of an adversary A in this game is defined as $\left| \Pr\left[k' = k \wedge l' = l\right] - \frac{1}{4} \right|$.

Definition 2. An anonymous IBE system is (t, q, ε)-ANON-IND-ID-CCA secure if all t-time ANON-IND-ID-CCA adversaries making at most q queries have advantage at most ε in winning the above game.

3   Anonymous IBE Scheme

Anonymous IBE can effectively guarantee that it will not disclose any identity information about the recipient in the ciphertexts, and has ANON-IND-ID-CCA security. In this section, we design an efficient anonymous IBE scheme, and prove its correctness and security.

Let G_1 and G_2 be multiplicative cyclic groups of prime order p, g is a generator of G_1, $e : G_1 \times G_1 \to G_2$ is the bilinear map.

Setup: In order to generate security parameters, we randomly select $\alpha \in Z_p^*$ and set $g_1 = g^\alpha, g_2 \in G_1$. The public parameters *params* and the secret master key MSK are given by

$$params = (g, g_1, g_2), MSK = \alpha. \tag{3}$$

Key generation: To generate private key d_{ID}, we randomly select $r \in Z_p^*$, input master secret key MSK and an identity $ID \in Z_p^*$ and output

$$d_{ID} = (d_1, d_2) = \left(g_2^\alpha g_1^{ID \cdot r}, g^{-r}\right). \tag{4}$$

Encryption: To encrypt a message $m \in G_2$ under public key ID, pick a random $t \in Z_p^*$ and we output

$$C = (C_1, C_2, C_3) = \left(e(g, g_2)^{\alpha t} \cdot m, g^t, g_1^{ID \cdot t}\right). \tag{5}$$

Decryption: To decrypt a ciphertext $C = (C_1, C_2, C_3)$ using private key $d_{ID} = (d_1, d_2)$, output

$$m = C_1 \cdot \frac{1}{e(C_2, d_1) e(d_2, C_3)}. \tag{6}$$

4   Lightweight Anonymous Communication Model Based on Anonymous IBE

In this section, we design a lightweight anonymous communication model based on anonymous IBE, which is proposed in Sect. 3.

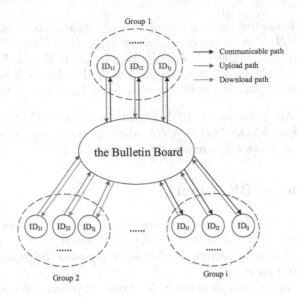

Fig. 1. Lightweight anonymous communication model (Color figure online)

When a user enters the model, the model automatically distributes a unique and fixed identity ID to the user. At the same time, the private key generation (PKG) in the model generates the system's secret master key and the private key corresponding to each user according to the previous IBE encryption mechanism. On the other hand, PKG is responsible for grouping all the users and dividing the users into M groups, where each group is of N members. To prevent traffic analysis attacks, the number of N should be large enough. An ID corresponds to a unique group number i and a serial number j in the group (i, j are randomly selected, and $0 < i \leq M, 0 < j \leq N$). We notate the user as ID_{ij}, and every trusted user knows the identities and group numbers of other users in the system.

In the communication phase, users divide time slices to encrypt messages, upload ciphertext, download ciphertext and decrypt ciphertext. During time T_1, the sender encrypts the message to be sent by using the anonymous IBE scheme. It is worth mentioning that in order to reduce memory consumption on the basis of ensuring security, we add the group number of the recipient as a mark. During time T_2, all the users upload the ciphertext to the bulletin board and the bulletin board is provided for users to upload and download ciphertexts. This process is indicated by the red line in Fig. 1. During time T_3, if the mark in the ciphertext is equal to the group number in the model, then all users in the group must download the ciphertext to the local host, other groups will not download the ciphertext. This downloading process is indicated by the green line in Fig. 1, and the black line indicates the available communication path in the model. During time T_4, the user decrypts the downloaded ciphertext with his/her private key.

5 Model Performance Analysis

5.1 Anonymity of Messages

In our model, the public key of the recipient does not need to be queried by the sender, because the public key is the identity of the receiver that every user knows. We consider that all the users perform upload operations in time T_2. The adversary cannot determine which users are the real senders through the traffic analysis attack, which can ensure the sender's anonymity. Because the recipient's identity is used as the public key to encrypt the ciphertext, the anonymous IBE scheme ensures that the adversary cannot extract the receiver's identity from the ciphertexts. During time T_3, all the members of the real receiver's group download the ciphertexts. On the other hand, there are relatively many members in the group, and the adversary does not know which member of the group is the real receiver, thus ensuring the receiver's anonymity.

5.2 Efficiency Analysis

Our scheme has no limit on the number of ciphertexts that need to be sent in each round. Compared with the communication model that can only send one message in each round [7], the more messages we send in each round, the more efficient our model is. Similarly, compared to the anonymous communication model designed by Jiang et al. [11], our model manages users in groups. Before users download the ciphertexts, they need to be screened, which greatly reduces the number of ciphertexts that users download and need to decrypt. When delivering the same amount of messages, our solution saves time and memory on the basis of security.

6 Conclusion

With the development of mobile Internet and cloud computing, the previous anonymous communication model had large requirements on network bandwidth and memory, which cannot meet its development needs. And using a large-scale anonymous communication model in the group is inefficient, expensive, and insecure. In this paper, we design a lightweight anonymous communication model based on IBE, which is suitable for small and medium-sized groups. In the proposed model, we design an anonymous IBE scheme, modify the ciphertext structure, and simplify the encryption process while ensuring security. Furthermore, all the users are organised in groups and all the ciphertexts are filtered before the downloading practice. The operations reduce the workload of users to download the ciphertexts and the number of the decrypted ciphertexts. Analysis results show that the communication model has better performance while ensuring security and anonymity. In the future, we will consider applying this model to user authentication and application scenarios in the Internet of Things.

References

1. Aaron, J., Chris, W., Rob, J., Micah, S., Paul, S.: Users get routed: traffic correlation on tor by realistic adversaries. In: Proceedings of the 2013 ACM SIGSAC Conference on Computer & Communications Security, pp. 337–348 (2013)
2. Abusukhon, A., Bilal, H.: A secure network communication protocol based on textto barcode encryption algorithm. Int. J. Adv. Comput. Sci. Appl. 6(12), 64–70 (2015)
3. Joux, A.: A one round protocol for tripartite diffie–hellman. In: Bosma, W. (ed.) ANTS 2000. LNCS, vol. 1838, pp. 385–393. Springer, Heidelberg (2000). https://doi.org/10.1007/10722028_23
4. Antonela, D., Roger, D., Arthur, E., Finkel, M.: Addressing denial of service attacks on free and open communication on the internet. The Tor Project, Technical report (2018)
5. Boneh, D., Gentry, C., Waters, B.: Collusion resistant broadcast encryption with short ciphertexts and private keys. In: Shoup, V. (ed.) CRYPTO 2005. LNCS, vol. 3621, pp. 258–275. Springer, Heidelberg (2005). https://doi.org/10.1007/11535218_16
6. Boneh, D., Franklin, M.: Identity-based encryption from the weil pairing. In: Kilian, J. (ed.) CRYPTO 2001. LNCS, vol. 2139, pp. 213–229. Springer, Heidelberg (2001). https://doi.org/10.1007/3-540-44647-8_13
7. David, C.: The dining cryptographers problem: Unconditional sender and recipient untraceability. J. Cryptology 1(1), 65–75 (1988)
8. Fatemeh, S., Milivoj, S., Rizwan, A.M., Michael, B., Claudia, D.: A survey on routing in anonymous communication protocols. ACM Comput. Surv. (CSUR) 51(3), 1–39 (2018)
9. Reed, M.G., Syverson, P.F., Goldschlag, D.M.: Anonymous connections and onion routing. IEEE J. Sel. Areas Commun. 16(4), 482–494 (1998)
10. Gentry, C.: Practical identity-based encryption without random oracles. In: Vaudenay, S. (ed.) EUROCRYPT 2006. LNCS, vol. 4004, pp. 445–464. Springer, Heidelberg (2006). https://doi.org/10.1007/11761679_27
11. Jiang, L., Li, T., Li, X., Atiquzzaman, M., Ahmad, H., Wang, X.: Anonymous communication via anonymous identity-based encryption and its application iniot. Wireless Commun. Mob. Comput.2018, 8 (2018)
12. Kevin, B., Damon, M., Dirk, G., Tadayoshi, K., Douglas, S.: Low-resource routing attacks against tor. In: Proceedings of the 2007 ACM Workshop on Privacy in Electronic Society, pp. 11–20 (2007)
13. Chaum, D.L.: Untraceable electronic mail, return addresses, and digital pseudonyms. Commun. ACM 24(2), 84–90 (1981)
14. Liu, Z., Liu, Y., Winter, P., Mittal, P., Hu, Y.C.: Torpolice: towards enforcing service-defined access policies for anonymous communication in the tor network. In: 2017 IEEE 25th International Conference on Network Protocols (ICNP), pp. 1–10. IEEE (2017)
15. Nicholas, H., Y, V.E., Eric, C.T.: How much anonymity does network latency leak? ACM Trans. Inf. Syst. Secur. (TISSEC) 13(2), 1–28 (2010)
16. Goldschlag, D., Reedy, M., Syverson, P.: Onion routing for anonymous and private internet connections. Commun. ACM 42(2), 5 (1999)
17. Sambuddho, C., Angelos, S., Keromytis, A.D.: Identifying proxy nodes in a tor anonymization circuit. In: 2008 IEEE International Conference on Signal Image Technology and Internet Based Systems, pp. 633–639. IEEE (2008)

Research on Distributed Trust Management in IoT

Ying Wang, Dongfeng Wang, and Fengyin Li[✉]

School of Computer Science, Qufu Normal University, Rizhao 276826, China
Lfyin318@126.com

Abstract. Widely used Internet of Things (IoT) has led to close cooperation between electronic devices. It requires strong reliability and trustworthiness of the devices involved in the communication. However, current trust mechanisms have the following issues: (1) Heavily relying on a trusted third party, which may incur severe security issues if it is corrupted. (2) Malicious evaluations on the involved devices may bias the trustrank of the devices. By introducing the concept of risk management into the trust mechanism, we propose a trust mechanism for distributed IoT devices in this paper. In the proposed trust mechanism, trustrank is quantified by normative trust and risk measures. Performance analysis shows that the proposed trust mechanism has a higher probability of high trust device being selected and higher success rate of cooperation.

Keywords: Internet of Things · Trust management · Normative trust · Risk

1 Introduction

In recent years, IoT has been widely implemented. It is estimated that by 2025, the number of global IoT connections will reach 25.1 billion, and the market size will exceed 10 trillion Chinese yuan. Emerging technologies such as data mining, artificial intelligence and natural language processing are also increasingly being extended to IoT applications [1–3]. Therefore, the need for cooperation between IoT devices has been significantly increased [4]. However, the performance of IoT devices in the process of cooperation is uncertain. How to measure the performance of devices through trust data, so as to understand the recent performance of IoT devices, has become the focus of recent research.

An IoT device is expected to cooperate with the devices of high reliability. It is necessary to ensure not only the performance of the other devices, but also the trustworthiness of them, which is the criterion to examine the reliability of the devices before cooperation [5,6]. Because existing trust mechanisms heavily rely on the trusted third parties or additional trust assumptions, there are hidden security risks such as malicious modifications to the trusted data [7]. Moreover, most distributed trust systems have not considered the malicious evaluation on the IoT devices. Saied et al. proposed a trust management method using

© ICST Institute for Computer Sciences, Social Informatics and Telecommunications Engineering 2021
Published by Springer Nature Switzerland AG 2021. All Rights Reserved
L. Qi et al. (Eds.): CloudComp 2020, LNICST 363, pp. 111–119, 2021.
https://doi.org/10.1007/978-3-030-69992-5_9

environment-awareness [8]. From nodes' historical behaviors in different cooperation types, they obtained a comprehensive trustrank to handle any new task, but this process relies on a reliable trust management institution. By caching previous interaction summaries, Liu et al. proposed a verifiable method to solve the hierarchical trust problem of IoT systems [9], but this method needs to establish additional trusted third parties over different domains. Benkerrou et al. proposed an IoT trust evaluation method based on trust and honesty [10], but they assume that all master nodes in the domain are completely trusted. Based on blockchain technologies, Ren et al. proposed a trust management method suitable for distributed Internet of Things, but they did not consider the irresponsible malicious evaluation problems between malicious devices [11].

By introducing the theory of risk into trust management, we propose a trust management method for distributed IoT. The new mechanism does not rely on any trusted third party, and the process of trust establishment and management are entirely independent maintained by each IoT domain manager. The main contributions of our method are as follows:

Aiming at the problem of dependence on trusted third-party, an IoT trust mechanism based on normative trust and risk trust is proposed. This trust mechanism does not depend on any trusted third party, and all trust establishments and trust managements are completely managed and maintained by IoT domain managers and IoT devices.

2   Trust Management Model in Distributed Internet of Things

2.1   The Structure of System

According to the distributed IoT environment, we here design a decentralized distributed IoT architecture (as shown in Fig. 1). There are many different IoTs in the real environment, and each IoT has a management domain. Each management domain consists of a domain manager and all subordinate IoT devices. The domain manager manages all the IoT devices in the domain. IoT devices can communicate and cooperate with others in any management domain. Domain managers can collaborate with others on the exchanging data.

For each cooperation between domain managers and devices, a two-way evaluation is conducted based on the other party's performance. The gist for evaluation includes the device's communication success rate, data processing capability, transmission range, and network stability. The device can be evaluated based on the other party's overall performance. The communication success rate between the devices is considered as the main indicator of the devices' performance in this paper.

The architecture of the Internet of Things is generally divided into three layer: a perception layer, a network layer, and an application layer. The perception layer includes some wireless sensors and other smart terminal devices with data processing capabilities. We denote wireless sensors with the devices $D(x_i, y_n)$, and denote Smart terminal devices with the domain manager $H(x_i)$ in this paper. Data exchange and communication between the device and the domain manager are implemented via the network layer.

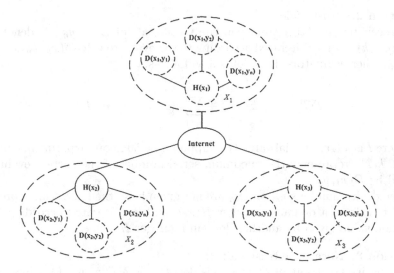

Fig. 1. Architecture of distributed IoT

In Fig. 1, x represents the IoT domain identifier, x_1, x_2, x_3 represent different IoT domain identifiers, $H(x)$ represents the domain manager of IoT domain x , $D(x, y_i)$ represents different IoT devices in the domain x, which is managed by $H(x)$, where $y_i \epsilon N^*(i = 1, 2, ..., n)$.

2.2 Trust Model

In order to describe the trustworthiness of IoT devices, this paper uses normative trust and risk measures to quantify trustrank. Normative trust defines the ability of a specific entity to earn credit by other entities, and the risk measure defines the stability level of a specific entity's credit performance in the past period. The concrete definition of the trust model is as follows.

Definition 1. Evaluation value
The evaluation value of $D(x_i, y_m)$ is denoted as $\delta(x_i, y_m, x_j, y_n, l)$, which refers to the evaluation of a given IoT device $D(x_i, y_m)$ by another IoT device $D(x_j, y_n)$. It is defined as follows.

$$\delta(x_i, y_m, x_j, y_n, l) = \begin{cases} 1 & Good\ performance \\ 0 & Ordinary\ performance \\ -1 & Poor\ performance \end{cases} \tag{1}$$

Where l indicates the serial number of the evaluation currently received by $D(x_i, y_m)$.

If the device numbers y_m and y_n are not given here, the evaluation value represents the evaluation value of $H(x_i)$, which refers to the evaluation of a domain manager $H(x_i)$ by another domain manager $H(x_i)$.

Definition 2. Trust scale
When receiving the kth evaluation, the trust scale of $D(x_i, y_m)$ is denoted as $TC(x_i, y_m, k)$, and it is iterated according to the evaluate value $\delta(x_i, y_m, x_j, y_n, l)$ given by other evaluators. It is defined as follows.

$$TC(x_i, y_m, k) = I + \sum_{i=1}^{k-1} \delta(x_i, y_m, x_j, y_n, l) \tag{2}$$

Where I is a trust initial value (we suppose $I = 50$ in our experiments for simplicity), $k \epsilon N^*$ represents the maximum serial number of the current evaluation received by $D(x_i, y_m)$.

If the device numbers y_m and y_n are not given here, the trust scale represents the trust scale of a domain manager $H(x_i)$, and it is iterated according to its evaluation value given by another domain manager $H(x_i)$.

Definition 3. Normative trustrank
The normative trustrank of $D(x_i, y_m)$ is denoted as $NT(x_i, y_m, k)$, which represents the standardized trustrank of device $D(x_i, y_m)$. It is defined as follows.

$$NT(x_i, y_m, k) = f(TC(x_i, y_m, k)) = \frac{1}{1 + e^{(-TC(x_i, y_m, k))}} \tag{3}$$

Where $x_i, x_j (i \neq j)$ represent different IoT domain identifiers, $y_i, y_j (i \neq j)$ represent different IoT devices and represents the $k \epsilon N^*$ maximum serial number of the current evaluations received by $D(x_i, y_m)$.

If the device numbers y_m and y_n are not given here, the normative trustrank represents the normative trustrank of a domain manager $H(x_i)$.

Definition 4. The mean value
The mean value of the trust of $D(x_i, y_m)$ is denoted as $MT(x_i, y_m, k, r)$, which represents the average value of the latest r normative trust of $D(x_i, y_m)$. It is defined as follows.

$$MT(x_i, y_m, k, r) = f(TC(x_i, y_m, k)) = \frac{\sum_{k'=k-r+1}^{k} NT(x_i, y_m, k')}{r} \tag{4}$$

Where $k \epsilon N^*$ represents the maximum evaluation serial number received by $H(x_i)$, and $r \epsilon N^*$ represents the number of $CD(x_i, y_m, k')$ included in the risk assessment.

If the device numbers y_m and y_n are not given here, this value represents the mean value of a domain manager $H(x_i)$, which represents the average value of the latest r normative trust of $H(x_i)$.

Definition 5. Risk value

The risk value of $D(x_i, y_m)$ is denoted as $RV(x_i, y_m, k, r)$, which is used to measure the risk of the credit performance of $D(x_i, y_m)$ in the history. Up to the maximum evaluation serial number k , the most recent r normative trustranks are taken into consideration, and the risk measure of definition $D(x_i, y_m)$ is as follows.

$$RV(x_i, y_m, k, r) = \sqrt{\frac{\sum_{k'=k-r+1}^{k}[NT(x_i, y_m, k') - MT(x_i, y_m, k, r)]^2}{r}} \tag{5}$$

Where $k \epsilon N^*$ represents the maximum evaluation serial number received by $D(x_i, y_m)$, and $r \epsilon N^*$ represents the number of $NT(x_i, y_m, k')$ included in the risk assessment.

If the device numbers y_m and y_n are not given here, this value represents the risk value of a domain manager $H(x_i)$, which is used to measure the risk of the credit performance of $H(x_i)$ in the past.

Definition 6. Harmonic trustrank

The harmonic trustrank of $D(x_i, y_m)$ is denoted as $HT(x_i, y_m, k, r)$, which is used to represent the comprehensive trust evaluation of $D(x_i, y_m)$. Considering the normative trustrank and risk measure of $D(x_i, y_m)$, we define $HT(x_i, y_m, k, r)$ as follows.

$$HT(x_i, y_m, k, r) = \frac{NT(x_i, y_m, k)}{1 + NT(x_i, y_m, k) \times RV(x_i, y_m, k, r)} \tag{6}$$

If the device numbers y_m and y_n are not given here, this value represents the harmonic trustrank of a domain manager $H(x_i)$, which is used to represent the comprehensive trust evaluation of $H(x_i)$.

The architecture of the trust management model is shown in Fig. 2.

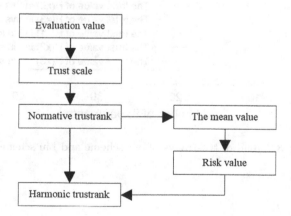

Fig. 2. Trust management model

3　Performance Evaluation

3.1　Trust Value Update

In order to test the effectiveness of the proposed scheme, simulation experiments are carried out to analyze the update rate of trustranks, the probability of the high trustrank equipment being selected and the success rate of the cooperation.

The experiment simulates three scenarios of the IoT domains and the corresponding IoT devices. The domain manager set is $H = \{H(x_1), H(x_2), H(x_3)\}$, including one malicious device and two benign devices. We used MATLAB to generate evaluation data for 50 device-to-device evaluations, simulating the trend of the trust data in the IoT trust model, the probability of high-trustrank devices being selected, and the success rate of cooperation between IoT devices. All the data are obtained by averaging the results of 10 iterations. The experimental results are shown in Figs. 3-7.

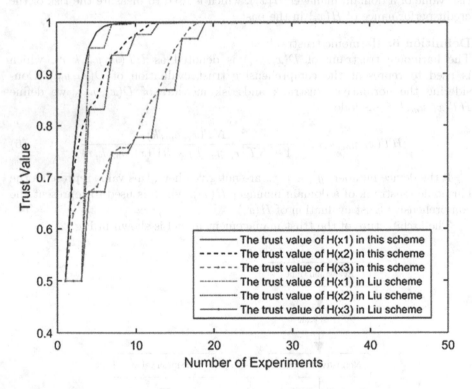

Fig. 3. Trend of trustranks of our scheme and Liu scheme.

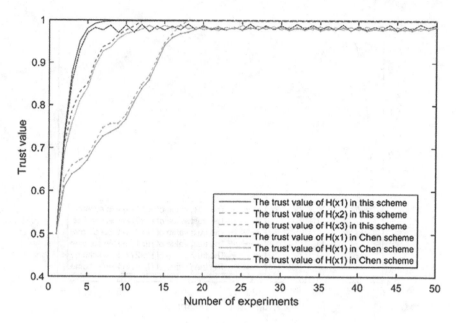

Fig. 4. Trend of trustranks of our scheme and Chen scheme

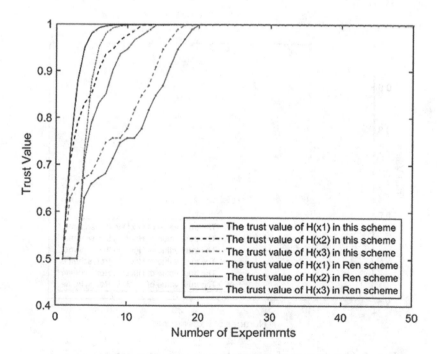

Fig. 5. Trend of trustranks of our scheme and Ren scheme

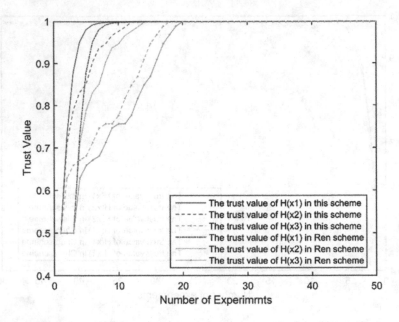

Fig. 6. Comparison of the probability of a high-trust device being selected

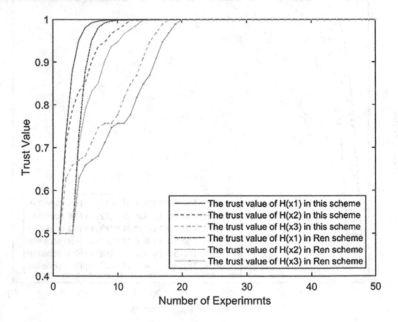

Fig. 7. Comparison of cooperation success rates between devices

4   Conclusion

To address the problems that a trust mechanism relies on the trusted third party or additional trust assumptions, and that the trust data is vulnerable to malicious attacks currently, in this paper, we quantified trust into normative trust and risk measure, which can construct a comprehensive review of normative trust, and we proposed a trust mechanism for distributed IoT, which realizes the identification and shielding of malicious evaluations between IoT devices, and can select the device that performs well and stable. Then it performs well in improving the success rate and reliability of cooperation on IoT devices. However, the mechanism in this paper has the problem of malicious evaluation on devices, and in this paper, how to work out this problem is the focus of the future work.

References

1. Yu, X., Wang, H., Zheng, X., Wang, Y.: Effective algorithms for vertical mining probabilistic frequent patterns in uncertain mobile environments. Int. J. Ad Hoc Ubiquit. Comput. **23**(3/4), 137 (2016)
2. Zheng, X., Hong, L.: A scalable coevolutionary multi-objective particle swarm optimizer. Int. J. Comput. Intell. Syst. **3**(5), 590–600 (2010)
3. Yu, X.-M., Feng, W.-Z., Wang, H., Chu, Q., Chen, Q.: An attention mechanism and multi-granularity-based Bi-LSTM model for Chinese Q&A system. Soft Comput. **24**(8), 5831–5845 (2019). https://doi.org/10.1007/s00500-019-04367-8
4. Wang, J.: Study of quantitative trust management model for the internet of things. Network Security Technology and Application (2014)
5. Feng, Y., Liu, Y., Gong, Y.: Trust system based on node behavior detection in internet of things. J. Commun. **35**(5), 8–15 (2014)
6. Li, X.: Design and analysis of revisable reputation evaluation system based on blockchain. Xi'an University of Electronic Science and Technology (2018)
7. Gu, L., Wang, J., Sun, B.: Trust management mechanism for internet of things. Chin. Commun. **11**(2), 148–156 (2014)
8. Saied, Y.B., Olivereau, A., Zeghlache, D., Laurent, M.: Trust management system design for the internet of things: a context-aware and multi- service approach. Comput. Secur. **39**, 351–365 (2013)
9. Liu, W.M., Yin, L.H., Fang, B.X., Zhang, H.L.: A hierarchical trust model for the internet of things. Chin. J. Comput. **35**(5), 846–855 (2012)
10. Benkerrou, H., Heddad, S.: Credit and honesty-based trust assessment for hierarchical collaborative IOT systems, pp. 295–299. IEEE (2017)
11. Ren, Y., Li, X., Liu, H., Cheng, Q., Ma, J.: Blockchain-based trust management framework for distributed internet of things. J. Comput. Res. Dev. **55**(7), 1462 (2018)

Cost-Aware Big Data Stream Processing in Cloud Environment

Ahmed Al-Mansoori$^{(\boxtimes)}$, Jemal Abawajy, and Morshed Chowdhury

School of Information Technology, Faculty of Science, Engineering and Built
Environment, Deakin University, Geelong, Australia
{ajalma,jemal.abawajy,morshed.chowdhury}@deakin.edu.au

Abstract. The increasing size of big data and the speed with which it
is generated have put a tremendous burden on cloud storage and communication systems. Network traffic and server capacity are crucial to
having systems that are cost aware during big data stream processing in
Software-Defined Network (SDN) enabled cloud environment. The common approach to address this problem has been through various optimization techniques. In this paper, we propose SDN based cost optimization approach to address the problem. Although SDN has been shown
to improve cloud system performance, there is little attention given to
SDN-based cost optimization approach to address the challenges of the
increasing big data. To this end, we used Spark Streaming Processing
approach (SSP). The proposed cost optimization approach is based on
SDN within the cloud environment and focuses on optimizing the communication and computational costs. We performed extensive experiments to valid the approach and compared it with a Spark Streaming
approach. The results of the experiment show that the proposed approach has better cost optimization than the baseline approach.

Keywords: Big data stream processing · Cloud computing · SSP ·
Cost-aware

1 Introduction

Big data is generated by a wide variety of resources such as Global Position-
ing System (GPS), Internet of Things (IoT) and social media systems [1]. With
its potential to derive high-quality insights and improve data-driven decision-
making, big data as a new paradigm has attracted increasing attention from
researchers and practitioners. Appropriately exploited, big data will enable
organisations to extract valuable insights, innovate growth and improve pro-
ductivity. Therefore, Cloud computing has become the backbone for processing
and analysing big data promptly. Cloud computing offers elastic on-demand
resources such as computing, storage, networking and software [2,3]. This pool
of resources is suitable for processing big data in real-time applications that
demand real-time processing. With recent attention to big data stream processing (BDSP), how to handle data traffic and volume in cloud data centre has
become a significant challenge. Especially the BDSP requirement for latency

L. Qi et al. (Eds.): CloudComp 2020, LNICST 363, pp. 120–136, 2021.
https://doi.org/10.1007/978-3-030-69992-5_10

and bandwidth issues brings new obstacles to cloud data centres. Moreover, the increasing size of big data and the speed with which it is generated has put a tremendous burden on cloud data centres. Besides, cloud data centres support numerous users, simultaneously causing a rapid increase in network traffic to the data centre, which also increases energy consumption [4]. Most importantly, the conventional network technologies and architectures that are most visible in the contemporary cloud data centres pose a severe challenge to the prospect of handling large volumes of data in real-time in cloud data centres [5]. Therefore, the need to meet traffic management for BDSP has raised interest for developing a mechanism that ensures the Quality of Service (QoS) to end-users such as delivering optimal services with as many minimal costs as possible [6]. A significant challenge is how to ensure the QoS for big data stream processing. A variety of approaches have been proposed to address these challenges. The primary practice is to push the data streams straight to a cloud data centre to optimise the processing the data when it reaches the data centre through approaches such as allocation of virtual machines [7] and optimisation techniques such as machine learning [8–10]. These approaches rarely consider the inherent BDSP issues that include a high level of latency, high level of data rates, and the infinite order of incoming streams [11]. Therefore, a robust framework that ensures QoS for big data stream processing is necessary [12].

A possible approach to address these challenges is to deploy a SDN. [13] shows that the data centres based on conventional network technologies and architectures are inferior to SDN-based cloud data centres because the later allows for the network to be managed dynamically and thus greatly enhance the efficiency of the network. As a result, interest in SDN-based cloud data centres has recently increased. SDN-enabled distributed open exchange framework for dynamic optimisation of end-to-end (E2E) and QoS paths selection has been discussed in [14].

[15] discuss a software-defined network (SDN) for big data stream processing. [12] propose an SDN-enabled network service for big data science suitable for campus or local area networks. [5] propose an SDN-based traffic management method for cloud data centre. Although an approach that utilises a software-defined network (SDN) for big data stream processing has started appearing [15], it is still at its infancy. Moreover, the challenges of cost optimisation while at the same time, ensuring that performance levels are highly maintained remains. To address these challenges, we propose an SDN-based framework that provides QoS in terms of cost optimisation for big data stream processing. We make the following contributions:

- A mathematical formulation of the cost optimisation while ensuring efficient performance.
- An SDN-based framework that ensures QoS in terms of cost optimisation for big data stream processing Results of the experimental evaluation to validate the proposed approach and its performance.

The rest of the paper is organised as follows. Section 2 covers the review of related works while Sect. 3 covers the problem formation. In Sect. 4, the system model is discussed while Sect. 5 presents the proposed stream big data processing framework. Section 6 covers the validation of results found, and Sect. 7 covers the conclusion.

2 Related Work

Cloud computing and big data stream processing have emerged as important areas of research, and they continue to receive a lot of attention among researchers. There have been several attempts to investigate cost optimisation issue in the SDN enabled cloud environment. Several researchers have tried to come up with efficient scheduling methods aimed at ensuring cost optimisation. Below is a review of the researchers that have performed an investigation on the issue and the shortcomings of their studies that determine the improvements that we shall make.

[9] described an approach that could be used to minimise cost for big data processing in data centres distributed in various locations. The author characterised data processing using "two-dimensional Markov chain" and derived the time to completion closed-form. Using this, the author computed a joint optimisation as an MINLP problem. The model was further based on graph construction using the function $G_v = (V_v, E_v)$. In the function, V_v stands for the tasks while E_v represents the data links. The authors covered several costs, including communication, server, and operation costs. They also focused on determining the time taken to complete a given task by taking into account computation and data transmission to determine the average time it takes to complete. Also modelled their problem as a mixed "integer non-linear programming" and proposed a way their problem could be linearised. This gives an insight into the areas where cost optimisation can be looked at so that the optimisation goals can be met. The shortcoming of this approach is that it never takes into account the fact that the servers have calculation and capacity limit limitations.

[7] defined a task flow graph algorithm denoted by Gt = (Vt, Et) where Vt represented all the tasks while Et denoted that data flow links that existed among the tasks. The algorithm helped the authors to determine the way of minimising communication cost in data centres that are distributed widely. The modelling framework proposed by the authors described "representative intertrack relationship semantics" in BDSP. The authors also formulated the "communication cost minimisation problem" for BDSP and came up with mixed-integer linear programming (MILP) and proved that the problem was NP-hard. Using the MILP, the authors came up with their solution. The shortcoming of this work is that the authors never took into consideration how the placement of the VMs will affect their solution. They assumed that the solution would work well under all conditions. However, VM placement is a crucial issue to the MILP solution that they proposed.

[16] proposed an ORCP algorithm for cost optimisation in cloud computing. The authors note that before ORCP algorithm, OVMP algorithm was already being used. OVMP algorithm helped in solving the problem of provisioning resources for cloud consumers and placement of VMs. With the ORCP algorithm, the researchers hoped to improve the number of stages involved in provisioning and reduce costs. Even though the authors never define an actual formula, they argue that using the ORCP algorithm is a right approach for large sets of scenarios. ORCP algorithm has been shown to be capable of performing in many studies. The authors formulated the stochastic programming model and took into consideration the price and demand uncertainty. They consider the demand uncertainty by the consumers and the price uncertainties from the cloud service providers. The authors hold that limiting these uncertainties is crucial to cost optimisation. The authors solved the ORCP problem using "simple average approximation approach" and this enhanced their ability to arrive at an optimum solution. The work was not without its shortcomings, the greatest of which the complexity of the programming language used. It is not easy to follow this algorithm to the conclusion and make sense of the entire solution.

Chen et al. [17] defined a model that was aimed at minimising computation and communication costs during big data stream processing. In the attempt to find the "optimal solution", the authors started with structuring an "ESWG" using the task "semantics of streaming workflows" and the diversity of prices of "geo-distributed data centres." The authors also formulated the "streaming workflow allocation problem" often known as MILP. Additionally, the authors pressed streaming workflow algorithms based on DC-ESWG and TC-ESWG and proved that their approach could work out better with lower costs. However, the shortcoming of the solution the authors provided was that it had a longer execution time with limited its efficiency. The algorithm has also not been tested in a real-world problem, and there is a lot of doubt on its workability. In other work Chen et al. [18] focused on cost-minimization in using transformation-based streaming workflow allocation where data centres are geographically distributed. They used streaming workflow allocation as the problem and addressed it with their proposed solution.

Zhao et al. [19] proposed a cost-aware scheduling algorithm on the cloud environment. The algorithm determined cost based on the total processing time. The algorithm determining time-based on the cost of resources and the number of processing tasks. The authors argued that to reduce the time; there is a need to ensure the cost remains low and the number of tasks processed at a time is also kept as minimum as possible. The function was: $T_{total} = max\Sigma_{t=1}^{n}T_{(r,t)}$. Where $T_{(r,t)}$ stands for the time cost of resources r to process task t and n is the number of tasks that have been assigned to r. The shortcoming of this research is that it never addresses the influence that the distribution of data has on schedule. Therefore, it would be difficult to ascertain the result gotten or even confirm that it is accurate or not.

In [20], the authors defined a big data processing architecture known as RedEdge, which used the principle of "data reduction" on edge to facilitate big data new the edge. The algorithm used mobile IoT-devices as the primary processing platforms. The authors established that the model could reduce "big data streams" by up to 92.8% while optimising memory and energy consumptions on mobile devices. The biggest shortcoming of this model is that it never takes security and privacy into account. Therefore, there is no way of guaranteeing the protection of data that is streamed. This is a significant flaw that needs to be addressed because security must be given a priority regardless of the model that is used.

The models described above aim at providing an effective way of managing big data. They aim at improving the computation and storage process as a way of optimising costs. The issue that should be addressed in data processing is ensuring adequate and reliable data placement. SDN is a concept that is being embraced in the cloud environment. Without SDN, managing and provisioning networks was always a labour intensive and challenging process. SDN eliminates this pain by enabling administrators to use virtual resources in their network administration. Even though the several algorithmic developments have come with their benefits, their failures have also been well documented. Most of the algorithms that have been developed face issues of scalability after they have left the laboratory or simulation environment. Most of the algorithms developed are not fault-tolerant, and they lack the stability of a system that is ready to be deployed in the production environment. Additionally, those of the models that are developed assume that they will be executed offline. Some have also considered that their execution will be on a big batch of data. Most importantly, most of the algorithms to not provide for knowledge exchange to ensure that they can provide optimum solutions. The models designed have not been able to make use of the power of SDN. However, coming up with a model that is based on SDN supported cloud environment can help solve the shortcomings addressed above and increase scalability. The proposed model will aim at using the power of SDN to increase availability and scalability dynamically.

3   Problem Formulation

The problem being investigated in the research work is based on the establishment of a mechanism that ensures that BDSP in a cloud environment is enhanced using an elaborate and robust method of resource allocation. It is noteworthy that the existing methods of allocating resources in a BDSP environment need to have a balance between performance and the cost of resources incurred by the end-user. Majority of cloud implementations utilises implementation approaches that focus on the strategic placement of virtual machines. Numerous literature materials focus on the best strategies for placing virtual resources in a BDSP environment to ensure that performance is enhanced while at the same time cost utilisation is optimized. It is noteworthy that the placement strategies of VM resources should be based on the understanding of the cloud environment as well as the traffic requirements. Fundamentally, there lacks a comprehensive framework aimed at enhancing cost optimisation in BDSP based on a cloud utilising SDNs for the processing of real-time data. There is a need to develop a comprehensive cost optimisation model that will ensure that BDSP in a cloud environment that uses SDN is optimized for maximum performance.

There is a excessive concern in ensuring that "big data stream processing" in the cloud environment is cost-effective. Adding SDN to control the entire process comes with added benefits, and there is a need to ensure that cost-benefit is also guaranteed. The issue is ensuring the challenge of cost optimisation is met in the long run.

To explain the problem, let us assume that we have S servers each having different capacity. The servers for a set $S = \{1, 2, 3, 4, 5......s\}$. All these servers work at the same time, holding data that users may need during streaming. It is possible that these servers will have different computation capacities and powers, and they will, in turn, have different cost variations. Therefore, we will model the cost of streaming data. Let $C^i = \{1, 2, 3, 4, 5.....c^i\}$ processing costs, where C^i is the streaming cost for a given quantity of streamed data Q. We consider the resource consumption by CPU for every streaming job. This is necessary to establish the problem and determine how best it can be solved. We assume that every server has a capacity K and a processing speed P and takes time t to stream the data needed. A single server may need to handle multiple stream requests. Our primary interest is on cost optimisation. Therefore, we may want to know the time and cost of streaming a given quantity of information on each server and the resources used during this streaming. In simple terms, we want to know the cost of resources taken to stream data on a server concerning server capacity, the total number of streaming tasks, and the time taken to stream this data. We define the following equation to help model the cost issue:

$$C^i = Q_{si}K_{sn}P_{si}t_{si} \tag{1}$$

Therefore, we compute the different parameters for each server that leads to a reduction in the cost to be able to solve this problem. We want to reduce the total communication cost so that we can reduce the congestion on the network We will use the data gathered to draw up several cost components against each server. First, we will determine the server cost against the rate at which tasks arrive. We will also determine how communication costs compare with the number of SDN enabled servers that are being used. We will further examine the communication cost with the task arrival rate. Another cost component that will be determined is the operation cost, and it will also be compared with the number of servers and the task arrival rate. All these will be plotted in a graph to give a better comparative analysis that can be used to draw up meaningful conclusions. For us to be able to assign workflow streaming tasks in SDN supported cloud environment, we should consider several constraints. First, to total requests, data flow for task ti to be processed in the entire cloud environment will have to be optimum to ensure that the data flow is maximum. Therefore, we shall have:

$$\Sigma_{k=i}^{n}x(t_i, d) = E(t_p) \tag{2}$$

where $E(t_p)$ represents the incoming data flow for t_i.

Secondly, we need to consider the total computational resources that are required for the streaming workflows are ensure that they are kept at the best possible level. Finally, we need to consider the total of the network flows that are incoming and ensure that there is a good flow all around. The overall goal is to ensure that the total cost is kept as low as possible.

4 Proposed Model

In this work, the Spark Streaming Processing (SSP) model was used; the SSP is an executable object-oriented language that can help to model distributed systems. In addition, the flexibility offered by SSP is better than that of other ad hoc simulators as it has "parallel run-time support" and, it can support CPU memory and resources. In this work, the experiments were performed using CloudSim SDN based prototype application. The observations were made on SDN-enabled big data stream processing in the cloud for resource optimisation. The results are presented in terms of the number of physical servers, processing time considered at three levels such as local, distributed and random. The number of service requests and the delay caused are also observed. The proposed SSP model has an ABS data type with an associated size and an identifier. In the definition of the data types, the manes of parameters used in the constructor become "accessor functions." In the proposed model, an EmptyBatch function helps in determining whether the batch is zero or not, as shown below:

- type BatchID=int;
- data Batch =Batch (BatchID bID, int bSize);
- def Bool isEmptyBatch (Batch batch)=(bSize(batch)==0

This work focuses on batch modelling so as to keep the modelling simple. In this regard, it is assumed that the batch interval specified by users is equal to the block interval. The focus is also on modelling allocations that can be used to stream data and different job levels. The stage level processing is achieved through Stage and STJob data types. "STJob" is used to define a job that is not empty, while "Stage" defines those constraints that care used for execution at every stage.

- type StageId=String;
- data STJob=STJob (List<StageID> stages);
- data Stage=Stage (StageID stID, List<StageID> constr);

The Fig. 1 shows the architecture of the proposed SSP model.

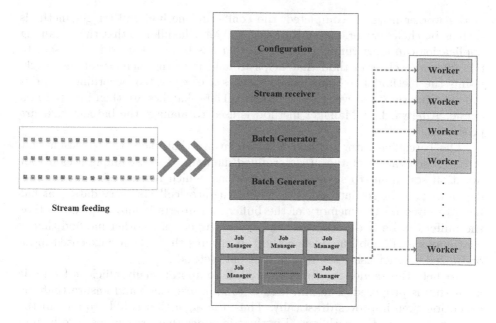

Fig. 1. SSP architecture

The architecture above has the main block on which users can configure their streaming applications. Figure 1 also has an underlying framework for Spark stream processing together with a "class SparkDriver" to help in modelling the Spark driver of the applications that are streamed. There is also a "class Worker" that can be used to model the work notes for applications that are used to process streams. The SSP has the following configuration parameters:

– The "job workflow specification" of the applications used for streaming.
– The cost of execution at every stage of data.
– The total number of worker nodes that are used in running applications.
– The resources that each worker node needs.
– The pattern for the data intervals
– The interval for the batches
– The maximum job numbers allowed to run concurrently.

The interface of the Spark driver has the following methods: jobScheduler, batchGenerator, streamReceiver, confSetup, and jobManager. When the SSP is launched, the confSetup method is invoked so that the number of worker nodes that have been requested can be created. It is the responsibility of the class worker to model every worker node. The class worker also has a method that is called exe. Using the modelling of the batch level, exe is executed by every stage of the streaming job. The cost expression that is used is e. The execution time of each step is determined by the expression "e" which denotes cost, and the speed of the CPU used for processing at the worker node. When the creation of the worker nodes is completed, the confSetup method will trigger methods such as batchGenerator, streamReceiver, and jobSchedular so that the streaming application can start running. The data that has been streamed is then sent to the streamReceiver method that helps to hold it in the memory of the spark. Using the method batchGenerator, batches are generated according to prior pre-configurations for every batch interval. These batches are then inserted in a queue. Afterwards, joManager method is used to manage the batches that are processed.

The batchGenerator method helps to ensure that there is a constant flow of batch generation at the predetermined intervals. The technique uses a wait duration statement to suspend its operations, which resume after some time, depending on the set interval. The batchGenerator collects every data that has been received on the memory of the buffer and inserts it into a queue so that the buffer can be free to continue the processing cycle. Another method that is continuous is the jobScheduler method. It ensures that jobs are executed in an organized manner using the first-in-first-out method.

To help the model the function well, a computationally efficient heuristic algorithm is proposed. The aim here is to minimize costs and ensure that the execution time improves drastically. Thus, the algorithm is able to stream the cloud servers and the workflows. Firstly, two nodes that are supposed to help in the streaming of data are defined. The first node is the "stream data source" s node and the second node is the "stream data sink node" t. The locations of these nodes are usually predetermined. A virtual node V_v can be created for task T_t. Subsequently, a link is created between these virtual nodes using the structures of the patterns created by the streaming workflows; Dc denotes the links. The associated costs between server i and j is determined so that the communication costs between D_{ci} and D_{cj}, and the computational costs between D_{ci} and D_{cj} can be calculated. The main focus here is the data nodes, rather than the task nodes.

The complexity of the proposed model p, and its ability to work well depends on the number of workflows, the number of tasks within the workflows and the number of servers within an SDN-enabled cloud environment. Therefore, another algorithm that takes the number of workflows W, together with the latency requirement is viable. Thus, an approach that can be used in combining the server's nodes and the tasks appropriately. If that can be achieved, then the computational time can be reduced effectively. Therefore, streaming workflows will have to be partitioned to reduce their size. To achieve this, the workflow is first partitioned. Firstly, the "streaming workflow" F is mapped into its adjacent matrix $A(F)$ with n vertices d_n. Where n refers to the total number of tasks in F and can be denoted as

$$An(F) = a_{ij}n_{xn} \tag{3}$$

Where a_{ij} is used to refer to the value of communication requirement between two tasks i and j.

Next, the adjacent matrix $A(F)$ was translated to $B(F)$ using a data-clustering algorithm. Using matrix decomposition, it was possible to map $B(F)$

into submatrices denoted by $\{B-1(F), B-2_F), B_3(F)..........B_k(F)\}$. The $B(F)$ matrix can then be used to divide F into several subgraphs that have smaller tasks. Finally, depending on the partitioning of the streaming workflow, we can have a definite graph for the algorithm.

5   Experiment

To evaluate the results of the proposed SSP model, a number of approaches were compared. The first approach was based on allocating workflows into SDN enabled cloud environment, and the next approach involved investigating the communication cost minimisation issue by comparing ow balancing and placement of virtual machines within the cloud environment. The focus is on communication and computational costs. Therefore, the performance metrics here are computational cost, which takes into consideration how much cost is incurred by a server in SDN-enabled cloud environment in executing streaming tasks. The cost was calculated as a total of all the tasks within the streaming flows. The next metric was the communication cost that determined how much traffic costs were incurred during the big data stream processing process within the cloud environment, especially following the SSP model. With these, the total costs that were incurred during the streaming process were determined. Here, the execution time for tasks during the streaming process was also taken into consideration.

The SSP model used over 300 streaming workflows which were made of different patterns. Every workflow had 50 tasks. The computation and communication costs were evenly distributed among these tasks, and they ranged from 0 to 50. The cloud environment chosen had close to 20 servers which each server is having a communication and computation capacity ranging from 10,000 to 100,000. There was a uniform distribution of communication and communication costs between the servers ranging from 0 to 0.2. It is essential to remember that the costs can vary depending on the server. For those streaming on the same network, the costs were set at 0.02, while those streaming from different networks was set at 0.1–0.2. The distribution was unequal.

In this work, the concept of spark streaming was employed, and a relatively stable computer with 8 GB RAM and 2.4 GHz processor speed was used. The computer was Intel (R) Core i7. The performance was evaluated using useful state approaches in terms of their abilities to achieve the required accuracy in terms of communication and computational costs. Tremendous efforts were made to ensure that close to 300 streaming workflows were averaged, while several parameters were varied including the type of the workflow, the requirement for data the capacity of the server, and the scale of the request of the workflow and the server.

6   Result and Dissection

First of all, the performance of the proposed model was evaluated by looking at the communication costs, computational costs and overall costs by averaging the 300 workflows. Also, the costs were compared with the spark streaming, and the Fig. 2 shows that the proposed approach worked best in terms of saving on costs.

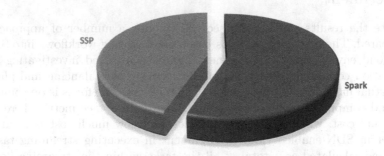

Fig. 2. Total cost

The result shows that the algorithm which was used helped in saving a significant portion of the total costs that were incurred in the entire process. Furthermore, the approaches were compared based on computational costs and communication costs independently, as shown in Figs. 3 and 4.

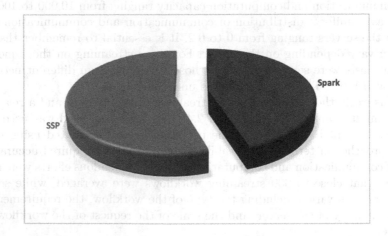

Fig. 3. Computation cost

Figure 3 show that the proposed approach performed well when only considering the communication costs, but the performance was poor in terms of computational costs. This indicates that the method which was used can lead to a lot of cost savings, if only the communication cost is taken into consideration.

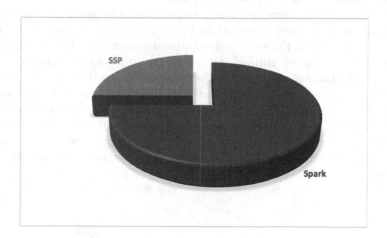

Fig. 4. Communication cost

The performances were also evaluated in terms of the time taken for execution. Figures 5 shows the batch processing time for both Spark Streaming and SSP.

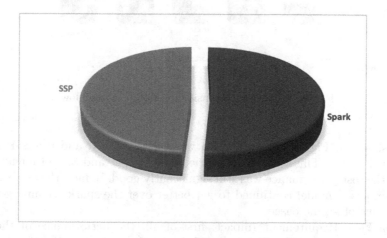

Fig. 5. Execution time

From the Fig. 5, it is evident that the proposed approach performed well in terms of the execution time, because it lowered the average batch execution time of Spark Streaming model. The performed better as it saved about 2,000 execution time compared with the spark streaming. Also, this approach reduced the computational space for latency requirements during stream processing. There-fore, the results reveal that, the proposed approach performs better by lowering the computational costs and processing time.

Considering the workflow type: data streaming can be performed for different types of data and in different quantities but using a small quantity of computa-tional power. It is with the used computational power that the communication cost incurred can be determined. Other streaming tasks can involve a small amount of data but still require a lot of power to be used in the computation. The value was varied in order to see the effect that it had on the communication and computational cost. The value was changed from 0.1 to 3. The results in the Fig. 6 show that our SSP model performed better at different values for all the values compared with the spark streaming. Also, the total cost was determined, and it was established that the SSP model performs better for all values, as shown below:

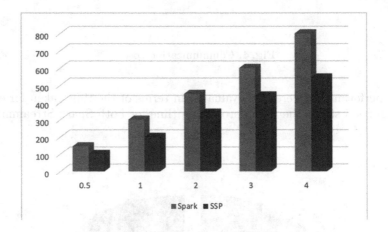

Fig. 6. Performance considering different workflow

As shown in Fig. 6, the value of a was varied at 0–1, and the SSP model performed better. This was further varied to 0.5, 1, 2, and 3, and for all those values, the cost performance was still significantly good. In fact, the performance of the proposed model continued to get better over the spark streaming model as the value of an increased.

Data Flow Requirement Impact: first of all, the performance of the pro-posed model was evaluated in terms of the two costs by varying the dataflow requirement between 5 and 25. It was observed that with an increase in the flow requirement, increase occurred in the processing time as more input data sets had to be processed. Therefore, the expectation was that the computational and communication costs had to increase. As shown in the Fig. 7, the total costs for both models increased as the data flow requirement increased. However, the

proposed SSP model achieved optimum performance with low data flow requirements. As the data flow requirements increased, the performance of the proposed
model became almost as worse as that of spark streaming.

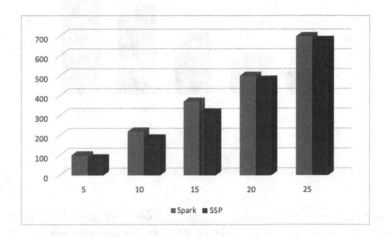

Fig. 7. Performance considering data flow requirement

Impact of the Requirement of VM: the requirements of the VMs were varied
from 10 to 40 so as to note the effect which that would have on the communication and computational cost. As the requirements on VM_s increased, the costs
were also expected to increase. The performance of the VM_s was almost the
same for both the spark streaming and the SSP model. This could be attributed
to the fact that the proposed model was not worked out to make the optimum
use of VM_s. However, the fact that it was able to match the performance of
spark streaming is considered as a big plus, and it showed that the VM_s could
further help to optimize costs. Increasing the VM requirement towards 40 led
to an increase in the total costs for both the communication and the computational costs. Also, the effect of increasing the VM requirement from 10 to 40 on
the execution time was determined. It was noted that there was no significant
change in the execution time, even as the VM requirement increased. In general,
the lower the execution time, the better the performance.

Impact of the Sever Capacity: As with the previous steps, this step began by
evaluating the effect that the capacity of the cloud servers had on the communication and computational costs, and afterwards, the impact on the execution
time was investigated. In addition, the DC capacity was varied from 10,000 to
100,0000. The results of the experiment show that the lower the DC capacity,
the higher the costs. This was true for both the proposed SSP model and spark
streaming. However, the efficiency of the SSP model meant that it had better
cost performances when compared with the spark streaming model.

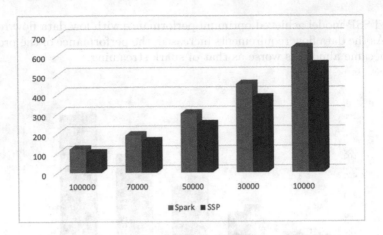

Fig. 8. Performance considering the Requirement of VM

As the Fig. 8, the performance of the proposed SSP model becomes better than the spark streaming model as the server capacity becomes lower. The gap in the total cost becomes more significant as the server capacity decreases. Therefore, it was concluded that the proposed model was more efficient at different capacity levels.

Further analysis which was performed focused on the impact on the scale of workflows and servers. All these, further revealed that the proposed model produced better performances overall, especially in terms of lower costs and better execution times. The evaluation focused on communication and optimisation costs. All the experiments performed revealed that the proposed model is better than the spark streaming model. It can be ascertained that the experiments were conducted with the utmost accuracy, and the results obtained were good. The model can therefore be taken as a viable solution to the issue of cost optimisation in the SDN-enabled cloud environment. In this regard, it has proven that this solution can indeed be taken into consideration and given some serious thoughts.

7 Summary

The SSP model was presented as an alternative to Spark Streaming with the aim of addressing the challenge of cost savings for big data stream processing in SDN-supported cloud environment. Also, the capabilities of the proposed model has been shown, and it has been established that the proposed model has the ability of help users adapt to the settings of their streaming applications, including stage execution cost and workflow. Apart from that, the model's ability to replicate the performance of Spark Streaming has been demonstrated, as well as its ability to provide users with a suitable alternative that enables them to save cost while maintaining the level of performance that they need. The experimental results showed that the proposed model could allow users to predict how their stream processing will perform under various conditions. Big data stream processing is growing in importance, and with the concept of software-defined networking growing, a lot of changes can be expected. As technology changes, people will want cost-effective performance. Big data looks like a simple concept, yet it is complicated. There are also not enough professionals in the field with the ability to handle the technology effectively. A lot of resources are needed to collect, analyse and store big data entities. For this reason, cost-saving has become a significant concern.

There are several methods of resource optimisation, but one of the commonly used one is the reduction of the processing delay and ensuring that the streaming process is faster. For this reason, the proposed model will be more suitable and adequate for the cloud environment, because it involves ways through which batch processing delays can be reduced. The results further indicated that the FIFO approach could be more suitable for the optimization of resources on the cloud environment in processing data packets. Specifically, it covers the time used for packet processing. Users on cloud-based environments can use the model proposed here without doubt, because it has been tested thoroughly and compared against Spark Streaming which is one of the best models out there. Despite the numerous benefits offered by the proposed model, it is accompanied by some limitations, and as such, it is hoped that in the future, it can be fine-tuned in a manner that allows its operation on all the popular platforms. Currently, it can only work on a few of those platforms.

Additionally, that a model which is capable of addressing the security and privacy demands can be developed in the future. One of the most significant shortcomings of SDN technology is that it has not been able to address the security issue effectively. Due to this fact, many people have shown reluctance in accepting technology as a whole. The success of this model depends on the ability of the SDN to address its security shortcomings. It would be difficult to achieve cost optimisation without addressing security demands.

References

1. Abawajy, J.: Comprehensive analysis of big data variety landscape. Int. J. Parallel Emergent Distrib. Syst. **30**(1), 5–14 (2015)
2. Chowdhury, M., Abawajy, J., Kelarev, A., Jelinek, H.: A clustering-based multilayer distributed ensemble for neurological diagnostics in cloud services. IEEE Trans. Cloud Comput. **8**, 473–483 (2016)
3. Shojafar, M., Canali, C., Lancellotti, R., Abawajy, J.: Adaptive computing-plus-communication optimization framework for multimedia processing in cloud systems. IEEE Trans. Cloud Comput. **8**(4), 1162–1175 (2020). https://doi.org/10.1109/TCC.2016.2617367
4. Zhou, Z., et al.: Minimizing SLA violation and power consumption in cloud data centers using adaptive energy-aware algorithms. Future Gener. Comput. Syst. **86**, 836–850 (2018)
5. Wang, Y., Wang, X., Li, H., Dong, Y., Liu, Q., Shi, X.: A multi-service differentiation traffic management strategy in SDN cloud data center. Comput. Netw. **171**, 107143 (2020)

6. Bouras, C., Ntarzanos, P., Papazois, A.: Cost modeling for SDN/NFV based mobile 5G networks. In: 2016 8th International Congress on Ultra Modern Telecommunications and Control Systems and Workshops (ICUMT), pp. 56–61. IEEE (2016)
7. Gu, L., Zeng, D., Guo, S., Xiang, Y., Hu, J.: A general communication cost optimization framework for big data stream processing in geo-distributed data centers. IEEE Trans. Comput. **65**(1), 19–29 (2015)
8. Abawajy, J., Chowdhury, M., Kelarev, A.: Hybrid consensus pruning of ensemble classifiers for big data malware detection. IEEE Trans. Cloud Comput. **8**(2), 398–407 (2020). https://doi.org/10.1109/TCC.2015.2481378
9. Sowmya, T.S.R.: Cost minimization for big data processing in geo-distributed data centers. Asia-Pac. J. Convergent Res. Interchange **2**(4), 33–41 (2016)
10. Bhattacharya, M., Islam, R., Abawajy, J.: Evolutionary optimization: a big data perspective. J. Netw. Comput. Appl. **59**, 416–426 (2016)
11. Cao, H., Wachowicz, M.: The design of an IoT-GIS platform for performing automated analytical tasks. Comput. Environ. Urban Syst. **74**, 23–40 (2019)
12. Shah, S.A.R., et al.: AmoebaNet: an SDN-enabled network service for big data science. J. Netw. Comput. Appl. **119**, 70–82 (2018)
13. Adami, D., et al.: An SDN orchestrator for cloud data center: system design and experimental evaluation. Trans. Emerg. Telecommun. Technol. **28**(11), e3172 (2017)
14. Bagci, K.T., Tekalp, A.M.: SDN-enabled distributed open exchange: dynamic QoS-path optimization in multi-operator services. Comput. Netw. **162**, 106845 (2019)
15. Vicentini, C., Santin, A., Viegas, E., Abreu, V.: SDN-based and multitenant-aware resource provisioning mechanism for cloud-based big data streaming. J. Netw. Comput. Appl. **126**, 133–149 (2019)
16. Poobalan, A., Selvi, V.: Optimization of cost in cloud computing using OCRP algorithm. Int. J. Eng. Trends Technol. **4**(5), 2105–2107 (2013)
17. Chen, W., Paik, I., Li, Z.: Cost-aware streaming workflow allocation on geo-distributed data centers. IEEE Trans. Comput. **66**(2), 256–271 (2016)
18. Chen, W., Paik, I., Hung, P.C.: Transformation-based streaming workflow allocation on geo-distributed datacenters for streaming big data processing. IEEE Trans. Serv. Comput. **12**, 654–668 (2016)
19. Zhao, G.: Cost-aware scheduling algorithm based on PSO in cloud computing environment. Int. J. Grid Distrib. Comput. **7**(1), 33–42 (2014)
20. Habib ur Rehman, M., Jayaraman, P.P., Malik, S.U.R., Khan, A.U.R., Medhat Gaber, M.: Rededge: a novel architecture for big data processing in mobile edge computing environments. J. Sensor Actuator Netw. **6**(3), 17 (2017)

Cloud Computing Applications

Research on the Development of Natural Human-Computer Interaction for Mobile Terminals

Qing Zhang[1] and Xiaoyong Lin[2]([✉])

[1] Computer Engineering College, Jimei University, XiaMen, China
[2] Xiamen University of Technology, XiaMen, China
qingzh_xm@163.com

Abstract. Human-Computer Interaction (HCI) technology, as an important part of computer systems, has developed rapidly in computer science. It has experienced a transition from humans adapting to computers, to computers constantly adapting to humans. With the development of human-computer interaction, users are more and more inclined to use natural communication methods such as natural language, gestures, and vision instead of traditional keyboard and mouse input. In today's era of the mobile Internet, mobile terminals have been widely used. Due to their portability and mobility, users expect their interactions with mobile terminals to be smooth and natural. The natural human-computer interaction of mobile terminals has become a research hotspot. Through the analysis of the evolution process of mobile terminal human-computer interaction, combined with the latest human-computer interaction technology, this paper discusses the hot issues in mobile human-computer interaction and concludes that the future human-computer interaction of mobile terminals has four development directions: 1) natural human computer interaction, 2) augmented reality interaction, 3) multi-modal fusion, 4) affective computing.

Keywords: Natural human-computer interaction · Mobile Terminals · AR · Multi-modal fusion · Affective Computing

1 Introduction

The term "mobile terminals" refers to computer devices that can be used in the mobile, that can provide digital information services or exchange data and information through the network. Mobile terminals include mobile phones, laptops, tablets, and other smart terminal devices.

With the emergence of the 5G network, mobile communication is becoming more and more broadband. In addition, most smart mobile terminals have strong computing power and have rapidly transformed from the original mobile network terminal to the key entrance of Internet business, becoming the main innovation platform in the mobile Internet era.

L. Qi et al. (Eds.): CloudComp 2020, LNICST 363, pp. 139–145, 2021.
https://doi.org/10.1007/978-3-030-69992-5_11

China Internet Network Information Center (CNNIC) released its 45th statistical report on the development of China's Internet. It shows that by March 2020, the number of Internet users in China had reached 904 million, including 897 million mobile Internet users accounting for 99.3%. Mobile Internet service scenarios are constantly enriching, the scale of mobile terminals is increasing rapidly, and the amount of mobile data is continuously expanding. It shows that Internet access through mobile terminals has become the most important access to the Internet. Human computer interaction for mobile applications has also become a research hotspot.

From the evolution process of mobile phone human-computer interaction, mobile human-computer interaction experienced the following three stages:

1. The human-computer interaction interface in the form of characters represented by MOTOROLA.
   In 1993, Motorola launched the Motorola 3200 in China, which only includes voice and text messaging functions. Since then, the mobile phones launched by various mobile phone manufacturers have used physical keyboard for input, including numbers 0–9 and several function keys. The mobile phone has simple functions, simple interaction mode and poor user experience.
2. Graphical user interface represented by Apple iPhone.
   The advent of Apple's iPhone in 2007 is a revolutionary product across the ages. The traditional physical-digital keyboard disappeared and was replaced by the touch screen interface. Instructions and information can be input through the direct touch of fingers or pens with the screen. The new touch screen interaction mode greatly facilitates the user's rapid human-computer interaction. The smooth operation experience of the iPhone also makes designers pay more attention to user experience, and user centered human-computer interaction design has become the mainstream.
3. Multi-modal human-computer interaction interface.
   With the development of multi-modal human-computer interaction technology, visual, auditory, tactile, and other sensory channels are used in human-computer interaction such as gesture interaction, voice interaction, and expression interaction. Users can interact with mobile phones in a variety of ways, which greatly improves the user experience.

At present, promoted by the new generation of information technology clusters such as artificial intelligence, big data, cloud computing, VR/AR, etc., the natural human-computer interaction technology of mobile terminals has also entered a new development stage.

In the second part, the directions of human-computer interaction in mobile situations will be discussed from four research hot spots.

2 Research Review

2.1 Natural HCI

At present, the human-computer interface of mobile terminals mainly adopts graphical user interface (GUI). The traditional graphical user interface uses keyboard or mouse to input user instructions. Users need to learn the operation methods set by software developers, and complete the interaction process according to the preset operation process in the operation process, which make users cost time for learning and is an unnatural human-computer interaction.

Natural human-computer interaction refers to a process in which users only use the existing cognitive habits and familiar behavior patterns to interact with the computer when they interact with the computer. It is usually imprecise and a natural behavior.

The goal of natural human-computer interaction is to get rid of the shackles of mouse and keyboard, allow users to use their own senses and existing life experience to operate, and reduce the cost and burden of learning as much as possible.

The common natural interaction technologies include multi-touch, gesture recognition, expression recognition, voice interaction and eye tracking. With the development of natural interaction technology, one or more natural interaction technologies are used in the interaction of mobile terminals, forming the prototype of natural user interface.

However, there are some usability problems in the use of natural user interface, such as limited use scenarios, lack of functional visibility, cognitive differences and so on. These usability problems will increase the learning cost of users and turn natural interaction into unnatural. Obviously, it is not enough to only apply natural interaction technology to human-computer interaction. From another aspect, interaction design should also adopt user centered design (UCD) method, design a natural interaction mode with the best user experience by considering user psychology, user habits, user types and use scenarios.

Besides, with the continuous breakthrough of brain-computer interface technology [5], it will be possible to directly control the computer with ideas, which will completely change the form of human-computer interaction in the future. Natural human-computer interaction will develop from tangible interface to invisible interface. The best interaction is natural, and the best interface is no interface [14]. The human-computer interaction of mobile terminals will gradually move towards a more humanized, more intelligent and more user-friendly level of natural experience.

2.2 HCI with AR Scenarios

Augmented Reality (AR) is developed on the basis of Virtual Reality (VR), it emphasizes the combination of virtual and real. It integrates the real environment of the real world and the virtual environment generated by computer in real time, to bring users a relatively realistic comprehensive feeling in hearing, vision and touch, and realize the natural integration of human and environment. Augmented reality oriented human-computer interaction has the characteristics of virtual reality superposition, three-dimensional, real-time interaction.

With the rapid development of mobile terminal devices, the products represented by high-performance smart phones and wearable devices (smart glasses, etc.) provide a carrier for the practical application of augmented reality in mobile terminals. If the AR system can be integrated into a mobile phone, the camera is responsible for collecting images, and the processing unit is responsible for analyzing and reconstructing the images, to realize the alignment of the coordinate system and the fusion calculation of the virtual scene. The processed images will be displayed on the screen of the mobile phone, to realize the realistic enhancement effect.

AR provides users with a new interaction mode, including motion capture, tactile feedback, eye tracking, EMG simulation, etc. Among them, eye control interaction technology could introduced into mobile augmented reality. Users only use line of sight to operate instead of VR device,interact with mobile phone by eyes, that is especially suitable for human-computer interaction of mobile terminal AR [2, 3].

An AR device that could replace the mobile may be developed in the future, make all products with screens a thing of the past. It could allow consumers to scroll through applications without obscuring visibility of the real world. Dreaming even bigger, the highest level of augmented reality is "what you see is what you think, what you think is what you can", to achieve a more immersive interactive experience.

2.3 HCI with Multi-modal Fusion

Mobile terminals are portable, users expect to input and output instructions quickly and conveniently, which makes it more urgent for people to improve the efficiency of human-computer information exchange through visual, auditory, tactile and other interactive ways. At present, although mobile terminals adopt various human-computer interaction modes of sensing modal technology, the information recognition and processing of each modal are mostly separated, and the real intention of users may not be accurately obtained.

Intelligent human-computer interaction requires the fusion of multiple sensory information, namely multi-modal fusion. When you see a picture, text could be generated, when you see the text, pictures and videos could be imaged. An agent should be able to complete the modal transformation between vision and semantics. Multi-modal human-computer interaction is actually the simulation of natural interaction between people. It transplants the interaction mode between people into the interaction between human and computer, aiming at reducing the gap between human and computer, and creating a natural and harmonious human-computer environment.

At present, multi-modal user interface uses new technologies such as eye tracking, speech recognition, gesture input, etc., users can use multiple sensory modals to conduct human-computer interaction in a natural, parallel and cooperative method. By fusing multi-modal accurate and imprecise information, the system can quickly capture the user's intention. This relies on the technology of "multi-modal deep learning", which enables the agent itself to understand the multi-modal signal. It needs to accommodate the auditory, visual and sensing signals for unified thinking, so that the machine can carry out multi-modal collaborative learning and truly "smart". The mobile terminals based on artificial intelligence technology will be a robot with various sensors such as vision, hearing, smell and taste [11–13].

In addition to perceptual intelligence, mobile applications on mobile phones can also connect to the cloud brain through the network and have cognitive intelligence. At present, most of the solutions of mobile artificial intelligence rely on cloud computing, but in the application scenarios which need high real-time response, the computing of mobile terminals is also essential. In addition, security and privacy also need to use the advantages of terminal computing to achieve. With the upgrading of mobile artificial intelligence chip and optimization of algorithm, part of the computing and processing functions of AI should be migrated from cloud to mobile terminals.

2.4 HCI with Affective Computing

Even if computer is given a variety of intelligents, it is still unable to understand and adapt to human emotions, it unable recognition human emotion, also unable to express emotions.

In 1997, Professor Rosalind W. Picard who is the founder of the Affective Computing Research Group at the MIT Media Lab proposed the concept of affective computing, which includes emotion recognition, emotion representation, Emotion Modeling and emotional interaction [15]. Using emotional computing, it is expected that computers will have the ability to observe, understand and generate various emotions similar to human beings, and finally make human-computer interaction as natural as human interaction.

Affective computing is a highly integrated research field, which combines computational science, psychological science and cognitive science. It can be used in the process of human-computer interaction. By studying the emotional characteristics of human interaction and human-computer interaction, a human-computer interaction environment with emotional feedback is constructed. The human-computer interaction not only has high perception and cognitive intelligence, but also has high emotional intelligence. In the future the computer will have high EQ, which can effectively solve the situation perception, emotional understanding and emotional expression in human-computer interaction, and make reasonable response.

At present, affective computing is still in its infancy, and most of the research hotspots and achievements are reflected in the level of emotion recognition. For example, in facial expression recognition or natural language processing, machine learning and convolution neural network can be used to identify anger, disgust, fear, happiness, calm, sadness, surprise and so on. Most of the intelligent applications based on mobile terminals use the powerful computing power of the cloud to realize emotion recognition. This type of emotion recognition needs to be from the mobile terminals to the cloud, and then back to the mobile terminals from the cloud. Under the limitation of network bandwidth, there may be delay. However, with the advent of 5G era, the cloud based emotion recognition which highly real-time response is still worth looking forward to.

On the other hand, during the continuous evolution of intelligent mobile terminals, it is also trying to improve the traditional processor computing architecture so as to support the high-speed computing and low-power consumption required by machine learning. Emotion recognition, emotional interaction will become the instinct of mobile terminals.

Emotional information is often expressed from multiple dimensions such as language, voice intonation, facial and limbs in face-to-face communication. In the process of human-computer interaction, emotional feature recognition also needs to be calculated from multiple dimensions, such as text emotion analysis, facial expression recognition, speech emotion recognition, posture recognition, and even through physiological pattern recognition, such as skin electric response, breathing, heart rate, body temperature, brain wave and so on [10]. Multi-modal emotion information fusion and combining the context information of the situation at that time would make computer recognize and understand the human emotion.

Human-computer interaction with affective computing is shown in the Fig. 1 below.

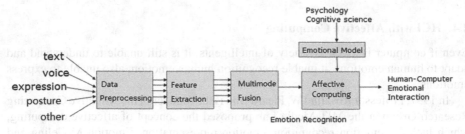

Fig. 1. HCI with affective computing

In addition, how to establish an emotional model based on psychology and cognitive science to express the relationship between emotion, cognition and will, which is suitable for machine implementation, will also be a great challenge.

3 Conclusion

The pervasiveness of mobile terminal services and applications fundamentally changed the way we access information and communicate with each other. With the continuous breakthrough of human-computer interaction technology, mobile human-computer interaction presents a trend of continuous development towards natural human-computer interaction, VR/AR, multi-modal fusion, and emotional human-computer interaction. The human-computer interaction of mobile terminals is gradually moving towards a more human-oriented, more intelligent, and more natural experience.

We can imagine the future through the comprehensive calculation of the user emotional model and generate empathy and emotionally interactive content through the addition of emotional factors to enhance user experience, establishing human-computer interaction with empathy, situational awareness, and natural harmony.

Acknowledgements. Major Research Topics of Social Science Base in Fujian Province: "Research on the future media industry and the development of strategic emerging industries in Fujian Province" (fj2018jdz055), 2018–2020.

References

1. Yi, X., Yu, C., Shi, Y.C.: Bayesian method for intent prediction in pervasive computing environments (in Chinese). Sci. Sin. Inf. **48**, 419–432 (2016). https://doi.org/10.1360/N11 2017-00228
2. Li, F.Y., Feng, J.P., Fu, M.S.: Research on natural human-computer interaction in virtual roaming. J. Phys. Conf. Ser. **1518**(1), 012022 (2020). https://doi.org/10.1088/1742-6596/ 1518/1/012022

3. Su, G.E., Sunar, M.S., Ismail, A.W.: Device-based manipulation technique with separated control structures for 3D object translation and rotation in handheld mobile AR. Int. J. Hum. Comput. Stud. **141**, 102433 (2020). https://doi.org/10.1016/j.ijhcs.2020.102433
4. Li, X., Zhang, M.: Emotion analysis for the upcoming response in open-domain human-computer conversation. In: U, L.H., Xie, H. (eds.) APWeb-WAIM 2018. LNCS, vol. 11268, pp. 352–367. Springer, Cham (2018). https://doi.org/10.1007/978-3-030-01298-4_29
5. Robert, L., Daniel, P.M.: Brain-computer interfaces and virtual reality for neurorehabilitation. In: Handbook of Clinical Neurology, vol. 168 (2020). https://doi.org/10.1016/B978-0-444-63934-9.00014-7.
6. Zhang, X.Y., Ban, X.J., Cheng, Z., Liu, T.: Modeling and recognition of human limbs cooperative interaction based on Random Increased Hybrid Learning Machine. Procedia Comput. Sci. **147**, 198–202 (2019). https://doi.org/10.1016/j.procs.2019.01.222
7. Alfaro, L., Linares, R., Herrera, J.: Scientific articles exploration system model based in immersive virtual reality and natural language processing techniques. Int. J. Adv. Comput. Sci. Appl. 9, 254–263 (2018). https://doi.org/10.14569/IJACSA.2018.090736
8. Bachmann, D., Weichert, F., Rinkenauer, G.: Review of three-dimensional human-computer interaction with focus on the leap motion controller. Sensors **18**(7), 2194 (2018). https://doi.org/10.3390/s18072194
9. Le, H.Y.: Modeling human behavior during touchscreen interaction in mobilesituations. In: MobileHCI 20'16 Adjunct. ACM (2016). https://doi.org/10.1145/2957265.2963113, 978-1-4503-4413-5/16/09
10. Patanè, A., Kwiatkowska, M.: Calibrating the classifier: siamese neural network architecture for end-to-end arousal recognition from ECG. In: Nicosia, G., Pardalos, P., Giuffrida, G., Umeton, R., Sciacca, V. (eds.) Machine Learning, Optimization, and Data Science. LOD 2018. Lecture Notes in Computer Science, vol. 11331, pp. 1–13. Springer, Cham (2019). https://doi.org/10.1007/978-3-030-13709-0_1
11. Cuzzocrea, A., Mumolo, E., Grasso, G.M.: An effective and efficient genetic-fuzzy algorithm for supporting advanced human-machine interfaces in big data settings. Algorithms **13**(1), 13 (2019). https://doi.org/10.3390/a13010013
12. Tsiourti, C., Weiss, A., Wac, K., Vincze, M.: Multimodal Integration of emotional signals from voice, body, and context: effects of (in)congruence on emotion recognition and attitudes towards robots. Int. J. Soc. Rob. **11**(4), 555–573 (2019). https://doi.org/10.1007/s12369-019-00524-z
13. Hobeom, H., Won, Y.S.: Gyroscope-based continuous human hand gesture recognition for multi-modal wearable input device for human machine interaction. Sensors (Basel, Switzerland) **19**(11) (2019). https://doi.org/10.3390/s19112562
14. Krishna, G.: The Best Interface is No Interface: The Simple Path to Brilliant Technology. Pearson Education Inc., New York (2015)
15. Rosalind, W.: Picard: Affective Computing. The MIT Press, Cambridge (1997)
16. Liu, G., Wang, Y., Orgun, M.A.: Finding K optimal social trust paths for the selection of trustworthy service providers in complex social networks, IEEE Trans. Serv. Comput. **6**(2) (2013)
17. Liu, G., Wang, Y., Orgun, M.A.: Optimal social trust path selection in complex social networks. In: Twenty-Fourth AAAI Conference on Artificial Intelligence (AAAI 2010), pp. 1391–1398 (2010)
18. Liu, G., et al.: MCS-GPM: multi-constrained simulation based graph pattern matching in contextual social graphs. IEEE Trans. Knowl. Data Eng. **30**(6), 1050–1064 (2018)
19. Liu, G., et al.: Multi-constrained graph pattern matching in large-scale contextual social graphs. In: IEEE 31st International Conference on Data Engineering (ICDE 2015), pp. 351–362 (2015)

Encoding Dual Semantic Knowledge for Text-Enhanced Cloud Services

Shicheng Cui[1], Qianmu Li[1,2]($\boxtimes$), Shu-Ching Chen[3], Jun Hou[4], Hanrui Zhang[1], and Shunmei Meng[1]

[1] School of Computer Science and Engineering,
Nanjing University of Science and Technology, Nanjing 210094, China
qianmu@njust.edu.cn
[2] Intelligent Manufacturing Department, Wuyi University, Jiangmen 529020, China
[3] School of Computing and Information Sciences, Florida International University,
Miami, FL 33199, USA
[4] Nanjing Vocational University of Industry Technology, Nanjing 210023, China

Abstract. Topic modeling techniques have been widely applied in many cloud computing applications. However, few of them have tried to discover latent semantic relationships of implicit topics and explicit words to generate a more comprehensive representation for each text. To fully exploit the semantic knowledge for text classification in cloud computing systems, we attempt to encode topic and word features based on their latent relationships. The extracted topical information reorganizes the original textual structures from two aspects: one is that the topic extracted by Latent Dirichlet Allocation (LDA) is viewed as a textual extension; the other is that the topic feature performs as a counterpart modality to the word. This paper proposes a Dual Semantic Embedding (DSE) method, which uses Convolutional Neural Networks (CNNs) to encode the dual semantic features of topics and words from the reorganized semantic structures. Experimental results show that DSE improves the performance of text classification and outperforms the state-of-the-art feature generation baselines on micro-F_1 and macro-F_1 scores over the real-world text classification datasets.

Keywords: Text classification · Dual Semantic Embedding · Convolutional Neural Networks

1 Introduction

Artificial Intelligence (AI) has been widely adopted in many real-world cloud computing services. Text classification [1] plays an important role in recent AI cloud computing platforms. For example, in some online recommendation systems [6,36], there are large quantities of reviews of items needed to be analyzed to estimate the sentiment [27] or to classify the items based on the textual information in cloud environments. Another interesting example is that in social networks [41], the techniques of text classification provided by some

© ICST Institute for Computer Sciences, Social Informatics and Telecommunications Engineering 2021
Published by Springer Nature Switzerland AG 2021. All Rights Reserved
L. Qi et al. (Eds.): CloudComp 2020, LNICST 363, pp. 146–159, 2021.
https://doi.org/10.1007/978-3-030-69992-5_12

social computing infrastructures, can help node classification [9,10,15,29] and link prediction [8,45]. With the rapid development of the deep learning techniques [13,21,22,31,32,38], plenty of AI applications have achieved great success. As a key component in intelligent cloud services, text classification still draws great attention. Thus, this study attempts to apply deep learning techniques to improve the effectiveness of text classification, which could help a large amount of intelligent data analytics in cloud computing systems.

In many Vector Space Model (VSM) [33] based methods, each text is represented as a vector in which each element indicates the frequency of a word appearing in the text. Although VSM is easy to comprehend and implement, there are some drawbacks in this model. The first drawback is the high dimensionality problem. VSM requires a dictionary that contains all words in a corpus. Usually, the form that represents a word is one-hot representation and the dimensionality of a dictionary is more than ten thousand magnitude, sometimes even higher. Next, it has the data sparseness problem, meaning that the words amongst a text only use a small portion of the vocabulary, but the whole dictionary is needed. Last but not the least, the format of the bag-of-words [16] in VSM causes semantic information loss. All of these result in high computational complexity, tremendous memory consumption, and lower accuracy of classification in VSM.

To deal with the aforementioned problems, dimensionality reduction methods were proposed. χ^2 statistics [43] and Information Gain (IG) [2,42] are two classical methods that select important terms in texts to build the vocabulary of keywords. These methods and their variants [34,37,40] indeed reduce the dimensionality and data sparseness to some extent. However, they still fail to consider the semantic relationships among words and phrases and only use the extrinsic structure of the texts. Hence, several semantic-based feature generation methods [5,7,11,18,30,35,39] have been proposed. Latent Dirichlet Allocation (LDA) [5,17] topic modeling method is one of the most classical semantic methods. It extracts latent topic features from words in the content with the assumption that each text is generated by a group of discriminative latent topics. Different from the aforementioned methods, the neural network based approaches [4,19,20,24,25,28,46] try to learn deeper semantics in the corpora. Continuous-Bag-Of-Words (CBOW) and skip-gram methods [24,25] are proposed for computing continuous vector representations of words from very large datasets and attempt to preserve the linear regularities among words. The Convolutional Neural Networks (CNNs) based methods [19,46] that represent the sentences or documents as a matrix perform efficiently in natural language processing.

However, to our best knowledge, most existing text classification approaches employed in popular intelligent cloud computing platforms neglect the latent semantic relationships of the topic and word features. Besides, the novel CNN-based ones lack the means of integrating features with diverse semantics, and fail to capture the cross semantic interactions among those extracted features. They only consider one single semantic information, such as word layer or sentence layer semantics, which might confine the usage of other meaningful textual features. Hence, this paper proposes Dual Semantic Embedding (DSE) method that attempts to extract the dual semantic features from topics and words for text classification using CNNs. Two structure-based fusion strategies are provided for reconstructing the textual information: one is that we directly extend the original contents by the topics; the other is that we generate the topic-based corpus by treating the topic as a counterpart feature to the corresponding word. We encode the dual semantic information into a shared representation from the reorganized semantic structures. Experimental results show that DSE can better represent the characteristics of each text.

The rest of the paper is organized as follows. Section 2 introduces text mining techniques that are involved in our method. In Sect. 3, the pipeline of the DSE method is presented. Next, DSE is evaluated over several state-of-the-art baselines and the detailed experiments are given in Sect. 4. Finally, we conclude our work and point out the future work in Sect. 5.

2   Preliminaries

In this section, we present the preliminaries of LDA [5,17] and skip-gram [24,25].

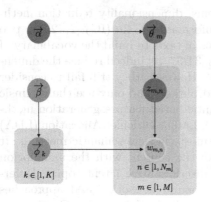

Fig. 1. The Bayesian network of LDA.   **Fig. 2.** Skip-gram framework.

2.1   LDA

To determine the distribution of latent topics, we need to construct a topic model. LDA is a probabilistic generative model that is able to estimate the probabilities of multinomial observations by utilizing the co-occurrence structure of words in documents to recover the latent topic structure without using any background knowledge [14]. It assumes that there are K independent topics shared by M documents, where document doc_m has N_m words ($m=1 \ldots, M$). Each topic is a polynomial probabilistic distribution of words, and each document is randomly generated by those topics. According to the Bayesian network of LDA shown in Fig. 1, the process of $\overrightarrow{\alpha} \rightarrow \overrightarrow{\theta}_m \rightarrow z_{m,n}$ denotes that a topic indicator $z_{m,n}$ is sampled by topic proportion $\overrightarrow{\theta}_m$ from a Dirichlet distribution with hyperparameter $\overrightarrow{\alpha}$, and the process of $\overrightarrow{\beta} \rightarrow \overrightarrow{\phi}_k \rightarrow w_{m,n}|k = z_{m,n}$ denotes that topic-specific word $w_{m,n}$ is emitted by the corresponding topic-specific term distribution $\overrightarrow{\phi}_k$ from a Dirichlet distribution with hyperparameter $\overrightarrow{\beta}$. For a corpus, $W = \{\overrightarrow{w}_m\}_{m=1}^M$, the joint distribution is defined as follows.

$$p(W|\Theta, \Phi) = \prod_{m=1}^M \prod_{n=1}^{N_m} \sum_{k=1}^K p(w_{m,n}|\overrightarrow{\phi}_k) p(z_{m,n} = k|\overrightarrow{\theta}_m), \quad (1)$$

where $\Theta = \{\overrightarrow{\theta}_m\}_{m=1}^M$ and $\Phi = \{\overrightarrow{\Phi}_k\}_{k=1}^K$. The gibbs sampling method is used for approximate inference in LDA. The dimension values z_i of the distribution are sampled once at a time, based on all the other dimension values $z_{\neg i}$. Let V be the vocabulary size, and then the estimations of parameters $\hat{\theta}_{m,k}$ and $\hat{\phi}_{k,v}$ are derived as follows.

$$\hat{\theta}_{m,k} = \frac{n_{m,\neg i}^{(k)} + \alpha_k}{\sum_{k=1}^K (n_{m,\neg i}^{(t)} + \alpha_k)},$$

$$\hat{\phi}_{k,v} = \frac{n_{k,\neg i}^{(v)} + \beta_v}{\sum_{v=1}^V (n_{k,\neg i}^{(v)} + \beta_v)}. \quad (2)$$

2.2 Skip-Gram

Given a corpus W, the objective under skip-gram is defined to maximize the following conditional probability and map each word w to a d-dimensional representation $x \in \mathbb{R}^{d \times V}$, where V is the vocabulary size.

$$\arg\max_{x} \prod_{w \in W} \prod_{\Gamma \in \mathcal{C}(w)} p(\Gamma|w; x) \quad (3)$$

where Γ is a context, and $\mathcal{C}(w)$ is the set of contexts of word w.

As shown in Fig. 2, there are three layers in the skip-gram framework: input, projection and output layers. The projection layer is the hidden layer of skip-gram that takes the embedding of w as the input and learns output embeddings of words in the contexts. Either hierarchical softmax or negative sampling can be applied to training process.

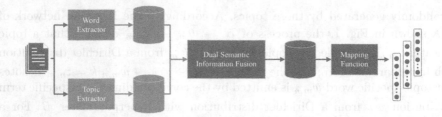

Fig. 3. An Illustration of DSE framework. At first, the topic and word extractors are used to preprocess the original text corpus. Then, the topic and word features are fused in the next step, where we pretrain the topic and word embeddings. After that, CNNs are applied to extract the dual semantic information by mapping the topic and word features into a shared representation.

3   Method

We present the detailed pipeline of DSE method that extracts the dual semantic features of topics and words. Figure 3 illustrates the framework of DSE.

3.1   Pretrained Embeddings

The pretrained word vectors have benefited a large number of applications. Inspired by that, we introduce skip-gram to pretrain the topic and word embeddings. Since applying LDA would be easy to obtain topics from a given corpus, we will focus on the strategy of generating embeddings with topic-word semantics. Suppose that after the LDA process, we have learned the topic set $\mathcal{T} = \{1, 2, ..., K\}$. We assign each word w the top_1 topic $t^w \in \mathcal{T}$ inferred by LDA.

$$\arg \max_k \bigcup_{k=1}^{K} \left(\frac{n_{k,\neg i}^{(w)} + \beta_w}{\sum_{v=1}^{V}(n_{k,\neg i}^{(v)} + \beta_v)} \right). \tag{4}$$

Two fusion strategies are provided to learn the embeddings with dual semantic knowledge for both topics and words based on the context-related structure. The key idea is that topics can be treated as words, which is commonly used in text enriching [23, 30, 44].

Mixed Strategy: As shown in Fig. 4, the mixed strategy makes the latent topic embedded directly after its corresponding word. For example, the topics of the content "a cat is sleeping" are $\{9, 5, 2, 7\}$. Based on the strategy, "a 9 cat 5 is 2 sleeping 7" would be fed into skip-gram.

Split Strategy: Figure 5 presents the split strategy. It simply yields topic sequences based on the word sequences and feeds two sequences into skip-gram separately.

We believe that these two strategies can generate meaningful embeddings for topics and words. Let τ denote both topics and words here. Due to the strategy of skip-gram which utilizes τ to predict $\mathcal{C}(\tau)$, the training set contains all the pairs of (γ, τ), where γ is a topic or a word in the context $\Gamma \in \mathcal{C}(\tau)$. That is, by applying the mixed strategy, we can conclude that a topic is affected by its surrounding topics and words, or vice versa. For the Split strategy, as the counterpart modal features to the words, the topic embeddings depict the sequential information of words and the semantic interactions among the topics. Hence, no matter which strategy is applied, the pretrained embeddings will learn the dual semantic information with the interactions among the topic and word features after the skip-gram process. In order to derive the pretrained embeddings more efficiently, negative sampling is applied.

$$\arg\max_{\lambda} \sum_{(\gamma,\tau)\in D} \log \sigma(\boldsymbol{v}_\gamma \cdot \boldsymbol{v}_\tau) + \sum_{(\gamma',\tau')\in D'} \log \sigma(-\boldsymbol{v}_{\gamma'} \cdot \boldsymbol{v}_{\tau'}), \tag{5}$$

where D denotes the set of pairs extracted using the strategies, D' denotes the generated set of random pairs which are assumed to be negative examples, $\sigma(x) = \frac{1}{1+e^{-x}}$, $\boldsymbol{v}_\gamma$ and $\boldsymbol{v}_\tau$ are the vectors of γ and τ respectively, and λ is the parameter in the neural network.

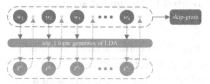
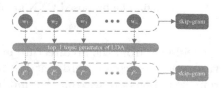

Fig. 4. The mixed strategy.   Fig. 5. The split strategy.

3.2   Encoding Dual Semantic Information

Two CNNs are designed to implement the aforementioned fusion strategies, with different structures of the shared representations. The multimodal joint representations based on multimodal deep learning [26] are used to form the shared representations. The key idea is that the technique of multimodal joint representations projects multimodal data into a common space, and is suited for scenarios when all of the modalities are present during inference [3]. Hence, we consider the topic and word features as different modalities and project them into a common feature space. Two architectures are shown in Fig. 6 and Fig. 7, respectively.

The inputs of the CNN in Fig. 6 are the shared representations, and the order of the sequence follows the description of the mixed strategy. That is,

$$\mathcal{I} = [\boldsymbol{w}_1, \boldsymbol{t}^{w_1}, \boldsymbol{w}_2, \boldsymbol{t}^{w_2}, ..., \boldsymbol{w}_l, \boldsymbol{t}^{w_l}]^\top, \tag{6}$$

where $\mathcal{I}$ is the 2-dimensional input, l is the length of the content. $\boldsymbol{w}_i$ and $\boldsymbol{t}^{w_i}$ are the pretrained embeddings of word w_i and topic t^{w_i} respectively, where t^{w_i} denotes the top-1 topic of w_i.

$$v_{shared} = v_w \oplus v_t. \tag{7}$$

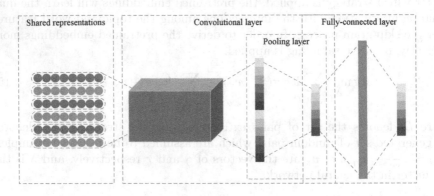

Fig. 6. The proposed CNN architecture related to the mixed strategy.

Different from the architecture in Fig. 6, Fig. 7 presents a Bi-CNN architecture, which processes word matrices and topic matrices respectively. The shared representations are used in the middle of the fully-connected layer, which combines the hidden vectors of words and topics. That is,

In general, a convolutional operation involves a kernel $\mathbf{k} \in \mathbb{R}^{n \times m}$, which is used to produce a new feature from $n \times m$ pixels. It is reasonable to use the kernels whose width is equal to the dimensionality d of the pretrained embeddings (i.e., $m = d$) because the rows in matrices represent the discrete topics and words. Suppose the kernel receives n adjacent rows of embeddings $\mathbf{x}_{i:i+n-1}$ each time, and the sub-matrix of $\mathbf{E}$ is $\mathbf{E}[i : i + n - 1]$. A feature c_i is generated by:

$$c_i = f(\mathbf{k} \cdot \mathbf{E}[i : i + n - 1] + \mathbf{b}), \tag{8}$$

where f is an activation function such as ReLU [12] and *tanh* (i.e., the hyperbolic tangent) [19,46], and $\mathbf{b}$ denotes a bias term.

To generate a better semantic representation from the text, a fully-connected layer is inserted into both CNN architectures. One is used for encoding the max-pooling results, while another one unifies the shared representations into a common space.

The cross-entropy loss function (as shown in Eq. (9)) is applied to optimize the CNNs for multi-class classification tasks.

$$\mathcal{L} = - \sum_{label=1}^{N} y_{label,o} \log(p_{label,o}), \tag{9}$$

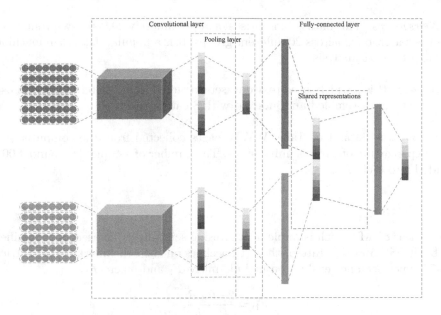

Fig. 7. The proposed CNN architecture related to the split strategy.

where $y_{label,o}$ denotes a binary indicator (0 or 1) representing whether class *label* is correct for observation o. $p_{label,o}$ is the predicted probability of observation o that how likely it belongs to class *label*.

4   Experimental Results

The performance of DSE is validated on several real-world datasets. The experimental results demonstrate the effectiveness of the proposed DSE for text classification tasks.

Table 1. Statistics of the datasets

Datasets	20 Newsgroups	Reuters-r8	WebKB
#Training samples	11,293	5,485	2,785
#Testing samples	7,527	2,189	1,383
#Labels	20	8	4

4.1   Datasets

The following datasets are used in the experiments. All datasets have been preprocessed and split into training sets and testing sets from the source, where some samples with missing textual values have been filtered. Table 1 lists the detailed statistics of these datasets.

20 Newsgroups. This dataset comprises of approximately 20,000 newsgroup documents, partitioned across 20 different groups. It is a popular dataset in machine learning for text analysis.

Reuters-r8. It is a widely used text dataset extracted from Reuters-21578. Those documents are assembled and indexed with 8 categories.

WebKB. This dataset contains WWW-pages collected from the computer science departments of various universities. The number of samples is around 4,000 divided into 4 classes.

4.2 Metrics

The Linear SVM (which is implemented using scikit-learn) is used as a classifier for both DSE and the state-of-the-art baselines on the benchmarks. The metrics used for performance evaluation include micro-F_1 and macro-F_1.

$$F_1 = \frac{2 \cdot P \cdot R}{P + R}, \tag{10}$$

where P denotes precision and R denotes recall.

- micro-F_1. This method sums up the individual true positives, false positives, and false negatives of the dataset for different classes, which can be used for imbalanced data problems.
- macro-F_1. It calculates the average of the precision and recall of the dataset on different classes, and finds their unweighted mean, which does not take label imbalance into account.

4.3 Baselines

The performance of DSE is compared with the state-of-the-art baseline methods as follows. In our experiments, for reducing the external factors and just focusing on the method itself, the word embeddings for all methods were pretrained.

- Doc2Vec [20]. This method aims at constructing a representation of a document, regardless of its length. It takes the documents in a corpus as the inputs and produces a vector space where each document in the corpus is assigned a corresponding vector in the space.
- TextCNN [19]. This method directly processes the intrinsic structure of each document using a CNN with little hyperparameter tuning and pretrained word vectors.

Table 2. Results of multi-classification in 20 Newsgroups on varying the dimensionality of document representations

	Dimensionality	DSE-m	DSE-s	Doc2Vec	TextCNN
micro-F_1 (%)	100	63.332	66.946	42.939	66.826
	200	63.226	66.401	33.479	66.109
	300	61.791	**67.743**	25.282	65.498
macro-F_1 (%)	100	63.065	66.555	42.223	66.091
	200	62.965	65.954	33.205	65.750
	300	61.409	**67.106**	25.021	65.305

Table 3. Results of multi-classification in Reuters-r8 on varying the dimensionality of document representations

	Dimensionality	DSE-m	DSE-s	Doc2Vec	TextCNN
micro-F_1 (%)	100	93.924	93.878	66.880	93.513
	200	94.381	92.005	62.814	93.741
	300	**95.021**	94.427	59.662	92.828
macro-F_1 (%)	100	81.468	78.695	37.008	76.342
	200	79.212	70.782	33.882	76.285
	300	79.690	**81.745**	30.503	74.354

Table 4. Results of multi-classification in WebKB on varying the dimensionality of document representations

	Dimensionality	DSE-m	DSE-s	Doc2Vec	TextCNN
micro-F_1 (%)	100	86.696	86.623	55.242	86.406
	200	86.623	85.900	48.301	86.551
	300	86.406	85.683	47.505	**86.913**
macro-F_1 (%)	100	85.029	85.021	50.683	85.159
	200	85.334	84.713	43.449	85.510
	300	84.435	83.799	43.398	**85.952**

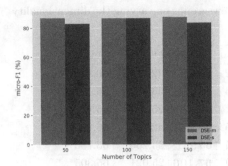
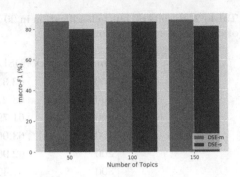

Fig. 8. The micro-F_1 scores on varying numbers of topics.

Fig. 9. The macro-F_1 scores on varying numbers of topics.

4.4 Text Classification

For comparison with the baselines, the values of the following parameters of DSE are set. The maximum length $L_{max} = 1000$ for each document, the number of topics $K = 100$, and the size of the pretrained embeddings is set to 100. The kernel size of CNN for the mixed strategy (DSE-m) is ($height = 20, width = 100$) with $stride = 20$, and half of $height$ and $stride$ parameters are used for the split one (DSE-s). Tables 2, 3, and 4 present the micro-F_1 and macro-F_1 scores of all methods by varying the dimensionality of document representations from 100 to 300 on three benchmarks, where the best scores are highlighted in bold.

On the 20 Newsgroups dataset, DSE-s with 300 dimensions achieves the highest micro-F_1 (67.743%) and macro-F_1 (67.106%) scores. Doc2Vec performs poorly on this dataset and shows an unstable trend with the increasing dimensionality values. The CNN-based methods have all achieved competitive results, but DSE with the split strategy outperforms TextCNN.

For the Reuters-r8 dataset, DSE also achieves the highest micro-F_1 (95.021%) and macro-F_1 (81.745%) scores. Doc2Vec is still affected by the feature dimensionality. TextCNN outperforms Doc2Vec, but there is a significant margin on macro-F_1 values between DSE and TextCNN, where our proposed method improves the results by more than 5%.

The WebKB dataset with four categories has fewer samples than the aforementioned datasets. In this scenario, DSE and TextCNN are considered indistinguishable by varying the dimensionality from 100 to 300. Since different numbers of topics may affect the semantic meaning of the pretrained embeddings, more experiments on the topic sensitivity is conducted in the next subsection.

4.5 Topic Sensitivity

Since DSE learns deep semantics partly from the latent topics, the numbers of topics are varied to evaluate its key parameter sensitivity on the WebKB dataset. The results are shown in Figs. 8 and 9.

It can be seen from the figures that DSE-s is somehow sensitive to the number of topics, while DSE-m seems to be quite stable. The highest micro-F_1 (87.419%) and macro-F_1 (86.179%) scores are achieved by DSE-m with the number of topics $K = 150$, which also outperforms the best results of TextCNN.

5 Conclusion and Future Work

In this paper, the Dual Semantic Embedding (DSE) method is proposed which attempts to encode dual semantic knowledge for text classification. Two CNNs are designed to implement the structure-based fusion strategies for capturing the dual semantic information. Experimental results demonstrate that the generated feature representations with topic-word semantics improve the effectiveness of text classification on micro-F_1 and macro-F_1 scores over the real-world datasets.

In the future, the strategy of coordinated representations will be considered, which learns separate representations for multiple features, instead of projecting the features together into a joint space. Furthermore, we also consider reframing the training process of DSE by applying distributed and parallel cloud computing techniques to improve its learning effectiveness.

Acknowledgment. This work was supported in part by the China Scholarship Council (201706840112), Fundamental Research Funds for the Central Universities (30918012204), Jiangsu province key research and development program (BE2017739), 2018 Jiangsu Province Major Technical Research Project "Information Security Simulation System" (BE2017100), the 4th project "Research on the Key Technology of Endogenous Security Switches" (2020YFB1804604) of the National Key R&D Program "New Network Equipment Based on Independent Programmable Chips" (2020YFB1804600), Military Common Information System Equipment Pre-research Special Technical Project (315075701) and Industrial Internet Innovation and Development Project in 2019 - Industrial Internet Security On-Site Emergency Detection Tool Project.

References

1. Aggarwal, C.C., Zhai, C.: A survey of text classification algorithms. In: Mining Text Data, pp. 163–222. Springer, Berlin (2012)
2. Aghdam, M.H., Ghasem-Aghaee, N., Basiri, M.E.: Text feature selection using ant colony optimization. Expert Syst. Appl. **36**(3), 6843–6853 (2009)
3. Baltrušaitis, T., Ahuja, C., Morency, L.P.: Multimodal machine learning: a survey and taxonomy. IEEE Trans. Pattern Anal. Mach. Intell. **41**(2), 423–443 (2018)
4. Bengio, Y., Ducharme, R., Vincent, P., Jauvin, C.: A neural probabilistic language model. J. Mach. Learn. Res. **3**, 1137–1155 (2003)
5. Blei, D.M., Ng, A.Y., Jordan, M.I.: Latent dirichlet allocation. J. Mach. Learn. Res. **3**, 993–1022 (2003)
6. Bobadilla, J., Ortega, F., Hernando, A., Gutiérrez, A.: Recommender systems survey. Knowl.-Based Syst. **46**, 109–132 (2013)
7. Chen, E., Lin, Y., Xiong, H., Luo, Q., Ma, H.: Exploiting probabilistic topic models to improve text categorization under class imbalance. Inform. Process. Manag. **47**(2), 202–214 (2011)

8. Cui, S., Li, Q., Chen, S.C.: An adversarial learning approach for discovering social relations in human-centered information networks. EURASIP J. Wireless Commun. Netw. **2020**(1), 172 (2020). https://doi.org/10.1186/s13638-020-01782-6

9. Cui, S., Li, T., Chen, S.C., Shyu, M.L., Li, Q., Zhang, H.: Disl: deep isomorphic substructure learning for network representations. Knowl.-Based Syst. **189**, 105086 (2020). https://doi.org/10.1016/j.knosys.2019.105086

10. Cui, S., et al.: Simwalk: learning network latent representations with social relation similarity. In: 2017 12th International Conference on Intelligent Systems and Knowledge Engineering, pp. 1–6. IEEE (2017)

11. Deerwester, S., Dumais, S.T., Furnas, G.W., Landauer, T.K., Harshman, R.: Indexing by latent semantic analysis. J. Am. Soc. Inform. Sci. **41**(6), 391–407 (1990)

12. Glorot, X., Bordes, A., Bengio, Y.: Deep sparse rectifier neural networks. In: Proceedings of the 14th International Conference on Artificial Intelligence and Statistics, pp. 315–323 (2011)

13. Goodfellow, I., Bengio, Y., Courville, A., Bengio, Y.: Deep Learning, vol. 1. MIT Press, Cambridge (2016)

14. Gregor, H.: Parameter estimation for text analysis. Technical report (2005)

15. Grover, A., Leskovec, J.: node2vec: scalable feature learning for networks. In: Proceedings of the 22nd ACM SIGKDD International Conference on Knowledge Discovery and Data Mining, pp. 855–864. ACM (2016)

16. Harris, Z.S.: Distributional structure. Word **10**(2–3), 146–162 (1954)

17. Hoffman, M., Bach, F.R., Blei, D.M.: Online learning for latent dirichlet allocation. In: Advances in Neural Information Processing Systems, pp. 856–864 (2010)

18. Hofmann, T.: Probabilistic latent semantic analysis. In: Proceedings of the 15th Conference on Uncertainty in Artificial Intelligence, pp. 289–296. Morgan Kaufmann Publishers Inc. (1999)

19. Kim, Y.: Convolutional neural networks for sentence classification. In: Proceedings of the Conference on Empirical Methods in Natural Language Processing, pp. 1746–1751 (2014)

20. Le, Q., Mikolov, T.: Distributed representations of sentences and documents. In: International Conference on Machine Learning, pp. 1188–1196 (2014)

21. LeCun, Y., Bengio, Y., Hinton, G.: Deep learning. Nature **521**(7553), 436–444 (2015)

22. Li, D., Li, Q.: Adversarial deep ensemble: evasion attacks and defenses for malware detection. IEEE Trans. Inform. Forensics Secur. **15**, 3886–3900 (2020)

23. Liu, Y., Liu, Z., Chua, T.S., Sun, M.: Topical word embeddings. In: AAAI, pp. 2418–2424 (2015)

24. Mikolov, T., Chen, K., Corrado, G., Dean, J.: Efficient estimation of word representations in vector space. arXiv preprint arXiv:1301.3781 (2013)

25. Mikolov, T., Sutskever, I., Chen, K., Corrado, G.S., Dean, J.: Distributed representations of words and phrases and their compositionality. In: Advances in Neural Information Processing Systems, pp. 3111–3119 (2013)

26. Ngiam, J., Khosla, A., Kim, M., Nam, J., Lee, H., Ng, A.Y.: Multimodal deep learning. In: Proceedings of the 28th International Conference on Machine Learning (ICML-11), pp. 689–696 (2011)

27. Pang, B., Lee, L., et al.: Opinion mining and sentiment analysis. Found. Trends® Inform. Retrieval **2**(1–2), 1–135 (2008)

28. Pennington, J., Socher, R., Manning, C.: Glove: global vectors for word representation. In: Proceedings of the 2014 Conference on Empirical Methods in Natural Language Processing (EMNLP), pp. 1532–1543 (2014)

29. Perozzi, B., Al-Rfou, R., Skiena, S.: Deepwalk: online learning of social representations. In: Proceedings of the 20th ACM SIGKDD International Conference on
Knowledge Discovery and Data Mining, pp. 701–710. ACM (2014)

30. Phan, X.H., Nguyen, C.T., Le, D.T., Nguyen, L.M., Horiguchi, S., Ha, Q.T.: A
hidden topic-based framework toward building applications with short web documents. IEEE Trans. Knowl. Data Eng. **23**(7), 961–976 (2011)

31. Pouyanfar, S., Chen, S.C., Shyu, M.L.: An efficient deep residual-inception network
for multimedia classification. In: Proceedings of the IEEE International Conference
on Multimedia and Expo, pp. 373–378. Hong Kong, China (2017)

32. Pouyanfar, S., et al.: Dynamic sampling in convolutional neural networks for imbalanced data classification. In: Proceedings of the First IEEE International Conference on Multimedia Information Processing and Retrieval, pp. 112–117. Miami,
FL, USA (2018)

33. Salton, G., Wong, A., Yang, C.S.: A vector space model for automatic indexing.
Commun. ACM **18**(11), 613–620 (1975)

34. Shang, C., Li, M., Feng, S., Jiang, Q., Fan, J.: Feature selection via maximizing
global information gain for text classification. Knowl.-Based Syst. **54**, 298–309
(2013)

35. Sidorov, G., Velasquez, F., Stamatatos, E., Gelbukh, A., Chanona-Hernández, L.:
Syntactic n-grams as machine learning features for natural language processing.
Expert Syst. Appl. **41**(3), 853–860 (2014)

36. Su, X., Khoshgoftaar, T.M.: A survey of collaborative filtering techniques. Adv.
Artif. Intell. **2009**, 4–22 (2009)

37. Sun, X., Liu, Y., Xu, M., Chen, H., Han, J., Wang, K.: Feature selection using
dynamic weights for classification. Knowl.-Based Syst. **37**, 541–549 (2013)

38. Tian, H., Zheng, H.C., Chen, S.C.: Sequential deep learning for disaster-related
video classification. In: Proceedings of the First IEEE International Conference on
Multimedia Information Processing and Retrieval, pp. 106–111. Miami, FL, USA
(2018)

39. Tomović, A., Janičić, P., Kešelj, V.: n-gram-based classification and unsupervised
hierarchical clustering of genome sequences. Comput. Methods Programs Biomed.
81(2), 137–153 (2006)

40. Uysal, A.K., Gunal, S.: A novel probabilistic feature selection method for text
classification. Knowl.-Based Syst. **36**, 226–235 (2012)

41. Wasserman, S., Faust, K.: Social Network Analysis: Methods and Applications,
vol. 8. Cambridge University Press, Cambridge (1994)

42. Yang, Y.: Feature selection in statistical learning of text categorization. In: Proceedings of 14th International Conference on Machine Learning, pp. 412–420 (1997)

43. Yang, Y., Pedersen, J.O.: A comparative study on feature selection in text categorization. ICML **97**, 412–420 (1997)

44. Zhang, H., Zhong, G.: Improving short text classification by learning vector representations of both words and hidden topics. Knowl.-Based Syst. **102**, 76–86 (2016)

45. Zhang, M., Chen, Y.: Weisfeiler-lehman neural machine for link prediction. In:
Proceedings of the 23rd ACM SIGKDD International Conference on Knowledge
Discovery and Data Mining, pp. 575–583. ACM (2017)

46. Zhang, Y., Wallace, B.: A sensitivity analysis of (and practitioners' guide
to) convolutional neural networks for sentence classification. arXiv preprint
arXiv:1510.03820 (2015)

Personalized Medical Diagnosis Recommendation Based on Neutrosophic Sets and Spectral Clustering

Mengru Dong[1], Shunmei Meng[1], Lixia Chen[2], and Jing Zhang[1(⊠)] (iD)

[1] School of Computer Science and Engineering, Nanjing University of Science and Technology, Nanjing 210094, China
1850193966@qq.com, jzhang@njust.edu.cn
[2] Jiangsu Second Chinese Medicine Hospital, Nanjing 210017, China

Abstract. With the development of cloud-based services and artificial intelligence technologies, the personalized diagnosis recommender system has been a hot research topic in medical services. An effective diagnosis recommendation model could help doctors and patients make more accurate predictions in clinical diagnosis. In this paper, we propose a novel personalized diagnosis recommendation method based on neutrosophic sets, spectral clustering, and web-based medical information to offer satisfied web-based medical service. Firstly, the neutrosophic set theory is adopted to formulate the patients' personal information and the symptom features into more interpretable neutrosophic sets with uniformly normalized values. Moreover, to make more accurate predictions, the spectral clustering scheme is integrated into a neutrosophic-based prediction approach to mining the similarity relationships between the undiagnosed diseases and the history disease records. Finally, a deneutrosophication operation is applied to recommend the final fine-grain diagnoses with interpretable clinic meanings. Experimental results on four real-world medical diagnosis datasets validate the effectiveness of the proposed method.

Keywords: Personalized diagnosis recommendation · Neutrosophic sets · Healthcare service · Spectral clustering

1 Introduction

Personalized recommender systems for medical diagnosis have become a hot research topic for healthcare service in the development of modern medical technology. It has been emerged as a valuable tool in healthcare service to assist doctors in dealing with overloaded web-based medical information and making more accurate predictions on medical diagnosis, which has received full attention from both industry and academia. As we know, disease diagnosis is still full of challenges for medical professionals because not only patient's symptoms are inherently uncertain, but also the relations between patients and symptoms as well as symptoms and diseases are vague and uncertain. For

L. Qi et al. (Eds.): CloudComp 2020, LNICST 363, pp. 160–174, 2021.
https://doi.org/10.1007/978-3-030-69992-5_13

example, a small number of symptoms and laboratory indicators are not sufficient to diagnose a disease, but waiting for the occurrence of a large number of symptoms or obtaining more laboratory indicators will place a heavy burden on patients. Therefore, for young doctors who lack clinical experience, auxiliary diagnostic systems can help them to use the experience in historical clinic cases to make a more accurate diagnosis.

For auxiliary diagnosis systems, the first issue that needs to be handled is the uncertainty of the data, which often has important clinical implications in the medical field. For example, an abnormal body temperature of 38.5 °C is not a high temperature for some diseases, and it does not require special attention, but for some other diseases, it may be high temperature and needs to be treated with caution. There have been some research focusing on dealing with uncertain information in medical diagnosis. Some studies used fuzzy set methods such as Intuitionistic fuzzy Soft Sets (IFSSs) and their extensions [4, 5] to deal with the uncertain information of symptoms. Neutrosophic Set, proposed by Smarandache [6], was utilized in the medical diagnosis field [7, 8], which is a three-dimensional set while the fuzzy set has only one dimension. Thus, neutrosophic sets can convert the features of patients into a uniform scale as well as provide more meaningful semantics. However, these theories still have some shortcomings in the deneutrosophication process [19], similarity measure [9, 10], and distance measure [13, 22].

In recent years, many diagnosis recommendation models have been proposed for medical services, such as hybrid recommender systems with picture fuzzy clustering and intuitionistic fuzzy sets [14], intuitionistic fuzzy recommender systems [19], the hybrid recommendation system for heart disease diagnosis based on multiple kernel learning [1]. The principle of these systems generally combines fuzzy sets or neutrosophic sets with traditional recommendation methods. Both fuzzy sets and neutrosophic sets follow a similar way to handle the uncertainty of objects' attributes.

To broaden the usage of neutrosophic sets in medical diagnosis, many techniques in machine learning and recommender systems [16, 26] (e.g., clustering [17]) are integrated with neutrosophic set theory to provide more meaningful and accurate predictions on diagnosis recommendations. For example, Ali and Son [3] proposed a hybrid method that combines neutrosophic sets and recommender systems for medical diagnosis. Although their method has a strong mathematical basis, it still has some defects in the similarity calculation for patients and symptoms, which is the key technical points in most recommender systems.

In this paper, we propose a novel personalized diagnosis recommendation method for medical service based on neutrosophic sets, spectral clustering, and web-based medical information to offer satisfied web-based medical service. Specifically, the neutrosophic set theory is adopted to formulate the patients' personal information and the symptom features into more interpretable neutrosophic sets with uniformly normalized values. Moreover, the spectral clustering scheme is integrated into the neutrosophic-based prediction method to enhance the similarity measure in the recommendation method. Experimental results validate the effectiveness of the proposed method.

The remainder of this paper is organized as follows: Sect. 2 reviews some related work. Then, a hybrid model that incorporates the neutrosophic recommendation method for medical diagnosis and spectral clustering is proposed in Sect. 3. Section 4 presents an empirical evaluation of the performance of the proposed method. Finally, Sect. 5 concludes the paper and provides an outlook on the continuations of our work.

2 Related Work

In recent years, a large number of web-based personalized healthcare applications have emerged dramatically [28], among which different types of recommender systems for medical diagnoses have also been proposed, such as neutrosophic recommender systems [3], hybrid recommender systems with picture fuzzy clustering and intuitionistic fuzzy sets [14], intuitionistic fuzzy recommender systems [19], and the hybrid recommendation system for heart disease diagnosis based on multiple kernel learning [1]. The principle of these systems generally combines fuzzy sets or neutrosophic sets with traditional recommendation methods. Both fuzzy sets and neutrosophic sets follow a similar way to handle the uncertainty of attributes. They extend an attribute to multidimensional ones accompanied by membership values. Moreover, the core of a recommender system is the similarity measure of items, which also provide users with information about predictive rating or preference. For example, Ye et al. [11] proposed a method that uses distance-based similarity measures of single-valued neutrosophic multisets for medical diagnosis. Davis et al. [26] proposed a recommendation engine that combines collaborative filtering with clustering to predict patients' most possible disease according to patients' symptoms and historical medical materials. Since neutrosophic sets have been widely used in medical diagnosis [7–10, 13, 21], our proposed recommendation method is also built on the neutrosophic sets.

Clustering has been widely used in recommender systems [18, 25] for computing similarity measures. Compared with some traditional clustering methods like K-means and K-medoids, spectral clustering [20], which is based on graph partition theory, has strong adaptability to the variety of data distributions and can generate more reasonable clusters. Therefore, many recommendation methods tend to employ spectral clustering for better performance. Li et al. [2] proposed a recommendation method that uses spectral clustering to group users and items in the original rating matrix. Xu et al. [12] proposed a spectral clustering based on intuitionistic fuzzy sets. In our study, spectral clustering is used for the calculation of the similarity between patients' demographic and symptom features.

3 The Proposed Method

3.1 Recommender System for Medical Diagnosis

A medical diagnosis recommender system reads the demographical features and clinical symptoms of a patient and then predicts potential diseases, which can help doctors make decisions in their clinical diagnosis. In the recommender system, we use a vector $r = [r_1, ..., r_M] \in R^M$ to represent M demographical features of patients, a vector $s = [s_1, ..., s_N] \in S^N$ to represent N clinical symptoms, and a set $D = \{ d_1, ..., d_K \}$ to represent K diseases. Each element of r, s, or D is a positive real number or zero when the element is not specified.

Definition 1: (A medical diagnosis recommender system) uses a utility function $\mathfrak{R}$ to map patients and their symptoms onto diseases, i.e., $\mathfrak{R} : (R \times S) \to D$.

The utility function $\mathfrak{R}$ determines an optimal mapping from $R \times S$ to D by calculating some measure (usually similarity) on a diagnosis database. A diagnosis database has the form $B = \{[r^{(i)}, s^{(i)}, d^{(i)}]\}_{i=1}^{I}$, where each entry is called a *diagnosis*.

Definition 2: (A diagnosis) is a triple tuple $[r, s, d]$, where r and s together comprise the features of a patient, and the non-zero d is a disease. If d is zero, we call it an *undecided* diagnosis.

Therefore, in the system, each diagnosis is a non-negative real-number vector. A recommendation is to predict a d to substitute 0 in an undecided diagnosis $[r, s, 0]$. Typically, this goal is achieved by calculating the similarity among the diagnoses (including undecided diagnosis). Obviously, elements in a diagnosis vector have different scales and types. For example, "age" is in the range of [0, 120] and usually an integer, while "temperature" is in the range of [35.0, 42.0] and usually a real number. Thus, directly computing similarity on these elements (also called "attribute" in this study) may result in poor performance. To address this issue, we use neutrosophic sets, which can convert attributes into a more meaningful space with a uniform scale.

3.2 Neutrosophic Set, Neutrosophication, and Deneutrosophication [15]

For each positive real number attribute x, we can define a set of linguistic labels $L^{(x)} = \{l_1, ..., l_C\}$ on it to represent some concepts. For example, if x is the age of a patient, we can define $L^{(x)} = \{infant, child, adolescent, youth, middle, senior\}$. We can use function $L(x, c)$, $(1 \le c \le C)$ to retrieve the c-th linguistic label of attribute x. Without ambiguity in the context, we can directly use c to represent its c-th label. For attribute x, we can define its neutrosophic set.

Definition 3: (A neutrosophic set) of the c-th linguistic label of attribute x is a triple tuple $[T_c(x), I_c(x), F_c(x)]$, where $T_c(x)$, $I_c(x)$, and $F_c(x)$ are membership functions that measure the degrees of the truth membership, indeterminate membership, and false membership of attribute x belonging to the c-th concept, respectively.

Definition 4: (Membership functions T, I, and F) are defined on the partitions of the real number attributes on the linguistic label (concept) l_c. For each membership function, the range of attribute x is divided into three intervals, saying that the range of x is divided into $[\alpha_1^{(c)}, \alpha_2^{(c)})$, $[\alpha_2^{(c)}, \alpha_3^{(c)})$, $[\alpha_3^{(c)}, \alpha_4^{(c)})$ for T, $[\beta_1^{(c)}, \beta_2^{(c)})$, $[\beta_2^{(c)}, \beta_3^{(c)})$, $[\beta_3^{(c)}, \beta_4^{(c)})$ for I, and $[\gamma_1^{(c)}, \gamma_2^{(c)})$, $[\gamma_2^{(c)}, \gamma_3^{(c)})$, $[\gamma_3^{(c)}, \gamma_4^{(c)})$ for F, membership functions T, I and F are defined as follows:

$$
T_c(x) = \begin{cases} \frac{x - \alpha_1^{(c)}}{\alpha_2^{(c)} - \alpha_1^{(c)}}, & x \in [\alpha_1^{(c)}, \alpha_2^{(c)}) \\[2mm] \frac{\alpha_3^{(c)} - x}{\alpha_3^{(c)} - \alpha_2^{(c)}}, & x \in [\alpha_2^{(c)}, \alpha_3^{(c)}) \\[2mm] \frac{x - \alpha_3^{(c)}}{\alpha_4^{(c)} - \alpha_3^{(c)}}, & x \in [\alpha_3^{(c)}, \alpha_4^{(c)}) \\[2mm] 0, & \text{otherwise} \end{cases}
\tag{1}
$$

$$
I_c(x) = \begin{cases} \dfrac{\beta_2^{(c)} - x}{\beta_2^{(c)} - \beta_1^{(c)}}, & x \in [\beta_1^{(c)}, \beta_2^{(c)}) \\[2ex] \dfrac{x - \beta_2^{(c)}}{\beta_3^{(c)} - \beta_2^{(c)}}, & x \in [\beta_2^{(c)}, \beta_3^{(c)}) \\[2ex] \dfrac{\beta_3^{(c)} + \beta_4^{(c)} - x}{\beta_4^{(c)} - \beta_3^{(c)}}, & x \in [\beta_3^{(c)}, \beta_4^{(c)}) \\[2ex] 1, & \text{otherwise} \end{cases}
\tag{2}
$$

$$
F_c(x) = \begin{cases} \dfrac{\gamma_2^{(c)} - x}{\gamma_2^{(c)} - \gamma_1^{(c)}}, & x \in [\gamma_1^{(c)}, \gamma_2^{(c)}) \\[2ex] \dfrac{x}{\gamma_3^{(c)}}, & x \in [\gamma_2^{(c)}, \gamma_3^{(c)}) \\[2ex] \dfrac{\gamma_4^{(c)} + \gamma_3^{(c)} - x}{\gamma_4^{(c)} - \gamma_3^{(c)}}, & x \in [\gamma_3^{(c)}, \gamma_4^{(c)}) \\[2ex] 1, & \text{otherwise} \end{cases}
\tag{3}
$$

Here, the value of each membership function is in the range of [0, 1].

Definition 5: (Neutrosophication operation) Ψ extends each attribute x to $3C$ attributes, given its linguistic labels $L^{(x)} = \{l_1, \ldots, l_C\}$. That is,

$$
\Psi(x) = [T_1(x), I_1(x), F_1(x), \ldots, T_C(x), I_C(x), F_C(x)].
\tag{4}
$$

For a M-dimensional vector x with different linguistic labels $L^{(x_1)}, L^{(x_2)}, \ldots, L^{(x_M)}$, sized $C_1, C_2, \ldots, C_M$ on each element, we have:

$$
\begin{aligned}
\Psi(x) = [&T_{L(x_1,1)}(x_1), I_{L(x_1,1)}(x_1), F_{L(x_1,1)}(x_1), T_{L(x_1,2)}(x_1), \\
&I_{L(x_1,2)}(x_1), F_{L(x_1,2)}(x_1), \ldots, T_{L(x_M,C_M)}(x_M), \\
&I_{L(x_M,C_M)}(x_M), F_{L(x_M,C_M)}(x_M)]
\end{aligned}
\tag{5}
$$

Definition 6: (Deneutrosophication operation) $\overline{\Psi}$ first transforms the membership functions of neutrosophic set into the membership function of a fuzzy set A:

$$
\mu_A(x) = \kappa T_c(x) + \tau \frac{F_c(x)}{4} + \upsilon \frac{I_c(x)}{2},
\tag{6}
$$

where $\kappa, \tau, \upsilon \in [0, 1]$ and $\kappa + \tau + \upsilon = 1$. Then, a typical deneutrosophicated value $den(\mu_A(x))$ can be calculated by the centroid or center of gravity method below:

$$
den(\mu_A(x)) = \frac{\int_x \mu_A(x)x dy}{\int_x \mu_A(x)dy}.
\tag{7}
$$

3.3 Neutrosophic Recommender System for Medical Diagnosis

Our neutrosophic recommender system directly extends each attribute in diagnoses to three membership functions. On these new attributes, the system calculates the membership functions of diseases in those undecided diagnoses. Then, it uses deneutrosophication to recover the original value of the predicted diseases.

Definition 7: (A neutrosophic recommender system) defines a utility function $\Re$ on neutrosophication operations, i.e., $\Re : \Psi(R) \times \Psi(S) \to \Psi(D)$.

Therefore, two essential functions of a neutrosophic recommender system are [3]:

(1) Prediction: given $[\Psi(r), \Psi(s), 0]$, computing $\Psi(d)$, $d \in D$;
(2) Recommendation: given d, find a most meaningful clinical interpretation by

$$l_c = \arg\max_{l_c \in L^{(d)}} \{T_c(d) + T_c(d)(3 - T_c(d) - I_c(d) - F_c(d))\} \qquad (8)$$

Finally, we can use a deneutrosophication operation to obtain the specific value of d.

3.4 Recommendation Algorithm

The goal of the recommendation algorithm is to calculate the similarity between diagnoses and compensate missed d in those undecided diagnoses.

For each diagnosis $[r, s, d]$ in the dataset, we create its neutrosophic set as a vector $w = [\Psi(r), \Psi(s), \Psi(d)]$. Because some ds are unknown, we define the features of a diagnosis as $v = [\Psi(r), \Psi(s)]$. For two diagnoses $v^{(i)}$ and $v^{(j)}$, we calculate their similarity as follows:

$$s(v^{(i)}, v^{(j)}) = \frac{\sum_{m=1}^{M} SR_m^{(ij)} + \sum_{n=1}^{N} SS_n^{(ij)}}{M + N}, \qquad (9)$$

where SR_m and SS_n are similarities of a demographic feature and a symptom, respectively. That is, on the neutrosophic set space, they can be calculated through the similarity of each pair of corresponding attributes xs in two diagnoses as follows:

$$s(x^{(i)}, x^{(j)}) = \frac{1}{2C} \sum_{c=1}^{C} \max\Big\{ \Big| T_c(x^{(i)}) - T_c(x^{(j)}) \Big|,$$
$$\Big| I_c(x^{(i)}) - I_c(x^{(j)}) \Big|, \Big| F_c(x^{(i)}) - F_c(x^{(j)}) \Big| \Big\}, \qquad (10)$$

where $x^{(i)}$, $x^{(j)} \in R \cup S$. Then, we can construct a similarity matrix $P^{I \times I}$ for all I diagnoses on their features as follows:

$$P^{I \times I} = \begin{bmatrix} s(v^{(1)}, v^{(1)}) & \cdots & s(v^{(1)}, v^{(n)}) \\ \vdots & \ddots & \vdots \\ s(v^{(n)}, v^{(1)}) & \cdots & s(v^{(I)}, v^{(I)}) \end{bmatrix}. \qquad (11)$$

Although matrix P can measure the similarity of each pair of diagnoses, it is not good enough because all diagnoses have the same weights. That is, a large variance on a few features may result in considerable changes in similarity measure, leading to inaccurate predictions. To address this issue, we resort to spectral clustering [12].

The spectral clustering treats all the data as points in a uniform space, where related points are connected by edges. The edge weight between the two distant points is low, and that between the two close points is high. The algorithm cuts the graphs composed of all the data points, making the weights between different subgraphs after cutting are as low as possible, and the weights within subgraphs are as high as possible. Thus, a spectral clustering algorithm needs to construct a similarity matrix of data points. That is, a spectral clustering algorithm can have four types of input data, which are *data points*, *similarity matrix*, *base clustering algorithm*, and *the number of clusters*. Here, the data points are diagnosis features $[v_1; ...; v_I]^T$ and the similarity matrix is P.

Suppose the centroids of clusters are $\{\sigma_1, ..., \sigma_U\}$. We define the counter-similarity of a diagnosis v and a centroid σ_u as follows:

$$cs(v, \sigma_u) = 1 - \frac{v \cdot \sigma_u}{\|v\| \|\sigma_u\|}. \tag{12}$$

The probability of a diagnosis v belonging to cluster u is:

$$p(v, u) = 1 - \frac{cs(v, \sigma_u)}{\max\{cs(v^{(i)}, \sigma_u)\}_{i=1}^{I}} \tag{13}$$

Then, we construct a similarity measure between two diagnoses based on their positions in the clusters as follows:

$$s'(v_i, v_j) = \frac{1}{U} \sum_{u=1}^{U} |p(v_i, u) - \overline{p}(v_i)| |p(v_j, u) - \overline{p}(v_j)|, \tag{14}$$

where we have $\overline{p}(v) = \sum_{u=1}^{U} p(v, u) / U$. We make a linear combination of two similarity measures as follows:

$$s''(v_i, v_j) = \lambda s(v_i, v_j) + (1 - \lambda)s'(v_i, v_j), \tag{15}$$

where $\lambda \in [0, 1]$ is an adjustable coefficient.

Finally, we take the similarity of diseases of two diagnoses into account and obtain the final similarity measure of two diagnoses as follows:

$$s_{final}(v_i, v_j) = s''(v_i, v_j) + SD^{(ij)} - s''(v_i, v_j) \cdot SD^{(ij)}, \tag{16}$$

where $SD^{(ij)}$ can be calculated by Eq. (8). Also, we can construct a similarity matrix $Q^{I \times I}$ for all I diagnoses as $Q^{(ij)} = s_{final}(v_i, v_j)$. For an undecided diagnosis $w^{(i)}$, its neutrosophic set of the disease $d^{(i)}$ on the linguistic label c is calculated as following equation:

$$T_c(d^{(i)}) = \frac{\sum\limits_{j=1}^{I} Q^{(ij)} T_c(d^{(j)})}{\sum\limits_{j=1}^{I} Q^{(ij)}}, \tag{17}$$

$$I_c(d^{(i)}) = T_c(d^{(i)}) + \frac{\sum\limits_{j=1}^{I} Q^{(ij)} I_c(d^{(j)})}{\sum\limits_{j=1}^{I} Q^{(ij)}}, \tag{18}$$

$$F_c(d^{(i)}) = I_c(d^{(i)}) + \frac{\sum\limits_{j=1}^{I} Q^{(ij)} F_c(d^{(j)})}{\sum\limits_{j=1}^{I} Q^{(ij)}}. \tag{19}$$

Neutrosophic Recommendation with Spectral Clustering (NRSC). Algorithm NRSC presents the main steps of the proposed method. The input of algorithm 1 contains $B = \{[r^{(i)}, s^{(i)}, d^{(i)}]\}_{i=1}^{I}$, Δ, base_cluster_algo, U, λ. Here, $B = \{[r^{(i)}, s^{(i)}, d^{(i)}]\}_{i=1}^{I}$ represents the diagnosis database. Neutrosophication parameters Δ (such as $L^{(x)}$, $\alpha_1^{(c)}, ..., \alpha_4^{(c)}, \beta_1^{(c)} ..., \beta_4^{(4)}, \gamma_1^{(c)}, ..., \gamma_4^{(c)}, \kappa, \tau, \upsilon$) for each attribute x that will be used in Eqs. (1)–(7) are required a Neutrosophication Settings. Parameter U is the number of clusters. Parameter $\lambda \in [0, 1]$ is the adjustable coefficient that is used to calculate the final similarity measure.

First, the process of neutrosophication is that calculating the T, I, F values for each element including different linguistic labels to form $w^{(i)}$ and $v^{(i)}$ (Line 1). Then, constructing the neutrosophic similarity matrix P for all I diagnoses on their features according to each element's T, I, F values that are required to the neutrosophic algebraic operations (Line 2). Third, although P can measure the similarity of each pair of diagnoses, it is not good enough. Therefore, a spectral clustering algorithm is required to cluster the data points, and a base clustering algorithm (base_cluster_algo) such as K-means, which is chosen for spectral clustering (Line 3). After clustering, making a combination of two similarity measures and taking the similarity of diseases of two diagnoses into account and obtain the final similarity measure of two diagnoses (Line 4). Moreover, to predict the disease, the final similarity matrix Q is needed to calculate the neutrosophic set of the disease (Line 5), then find the most meaningful clinical interpretation from linguistic labels (Line 6). Finally, calculating the final result of disease according to the process of deneutrosophication (Line 7). Based on Algorithm 1, the predicted result is generated, which can be compared with other algorithms in our experiments.

Algorithm 1: Neutrosophic Recommendation with Spectral Clustering (NRSC)

Input: $B = \{[r^{(i)}, s^{(i)}, d^{(i)}]\}_{i=1}^{I}$, Δ, base_cluster_algo, U, λ
Output: d for an undecided disease
1: **For each** diagnosis $[r^{(i)}, s^{(i)}, d^{(i)}], i = 1, ..., I$
     Do neutrosophication to form $w^{(i)}$ and $v^{(i)}$ by Eq. (5)
2: Calculate similarity matrix P by Eqs. (9)-(11)
3: **Call** Spectral_Clustering($[v^{(i)}]_{i=1}^{I}$, base_cluster_algo, U)
4: Calculate the final similarity matrix Q by Eqs. (12)-(16)
5: For undecided diagnosis $w^{(i)}$, calculate its neutrosophic set by Eqs. (17-19)
6: Recommend a linguistic label $L(d^{(i)}, c)$ by Eq. (8)
7: Predict $d^{(i)}$ by deneutrosophication using Eqs. (6-7)

---

4 Experiment

In this section, we first introduce the experimental settings and the methods in comparison. Then, we focus on discussing experimental results.

4.1 Experimental Settings

Our experiments were conducted on four medical diagnosis datasets *Heart*, *Diabetes*, *RHC*, and *DMD*. Dataset *Heart* is from the UCI Machine Learning Repository [23] and consists of 270 medical records characterized by 13 attributes, such as chest pain type, resting blood pressure, fasting blood sugar and so on. Datasets *Diabetes*, *RHC*, *DMD* are all taken from [24]. Dataset *Diabetes* consists of 403 medical records characterized by 19 attributes and is often associated most strongly with obesity and hypertension. Dataset *RHC* consists of 5735 medical records characterized by 62 attributes and is associated with Mean Blood Pressure, white blood cell, heart rate, and so on. Dataset *DMD* consists of 209 medical records characterized by 9 attributes and is associated with Hemopexin, Pyruvate Kinase, Lactate Dehydrogenase and so on.

We implemented the proposed method based on the settings in [3] using MATLAB, where neutrosophication parameters are provided for the above datasets. We directly used their settings and conducted our spectral clustering only on the symptoms. In our spectral clustering implementation, we use K-means method as the base clustering algorithm.

We compared the proposed method (NRSC) with five state-of-the-art methods PFS, ICSM, NR, CARE, and DSM.

- PFS [27] presented an improved max-min-max composite relation using Pythagorean fuzzy sets for medical diagnosis.
- ICSM [9] presented an improved method based on the cosine similarity measures to solve medical diagnosis problems with simplified neutrosophic information.
- NR [3] designed a new hybrid method that combines the neutrosophic sets and traditional recommender systems for medical diagnosis.
- CARE [26] presented a recommendation engine that combines collaborative filtering with clustering to predict patients' most possible diseases.
- DSM [21] presented the dice similarity measure which was applied to medical diagnosis to deal with indeterminate and inconsistent information.

In this study, we use Root Mean Square Error (RMSE) and Mean Absolute Error (MAE) as evaluation metrics. MSE is the expected root of the square of the difference between the estimated value and the true value of the parameter and can evaluate the change degree of data. The smaller the value of MSE is, the better the accuracy of the prediction model to describe the experimental data is. MAE is the mean of absolute errors, which is not sensitive towards outliers and can better reflect the actual situation of the predicted value errors.

4.2 Experimental Results

1) Comparison of Proposed Method NRSC with NR, PFS, ICSM, DSM and CARE in RMSE and MAE

The comparison results of six state-of-the-art algorithms on the four datasets in terms of RMSE and MAE are shown in Fig. 1. From Fig. 1(a), we can find that RMSE of the proposed method (NRSC) is 0.225 on the *Heart* dataset, while that of PFS, NR, CARE, ICSM, and DSM are 0.243, 0.238, 0.250, 0.340, and 0.341, respectively. On the other hand, the MAE of NRSC is still smaller than the other methods. Therefore, NRSC outperforms all the previously above-mentioned methods.

From Fig. 1(b) and Fig. 1(d), we can find that NRSC consistently outperforms the other five methods in both evaluation metrices on both datasets *Diabetes* and *DMD*. Obviously, from Fig. 1(b), we can find that on dataset *Diabetes* the RMSE of NRSC is 0.167, while that of PFS, NR, ICSM, DSM and CARE are 0.179, 0.195, 0.329, 0.33, and 0.354, respectively. The MAE of NRSC is 0.14, while that of PFS, NR, ICSM, DSM and CARE are 0.153, 0.154, 0.289, 0.289, and 0.312, respectively. Similarly, from Fig. 1(d), we can find that on dataset *DMD*, the RMSE of NRSC is 0.215, while that of PFS, NR, ICSM, DSM and CARE are 0.231, 0.25, 0.258, 0.358 and 0.243, respectively. The MAE of NRSC is 0.315, while that of PFS, NR, ICSM, DSM and CARE are 0.371, 0.5, 0.358, 0.358, and 0.346, respectively. Therefore, NRSC still outperforms the other five methods.

From Fig. 1(c), on dataset *RHC*, we can find that the RMSE of the proposed NRSC (0.435) is slightly worse than ICSM (0.422) and DSM (0.422) in both evaluation metrics. However, differences between them are not statistically significant. Compared with the methods PFS, NR and CARE, the performance of NRSC is still significantly better, which suggests that the spectral clustering mechanism is still of effectiveness.

To sum up, in terms of both RMSE and MAE, the proposed NRSC achieves a better overall performance on the four datasets against all five state-of-the-art algorithms.

2) The performance of NRSC by tuning the parameters

Since there are several parameters in our proposed method, we need to investigate the robustness of the algorithm when tuning these parameters. Table 1 and Table 2 shows the RMSEs and MAEs, and running time of the proposed method (NRSC) when the parameters U, and λ are set to different values on four datasets. Parameter U is the number of clusters and parameter $\lambda \in [0, 1]$ is the adjustable coefficient that is used to calculate the final similarity measure. We find that the similarity degrees between patients derived from spectral clustering are supplemented into neutrosophic recommender similarity matrix to obtain the final similarity between items with similar demographic information and symptoms.

In the experiment, we can find that the values of RMSE and MAE change almost at the same time on each dataset as the parameters change. The running time also varies when we changed the values of parameters.

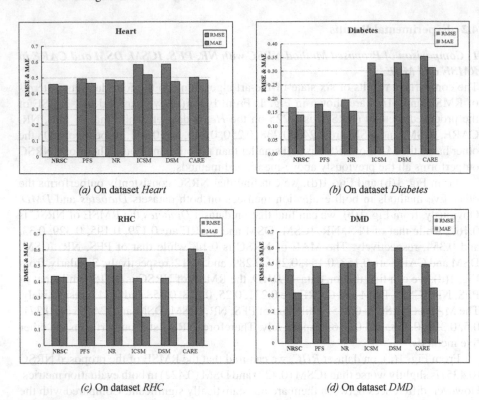

(a) On dataset *Heart*

(b) On dataset *Diabetes*

(c) On dataset *RHC*

(d) On dataset *DMD*

Fig. 1. Comparison of six state-of-the-art methods on four datasets in terms of RMSE and MAE

From the achieved results on Table 1, the value of λ should be larger than 0.5, ideally in the range of [0.6, 0.8] as expressed on four datasets. Besides, from Table 2, we find that the number of clusters is larger, the running time will be longer when we set λ = 0.6 and change the number of clusters U. Although the number of clusters U affects the running time, the increment is small and linear to U. At last, it is necessary to select appropriate parameters on four datasets. When we set the number of clusters $U = 3$ and λ = 0.6, the proposed method can consistently achieve its mostly best performance on the four medical datasets.

We also compared the proposed NRSC (setting $U = 3$ and λ = 0.6) with the five existing methods in running time, whose results are shown in Table 3. Compared with those simple methods, such as ICMS and DSM, the running time of our NRSC only slightly increases because of introducing spectral clustering. However, our method is still better than PFS and NR. Especially, when the size of the dataset is large (RHC), our method is as fast as ICSM and DSM. To sum up, the running time of the proposed NRSC is at least not worse than the state-of-the-art methods and sometimes better than some of the other methods, which is acceptable in a real-world environment.

Table 1. Performance of NRSC when tuning parameters on four datasets.

U	λ	Heart		Diabetes		RHC		DMD	
		RMSE	MAE	RMSE	MAE	RMSE	MAE	RMSE	MAE
2	0.2	0.233	0.480	0.037	0.157	0.201	0.440	0.218	0.321
2	0.4	0.226	0.470	0.034	0.151	0.198	0.440	0.216	0.317
2	0.5	0.225	0.469	0.032	0.150	0.196	0.435	0.215	0.315
2	0.6	**0.226**	**0.468**	**0.031**	**0.149**	0.196	0.434	**0.215**	**0.315**
2	0.8	0.226	0.470	0.032	0.149	**0.195**	**0.430**	0.216	0.315
3	0.2	0.230	0.475	0.035	0.154	0.198	0.438	0.218	0.318
3	0.4	0.225	0.468	0.033	0.150	0.197	0.435	0.215	0.314
3	0.5	0.226	0.468	0.033	0.149	0.195	0.435	0.215	0.315
3	0.6	0.224	0.464	<u>0.030</u>	<u>0.148</u>	<u>0.193</u>	<u>0.430</u>	<u>0.214</u>	<u>0.310</u>
3	0.8	<u>0.223</u>	<u>0.462</u>	0.033	0.149	0.195	0.433	0.214	0.311
4	0.2	0.230	0.473	0.038	0.154	0.198	0.443	0.221	0.321
4	0.4	0.227	0.469	0.036	0.152	0.196	0.438	**0.215**	**0.315**
4	0.5	0.227	0.470	0.037	0.152	0.195	0.436	0.217	0.318
4	0.6	0.230	0.470	**0.034**	**0.151**	**0.195**	**0.433**	0.216	0.316
4	0.8	**0.226**	**0.469**	0.035	0.151	0.195	0.433	0.217	0.315
5	0.2	0.235	0.475	0.040	0.160	0.214	0.452	0.225	0.323
5	0.4	0.232	0.471	0.038	0.157	0.201	0.446	0.220	0.320
5	0.5	0.228	0.470	0.038	0.155	0.198	0.440	0.218	0.320
5	0.6	**0.228**	**0.469**	0.036	0.153	0.197	0.439	0.217	0.318
5	0.8	0.228	0.469	**0.035**	**0.153**	**0.197**	**0.435**	**0.216**	**0.315**

Table 2. Running time (sec) of NRSC when tuning parameter U on four datasets.

U	2	3	4	5
Heart	1.651	2.173	2.673	3.152
Diabetes	3.621	3.788	4.963	5.324
RHC	175.282	253.667	282.376	302.231
DMD	1.104	1.37	1.620	1.962

Table 3. Comparison in running time (sec) on four datasets ($U = 3$ and $\lambda = 0.6$ for NRSC).

Algorithms	NRSC	PFS	NR	ICSM	DSM	CARE
Heart	0.173	1.050	0.218	0.126	0.154	0.185
Diabetes	0.802	1.638	0.753	0.289	0.362	0.553
RHC	253.667	420.379	380.456	247.189	254.254	280.821
DMD	1.071	2.842	1.157	0.934	1.191	1.329

5 Conclusion

In this paper, we concentrated on improving the performance of prediction in medical diagnosis. To address the problem that the features of patients' demographic information and symptoms have different scales and types, we resort to neutrosophic sets to convert these features into uniform-scaled values described by three membership functions. Then, we proposed a novel recommendation method that combines the neutrosophic recommendation method and spectral clustering. The spectral clustering can better group the items with similar demographic information and symptoms together and makes the similarity measures between items more accurate, which results in more accurate prediction and recommendation of diseases. And we compared the proposed method with four state-of-the-art methods on four medical diagnosis datasets. Experimental results demonstrate that the proposed methods outperform the others in terms of Root Mean Square Error and Mean Average Error.

This study is still preliminary. We only focus on predicting one disease. However, in real-world circumstances, relevant diseases usually happen together. Thus, the system should be able to predict a set of relevant diseases simultaneously. Moreover, constructing neutrosophic sets for the complicated datasets with large dimensions of features is time-consuming but essential to the development of the recommendation methods. In the future, we will keep our studies along with these directions.

Acknowledgments. This work has been supported by the National Natural Science Foundation of China under grants 62076130 and 91846104, and the National Key Research and Development Program of China under grant 2018AAA0102002.

References

1. Manogaran, G., Varatharajan, R., Priyan, M.K.: Hybrid recommendation system for heart disease diagnosis based on multiple kernel learning with adaptive neuro-fuzzy inference system. Multimedia Tools Appl. **77**(4), 4379–4399 (2017). https://doi.org/10.1007/s11042-017-5515-y
2. Li, X., Wang, Z.: A new recommendation algorithm combined with spectral clustering and transfer learning. Cluster Comput. **22**(1), 1151–1167 (2017). https://doi.org/10.1007/s10586-017-1161-4

3. Ali, M., Son, L.H., Thanh, N.D., Minh, N.V.: A neutrosophic recommender system for medical diagnosis based on algebraic neutrosophic measure. Appl. Soft Comput. **71**, 1054–1071 (2018)
4. Hu, J., Pan, L., Yang, Y., Chen, H.: A group medical diagnosis model based on intuitionistic fuzzy soft sets. Appl. Soft Comput. J. **77**, 453–466 (2019)
5. Khalil, S.M.: Decision making using algebraic operations on soft effect matrix as new category of similarity measures and study their application in medical diagnosis problems. J. Intell. Fuzzy Syst. **37**(2), 1865–1877 (2019)
6. Smarandache, F.: A Unifying Field in Logics. Neutrosophy: Neutrosophic Probability, Set and Logic, Rehoboth. American Research Press, Santa Fe (1998)
7. Guo, Y., et al.: Automated iterative neutrosophic lung segmentation for image analysis in thoracic computed tomography. Med. Phys. **40**(8), 081912 (2013)
8. Zhang, M., Zhang, L., Cheng, H.D.: Segmentation of ultrasound breast images based on a neutrosophic method. Opt. Eng. **49**(11), 117001 (2010)
9. Ye, J.: Improved cosine similarity measures of simplifield neutrosophic sets for medical diagnoses. Artif. Intell. Med. **63**(3), 171–179 (2015)
10. Ye, J., Fu, J.: Multi-period medical diagnosis method using a single valued neutrosophic similarity measure based on tangent function. Comput. Methods Programs Biomed. **123**, 142–149 (2016)
11. Ye, S., Fu, J., Ye, J.: Medical diagnosis using distance-based similarity measures of single valued neutrosophic multisets. Neutrosophic Sets Syst. **7**, 47–54 (2015)
12. Xu, D., Xu, Z., Liu, S., Zhao, H.: A spectral clustering algorithm based on intuitionistic fuzzy information. Knowl.-Based Syst. **53**, 20–26 (2013)
13. Broumi, S., Smarandache, S.: Extended hausdorff distance and similarity measure of refined neutrosophic sets and their application in medical diagnosis. J. New Theory **11**(7), 64–78 (2015)
14. Thong, N.T., Son, L.H.: HIFCF: an effective hybrid model between picture fuzzy clustering and intuitionistic fuzzy recommender systems for medical diagnosis. Exp. Syst. Appl. **42**(7), 3682–3701 (2015)
15. Wang, H., Smarandache, F., Zhang, Y.Q., Sunderraman, R.: Single valued neutrosophic sets. Multispace Multistruct. **4**, 410–413 (2010)
16. Duan, L., Street, W.N., Xu, E.: Healthcare information systems: data mining methods in the creation of a clinical recommender system. Enterp. Inf. Syst. **5**(2), 169–218 (2011)
17. Mahabaleshwar, S.: Kabbur : an efficient multiclass medical image CBIR system based on classification and clustering. J. Intell. Syst. **27**(2), 275–290 (2018)
18. Thanh, N.D., Ali, M., Son, L.H.: A novel clustering algorithm in a neutrosophic recommender system for medical diagnosis. Cogn. Comput. **9**(4), 526–544 (2017). https://doi.org/10.1007/s12559-017-9462-8
19. Son, L.H., Thong, N.T.: Intuitionistic fuzzy recommender systems: an effective tool for medical diagnosis. Knowl.-Based Syst. **74**, 133–150 (2015)
20. Yang, Y., Ma, Z., Yang, Y.: Multitask spectral clustering by exploring intertask correlation. IEEE Trans. Cybern. **45**(5), 1083–1094 (2015). https://doi.org/10.1109/TCYB.2014.2344015
21. Ye, S., Ye, J.: Dice similarity measure between single valued neutrosophic multisets and its application in medical diagnosis. Neutrosophic Sets Syst. **6**, 48–53 (2014)
22. Broumi, S.: F, Smarandache: serveral similarity measures of neutrosophic sets. Neutrosophic Sets Syst. **1**, 55 (2013)
23. UCI Repository of Machine Learning Databases, University of California (2007). https://archive.ics.uc.edu/ml
24. Department of Biostatistics. Vanderbilt University (2016). https://biostat.mc.vanderbilt.edu/DataSets

25. Lee, J., Noh, G., Oh, H., Kim, C.K.: Trustor clustering with an improved recommender system based on social relationships. Inf. Syst. **77**, 118–128 (2018)
26. Davis, D.A., Chawla, N.V., Blumm, N., Christakis, N., Barabási, A.L.: predicting individual disease risk based on medical history. In: Proceedings of the 17th ACM Conference on Information and Knowledge Management, pp. 769–778 (2008)
27. Ejegwa, P.A.: Improved composite relation for pythagorean fuzzy sets and its application to medical diagnosis. Granular Comput. **5**(2), 277–286 (2019). https://doi.org/10.1007/s41066-019-00156-8
28. He, S., Cheng, B., Huang, Y., Duan, L., Chen, J.: Proactive personalized services in large-scale IoT-based healthcare application. In: 2017 IEEE International Conference on Web Services (ICWS), pp. 808–813 (2017)

ECG Arrhythmia Heartbeat Classification Using Deep Learning Networks

Yuxi Yang, Linpeng Jin, and Zhigeng Pan[(⊠)]

School of Alibaba Business, Hangzhou Normal University, Hangzhou, China
`yuxiyang1027@163.com`, `20190014@hznu.edu.cn`, `443922077@qq.com`

Abstract. The electrocardiogram (ECG) records the process of depolarization and repolarization of the heart and contains many important details related to the condition of the human heart. In this paper, we designed four deep learning network structures and three electrocardiogram signal preprocessing methods, under the same dataset, explored the impact and performance of different preprocessing methods and models on the ECG arrhythmia classification work. For a fairer comparison, we used intra-patient and inter-patient evaluation for the final classification evaluation. In the evaluation of the intra-patient, the proposed network structures can achieve an accuracy of more than 95%. In the evaluation of inter-patient, all classification models can achieve an accuracy rate of more than 81.7%. During our research, we found convolutional neural network (CNN) is good at capturing spatial features of ECG. Long short-term memory networks (LSTM) is suitable for processing time-series signals. The combination of the two has a better classification performance than the sole network. Besides, the Attention mechanism can help the model do better on focusing on abnormal heartbeats also improve the interpretability of the model. Residual neural Network (ResNet) has good behavior in intra-patient, but not suitable for the inter-patient classification due to the vanishing gradient problem. Compared to the different preprocessing methods, we recommended using the raw signal in future work.

Keywords: ECG heartbeat classification · CNN · LSTM · Attention mechanism · ResNet

1 Introduction

Arrhythmia is a representative type of cardiovascular diseases (CVDs) that refers to any irregular change from normal heart rhythms. Although a single arrhythmia heartbeat may not have a serious impact on life, continuous arrhythmia beats can result in fatal circumstances [1]. The most widely applied solution for arrhythmia detection is electrocardiography (ECG). ECG shows the morbid status of the cardiovascular system by changes in its waveforms or rhythms [2]. The screening of arrhythmias requires careful study of the ECG records by

© ICST Institute for Computer Sciences, Social Informatics and Telecommunications Engineering 2021
Published by Springer Nature Switzerland AG 2021. All Rights Reserved
L. Qi et al. (Eds.): CloudComp 2020, LNICST 363, pp. 175–189, 2021.
https://doi.org/10.1007/978-3-030-69992-5_14

experienced cardiologists and this process is tedious and time-consuming. Moreover, there may be minute changes in the ECG that are overlooked by the naked eye [3]. Automatic arrhythmia detection based on ECG provides important assistance for doctors, and also helps common people to self-monitor their heart conditions using wearable devices. Accurate automatic arrhythmia detection plays as the foundation of machine-aided diagnosis and treatment of cardiovascular diseases [4].

With the improvement of computing power, deep learning has been successfully applied to many areas such as numbers, characters and face recognition, image classification. Deep learning methods are also used effectively in the analysis of bioinformatics signals. Kiranyaz et al. proposed an adaptive CNN model for the detection of ventricular ectopic beats (VEB) and supraventricular ectopic beats (SVEB). This model required small common patient-specific training data and achieved a superior classification performance. Acharya et al. developed a 9-layer deep CNN model to automatically identify five different categories of heartbeats in ECG signals. Their experiment obtained an accuracy of 94.03% in the diagnostic classification of the original ECG heartbeats [14]. Rajpurkar et al. proposed a 34-layer CNN model for arrhythmia detection [5]. It is reported that accuracy exceeds the level of cardiologists.

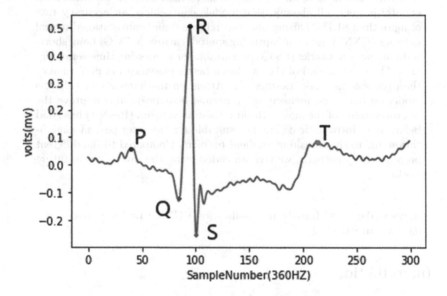

Fig. 1. An ECG heartbeat with P,Q,R,S and T waves.

In the last decades, there have been some works on ECG for different tasks promoting the application of ECG in clinical practice. Generally speaking, there are four main tasks: (1) ECG data preprocessing, (2) heartbeat segmentation, (3) feature extraction, (4) ECG classification. Among the four tasks, ECG feature

extraction and classification are the keys to successfully detect cardiac diseases
[7]. Although many researchers achieved almost optimal results for ECG classification and various filtering methods were proposed, owing to the diversities of
the ECG dataset and preprocessing methods, as well as the differences in evaluation indicators, there is a lack of horizontal comparison of such research works.
Thus, in this paper, we will focus on the comparison of commonly used ECG
preprocessing methods and mainstream deep learning networks to promote the
clinical practice of diagnosis by ECG (Fig. 2).

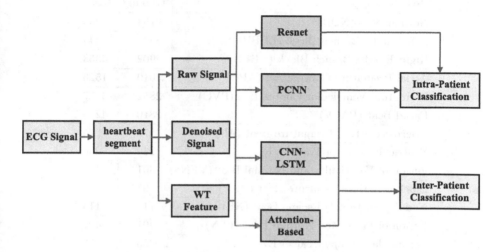

Fig. 2. Overall view of the proposed systems.

Major contributions of this research are as follows: 1) Referred to the previous application of deep learning networks structures in the detection of ECG
arrhythmia, we developed four mainstream networks such as an 11-layer pure
CNN model, a combination of CNN and LSTM model, Attention mechanism
model and ResNet model, separately trained to compare the final classification
performance. the same ECG dataset and preprocessing methods were used for
all reference models 2) Considering the comparison of preprocessing methods, we
chose three ECG presentations as the inputs of the classifier, there was a raw signal (without any preprocessing), denoised signal, and hand-crafted ECG features
which widely used in machine learning. 3) In this paper, we discussed two major
evaluations of heartbeat classification methods, intra-patient, and inter-patient
evaluation, presented the classification performance of existing approaches under
each evaluation.

2   Dataset

The ECG dataset used in our experiments is from the MIT-BIH arrhythmia
database [8] publicly available on PhysioNet. The MIT-BIH dataset contains 48

30-minutes long records from 47 patients. Each ECG record was digitized at 360 samples and annotated by cardiologists. The database is regarded as the benchmark database in arrhythmia detection and classification and has been extensively utilized for algorithm validation [9]. Hence, we used the MIT-BIH arrhythmia database to do contrast with different classification methods.

Table 1. Summary of training and testing datasets in intra-patient

Heartbeat type	Training	Test
Normal Beat (NOR)	9753	65265
Left Bundle Branch Block (LBBB)	3229	4843
Right Bundle Branch Block (RBBB)	2902	4353
Atrial Premature Contraction (APC)	1019	1526
Premature Ventricular Contraction (PVC)	2852	4277
Paced Beat (PACE)	2810	4215
Aberrated Atrial Premature Beat (AP)	75	75
Ventricular Flutter Wave (VF)	236	236
Fusion of Ventricular and Normal Beat (VFN)	401	401
Blocked Atrial Premature Beat (BAP)	97	96
Nodal (Junctional) Escape Beat (NE)	115	114
Fusion of Paced and Normal Beat (FPN)	491	491
Ventricular Escape Beat (VE)	53	53
Nodal (Junctional) Premature Beat (NP)	42	41
Atrial Escape Beat (AE)	8	8
Unclassifiable Beat (UN)	17	16
Total	24100	86009

For the sake of fairness, two types of evaluation approaches were investigated in this paper, namely, "inter-patient" and "intra-patient". In the "intra-patient" evaluation, all 48 records were used and heartbeat segments were provided by the annotated QRS position. The resulting heartbeat dataset was divided into 16 classes [9]. Specifically, 13% of the beats from the normal class, 40% of the beats from each of five bigger arrhythmia classes (i.e., "L," "R," "A," "V," "P"), and 50% of the beats from each of ten smaller arrhythmias classes were randomly selected to constitute the training dataset, for a total of 21.89% beats of the whole dataset. The remaining heartbeats were used as the test dataset. The details of the 16 heartbeat classes were summarized in Table 1. To be mentioned, in the "intra-patient" evaluation, the training and test dataset will contain heartbeats from the same people.

In consideration of it, the "intra-patient" evaluation is not a realistic measure. Therefore, the "inter-patient" evaluation is conducted in addition to a more realistic estimate of the generalization ability of the algorithm. According to ANSI/AAMI EC57:1998 standard [10], among the 48 records available in the MIT-BIH dataset the training and testing dataset contained 22 records each, the other four paced records (i.e., the records 102, 104, 107, 217) were excluded for experiments. The original 16 heartbeat classes were divided into the five bigger classes, namely "N", "S", "V", "F", and "Q". The mapping from the MIT-BIH arrhythmia database heartbeat classes to the AAMI heartbeat classes was shown in Table 2.

The purpose of ECG signal preprocessing is to reduce various types of noise that may be present in the ECG signal. Typical sources of noise in the ECG signal include baseline wander, artifacts caused by muscle contraction, and electrode movement [11]. In our research, the preprocessing of the ECG signal included baseline wander correction and band-pass filtering. The raw ECG signal was first processed to correct the baseline wander using a wavelet-based approach [12]. Following [13], the signal was band-pass filtered at 5–12 Hz to maximize the energy of the QRS complex, removing high-frequency and low-frequency artifacts. The denoised signals were used as one of the classifier inputs.

Table 2. Summary of training and testing datasets in inter-patient and the mapping from MIT-BIH classes to AAMI classes

Heartbeat type	MIT-BIH classes	Training	Test
N	NOR, LBBB, RBBB, AE, NE	45845	44238
S	APC, AP, BAP, NP	999	1973
V	PVC, VE, VF	4260	3220
F	VFN	414	388
Q	FPN, UN	8	7

ECG signals usually show changes over time or position. The classic Fourier transform (FT) can provide us with frequency-domain features, but a lack of analysis of time-domain features. Wavelet transform (WT) can satisfy these two characteristics. Until now, WT has been widely used in ECG signals [18–21], including denoising, heartbeat detection, and feature extraction. In traditional machine learning classification tasks, WT functions are often used for hand-crafted features as the classifier input. The performance of WT features is often better than using the raw ECG signal as the classifier input. In our paper, WT was used as one of the feature extraction methods. Daubechies wavelets of order 8 were selected due to their similarity with the most characteristic QRS waveform [9]. After applying four-level wavelet decomposition, we kept 114 coefficients (32 from A4, 32 from D4, and 50 from D3) as the wavelet features for one of the classifier inputs. In the heartbeat segmentation of ECG signals, we used the annotations of R-peak locations provided by the database. Each heartbeat segment consisted of 100 samples before the R peak location, R peak location, and 200 samples after the R peak, a total of 300 samples corresponding to 0.83 s.

3   Intra-Patient Model Architecture

3.1   PCNN Model

The PCNN (Pure-CNN) model used an 11-layer network structure [6], contained 4 convolutional layers, and the size of convolutional kernels was respectively 27, 14, 3, and 4. Structurally, each convolutional layer was followed by a max-pooling layer of stride 2. The last part of the model has consisted of 3 full-connected layers, the number of neurons of the first two layers were 30 and 10, the last layer neurons were determined by the number of output classes. We used a leaky rectifier linear unit as the activation function of the convolutional layers and the first two fully connected layers, also applied Xavier to initialize the weight of each layer. Softmax function was used for the last layer. During the training of the CNN model, we used Adam optimizer, the initial learning rate was set to 0.001, and the batch size was 20. The architecture for the PCNN model was illustrated in Fig. 3.

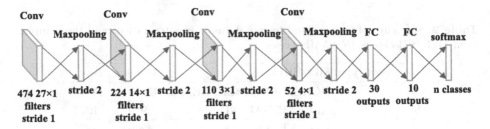

Fig. 3. The architecture of the proposed PCNN model.

3.2   CNN-LSTM Model

The model was composed of CNN and LSTM layers. The structure of CNN layers were designed with the reference to VGGNet developed by Visual Geometry Group [15]. VGGNet was chosen as it features smooth information flow and simple implementation. As shown in Fig. 4, the number of convolutional kernels continued to grow with increasing depth of network layers with the kernel size of 3. The stride size as well as kernel size of max-pooling layer is 3. Each convolutional layer were stepped by a batch normalization layer (BN) and a rectified linear unit activation function. The addition of the BN layer can make the distribution of the input data from each layer in the network relatively stable, which is conducive to improving the learning speed of the entire neural network [23]. The RELU function is a widely used activation function [16], which has the ability to prevent the gradient vanishing problem in deep neural networks. Following the convolutional layers were two LSTM layers, the input of the first LSTM layer was determined by the number of features which generated by the convolutional layer, and the output size of both LSTM layers were 32.

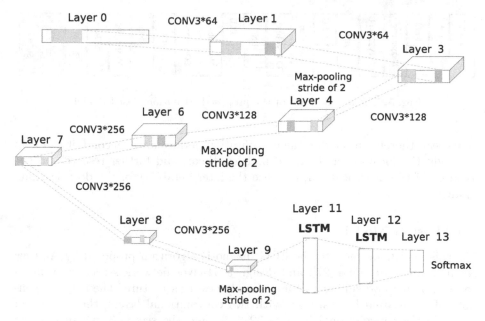

Fig. 4. The architecture of the proposed CNN-LSTM model.

The CNN-LSTM model was trained by Adam optimizer with an initial learning rate of 0.0001. Adam has the ability to balance gradient updates between different classes, so it can mitigate the adverse effects caused by data imbalance [24]. In a total of 90 periods of training, the learning rate was multiplied by 0.1 times every 30 periods. We used Kaiming to initialize the weight of each convolutional layer, and orthogonal to initialize the weight of the LSTM layer, which can greatly improve the convergence speed of the model parameters. To prevent overfitting [21], we multiplied the L2 loss of all parameters in the network by 0.004 to the training loss and used a 20% dropout rate in the LSTM layers.

3.3   Attention-Based Model

The Attention-Based model was constructed with CNN, LSTM, and Attention mechanism. The part of CNN and LSTM referred to the CNN-LSTM model. The size and number of kernel functions were consistent with the CNN-LSTM model. To give a fair comparison, the same hyperparameters including learning rate and batch size were used for the proposed model and kept in line with regularization strategies. The Attention-Based Model added the Attention layer after the LSTM layer as shown in Fig. 5 and the attention mechanism would generate a set of independent weights for each possible class in the N classes. Then for each class, the unique weighted average of the inputs was calculated, and finally, the probability of the ECG signal class was outputted.

The introduction of the attention mechanism in the network structure had two advantages. First, it can help the model to focus on the important part of the

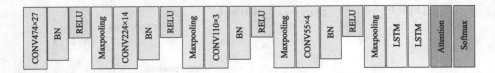

Fig. 5. The architecture of the proposed Attention-Based model.

heartbeat, thereby improving the classification performance. Second, it can help highlight the location of the abnormal heartbeat, and further research on the location of the heartbeat can increase the interpretability of the deep learning model.

3.4   ResNet Model

For this model, we refer to the ECG diagnosis algorithm proposed by Andrew Ng in Nature Medicine [27], and design a 34-layer network structure, using a connection method similar to the residual network structure. The network consists of 16 residual blocks, each with two convolutional layers, the number of filters in the convolutional layer is 32 * 2k, and the size is 3, where k starts from 1, and every 4 residual blocks Increase by 1. In the case of reaching the same receptive field, the smaller the convolution kernel, the less calculation of the parameter kernel required, so in the experiment, we prefer to use multiple small convolution kernels instead of using one alone. Large convolution kernel. Each spare residual block will subsample the input with a step size of 2. Before each convolutional layer, a batch normalization layer and activation function RELU layer is designed as a pre-activated block. In order to prevent over-fitting, the model adds a Dropout layer between the RELU layer and the convolutional layer, with a loss rate of 20.

In the training process, Adam optimizer is used, the initial learning rate is 0.0001, and the default parameters $\beta1 = 0.9$ and $\beta2 = 0.999$. The batch size is 128. We use the Xaiver to initialize the weight of each convolutional layer. In a total of 30 epochs of training, the learning rate is multiplied by 0.1 every 10 epochs.

4   Inter-Patient Model Architecture

Initially, we were consistent in choosing models for the inter-patient and intra-patient model, however, during the training process, we found the gradient vanishing problem by used intra-patient models to do the inter-patient classification. Hence, we referred to the PCNN model to simplify the network structure and parameters, and retraining. The CNN model selection was consistent with the above-mentioned A model. The difference is the construction of the CNN-LSTM framework, we add the two LSTM layers after the PCNN model, no longer applied modified VGGNet as the convolutional structure, and the output size were all 128, and 20% of the dropout rates were used.

5   Experimental Setup

Proposed models were deployed in Python 3.7.6 language with TensorFlow [25] which is an open-source software library for deep learning launched by Google. Since deep learning networks require a lot of free parameters to train, GPU support is strongly recommended to reduce the learning time of the model. Thus, our experimental setup was RTX2060-super GPU on the window10 system. With GPU, TensorFlow is accelerated by using CUDA and CUDNN [26]. Versions of each software are TensorFlowr2.1.0, CUDA 10.1, and CUDNN 7.6.4.

6   Experimental Results

6.1   Performance Metrics

In this research, typical classification metrics, including accuracy, precision, recall, and F1 score were used for each model. They were defined as:

$$Accuracy = \frac{TP + TN}{TP + FP + TN + FN} \tag{1}$$

$$Precision = \frac{TP}{TP + FP} \tag{2}$$

$$Recall = \frac{TP}{TP + FN} \tag{3}$$

$$F1 = \frac{2 \times (Precision \times Recall)}{Precision + Recall} \tag{4}$$

where TP refers to the number of correctly classified samples in a certain class, FN refers to the number of samples belonging to a certain class which was misclassified as in other classes, and FP refers to the number of samples misclassified as in a certain class when they belong to other classes.

6.2   Intra-Patient Performance

In the intra-patient experimental performance, from the view of various inputs, the performances of raw signal and manual WT feature were generally better than the denoised signal in Table 3, whether it is from the perspective of accuracy, or from the analysis of F1-score. But there was a special result here that the F1-score of the denoised signal which training on the PCNN and ResNet networks showed the highest performance in all groups.

We deliberately compared and analyzed the confusion matrix of the PCNN Denoised model and the lowest F1-score Attention Denoised model, and we found the recognition rate of the heartbeats of class6, class9, class13, class14, class15 in the Attention Denoised model was 0%. Considering that the sample numbers of these classes occupied a very low proportion of the total sample numbers of heartbeats (as shown in Table 1). On the other side, the recognition rate of the

Table 3. The intra-patient classification performance of three inputs and models

Model and inputs	Accuracy	F1-score	Recall	Precision
PCNN, Raw	0.971	0.698	0.755	0.660
PCNN, Denoised	0.947	0.856	0.875	0.845
PCNN, WT	0.974	0.707	0.736	0.683
CNN-LSTM, Raw	0.984	0.796	0.805	0.792
CNN-LSTM, Denoised	0.956	0.570	0.599	0.553
CNN-LSTM, WT	0.976	0.539	0.586	0.509
Attention, Raw	0.985	0.794	0.813	0.794
Attention, Denoised	0.950	0.535	0.585	0.501
Attention, WT	0.979	0.688	0.708	0.681
ResNet, Raw	0.974	0.801	0.805	0.792
ResNet, Denoised	0.979	0.912	0.932	0.908
ResNet, WT	0.977	0.757	0.762	0.751

PCNN Denoised model included the above-mentioned classes and exceeded 90% (excepted for classes 13).

From the framework point of view, the four mainstream deep learning frameworks can achieve an accuracy rate of more than 95%. Apart from denoising signals, almost all the frameworks can reach an accuracy rate of more than 97%. And in terms of overall performance, the Resnet model performs better than other frameworks but we need to point out that the intra-patient classification is not a real method for the actual evaluation of the performance of the classifier. The time-varying dynamics and the morphological characteristics of ECG signals show significant variations for different patients. Even for the ECG of a healthy subject, which appears to be deterministic, the shapes of QRS complex, P waves, and R-R intervals will not be the same from one beat to the other under different circumstances [17]. However, in real-world scenarios, the trained model must deal with heartbeats from patients that are unseen during training [22].

6.3   Inter-Patient Performance

In the inter-patient evaluation, according to the AAMI standard, 22 records were used for training and 22 records were used for testing. For the training set, we counted the heartbeats contained in each record according to the classes, and 21 records were used in the training process, one record for the validation. The validation data was derived from training data that had never been used before.

Table 4 compared the three reference models (PCNN, CNN-LSTM, Attention-Based Model) in the classification of arrhythmia. The results showed that the Attention-based model was superior to the PCNN and CNN-LSTM models in the F1-score of all classes. Besides, due to the sample imbalance of the

Table 4. The inter-patient classification performance of three inputs and models

Model and inputs	Accuracy	F1-score	Recall	Precision
PCNN, Raw	0.832	0.845	0.831	0.860
PCNN, Denoised	0.852	0.847	0.849	0.841
PCNN, WT	0.845	0.857	0.842	0.869
CNN-LSTM, Raw	0.843	0.836	0.841	0.828
CNN-LSTM, Denoised	0.870	0.846	0.872	0.831
CNN-LSTM, WT	0.853	0.841	0.850	0.832
Attention, Raw	0.821	0.821	0.819	0.820
Attention, Denoised	0.836	0.843	0.842	0.851
Attention, WT	0.817	0.839	0.824	0.870

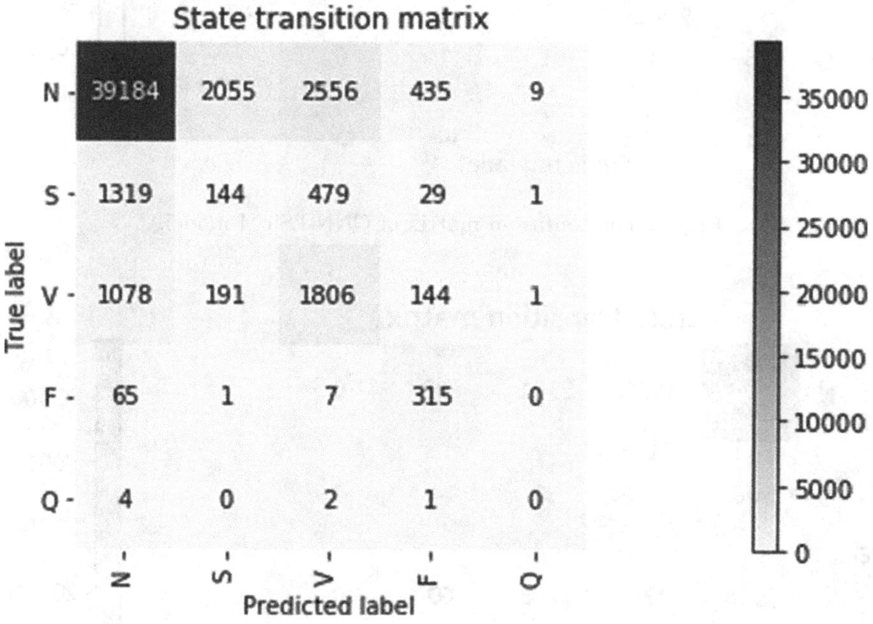

Fig. 6. The confusion matrix of CNN model.

MIT-BIH database, we used the weighted F1-score indicator. In terms of accuracy, the CNN-LSTM model was generally highest, up to 87.0%. On account the Attention-Based model was modified based on the CNN-LSTM model, the two were more comparable, it can be seen that as the introduction of attention mechanism, the model can help us improve the recognition rate of abnormal heartbeats. Observed Figs. 6, 7 and 8, in the recognition rate of "S" heartbeats, Attention-based model exhibited better performance than the CNN and CNN-LSTM networks. Compared to the classification performance of different signal

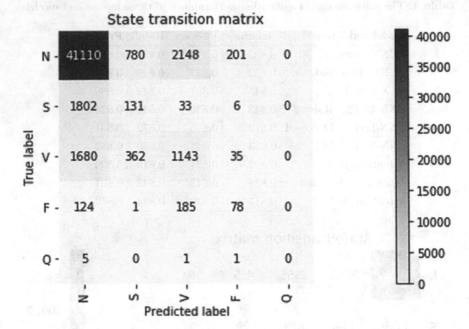

Fig. 7. The confusion matrix of CNN-LSTM model.

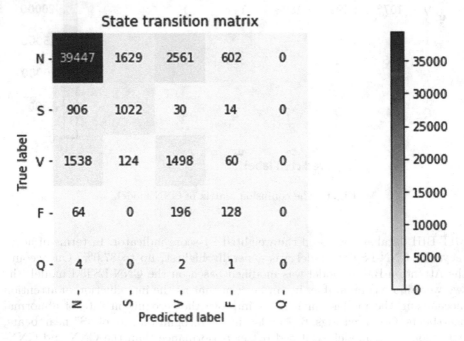

Fig. 8. The confusion matrix of Attention-Based model.

inputs, we are more inclined to recommend using the raw signal as the input of the inter-patient in the future arrhythmia classification research, because of its stable performance upon different deep learning network frameworks.

7   Discussion and Conclusion

As a result of the long history of ECG classification researches, these works used different datasets and detected different types of arrhythmia. It is unfair to compare it with them directly. In this paper, we proposed three different ECG signal inputs and used four different deep learning networks CNN, CNN-LSTM, Attention-Based model to do the intra-patient and inter-patient evaluation on the MIT-BIH dataset. The results showed that deep learning networks can generally achieve good classification performance on the MIT-BIH database. The CNN network is good at capturing spatial features, the LSTM network is suitable for processing time-series signals. Compared with the classification performance of CNN and CNN-LSTM, the combined performance of the two will be superior to the single CNN network. In addition, the introduction of the attention mechanism helps the model locate the important information part of the ECG signal and improve the interpretability of the model. The results of the Attention-Based model also showed that in future ECG classification research, it is important to focus on the subtle information part of the ECG signal. ResNet model has good behavior in intra-patient classification, but due to its complicated network structure and expensive training cost, we tend to recommend the simplified network (layers number did not exceed 15) in the heartbeats classification based on the MIT-BIH database. Due to the particularity of the MIT-BIH dataset, the numbers of normal heartbeats were far more than the abnormal. Therefore, experimental results with high accuracy were more inclined to the normal class. The phenomenon was obvious in the inter-patient experiments. It can be considered that keep a balance of the sample numbers between classes or using weighted evaluation indicators to compare performance more fairly. In this research, we used three different inputs, the raw signal, the denoised signal, and the handcrafted features, discussed the impact and significance of each input on the performance and applicability of our heartbeat classification method. It can be seen that the raw signal performance was more stable than the others. So we recommend using the raw signal in future works.

Acknowledgment. This work was supported by the Natural Science Foundation of Zhejiang Province, China (grant number LZ21F020008).

References

1. Jun, T.J., Nguyen, H.M., Kang, D., et al.: ECG arrhythmia classification using a 2-D convolutional neural network. arXiv preprint arXiv:1804.06812 (2018)
2. Van Mieghem, C., Sabbe, M., Knockaert, D.: The clinical value of the ECG in noncardiac conditions. Chest **125**(4), 1561–1576 (2004)

3. Oh, S.L., Ng, E.Y.K., San Tan, R., et al.: Automated diagnosis of arrhythmia using combination of CNN and LSTM techniques with variable length heart beats. Comput. Biol. Med. **102**, 278–287 (2018)
4. Yao, Q., Wang, R., Fan, X., et al.: Multi-class Arrhythmia detection from 12-lead varied-length ECG using Attention-based Time-Incremental Convolutional Neural Network. Inf. Fusion **53**, 174–182 (2020)
5. Rajpurkar, P., Hannun, A.Y., Haghpanahi, M., et al.: Cardiologist-level arrhythmia detection with convolutional neural networks. arXiv preprint arXiv:1707.01836 (2017)
6. Acharya, U.R., et al.: Automated detection of arrhythmias using different intervals of tachycardia ECG segments with convolutional neural network. Inf. Sci. **405**, 81–90 (2017)
7. Li, Y., Pang, Y., Wang, J., et al.: Patient-specific ECG classification by deeper CNN from generic to dedicated. Neurocomputing **314**, 336–346 (2018)
8. Mark, R., Moody, G.: MIT-BIH Arrhythmia Database Directory. http://ecg.mit.edu/dbinfo.html
9. Ye, C., Kumar, B.V.K.V., Coimbra, M.T.: Heartbeat classification using morphological and dynamic features of ECG signals. IEEE Trans. Biomed. Eng. **59**(10), 2930–2941 (2012)
10. Testing and Reporting Performance Results of Cardiac Rhythm and ST Segment Measurement Algorithms, ANSI/AAMI EC57:1998 standard, Association for the Advancement of Medical Instrumentation (1998)
11. Rajendra, A.U., Suri, J.S.: Advances in Cardiac Signal Processing, 1st edn. Springer, Heidelberg (2009). https://doi.org/10.1007/978-3-540-36675-1
12. Zhang, D.: Wavelet approach for ECG baseline wander correction and noise reduction. In: Proceedings of IEEE International Conference of the IEEE Engineering in Medicine and Biology Society, pp. 1212–1215 (2005)
13. Pan, J., Tompkins, W.J.: A real-time QRS detection algorithm. IEEE Trans. Biomed. Eng. **32**(3), 230–236 (1985)
14. Acharya, U.R., Fujita, H., Lih, O.S., et al.: Automated detection of arrhythmias using different intervals of tachycardia ECG segments with convolutional neural network. Inf. Sci. **405**, 81–90 (2017)
15. Simonyan, K., Zisserman, A.: Very deep convolutional networks for large-scale image recognition. arXiv preprint arXiv:1409.1556 (2014)
16. Nair, V., Hinton, G.E.: Rectified linear units improve restricted Boltzmann machines. In: ICML (2010)
17. Kiranyaz, S., Ince, T., Gabbouj, M.: Real-time patient-specific ECG classification by 1-D convolutional neural networks. IEEE Trans. Biomed. Eng. **63**(3), 664–675 (2015)
18. Sahoo, S., et al.: Multiresolution wavelet transform based feature extraction and ECG classification to detect cardiac abnormalities. Measurement **108**, 55–66 (2017)
19. Martis, R.J., Rajendra Acharya, U., Min, L.C.: ECG beat classification using PCA, LDA, ICA and discrete wavelet transform. Biomed. Signal Process. Control **8**(5), 437–448 (2013)
20. Yildirim, Ö.: A novel wavelet sequence based on deep bidirectional LSTM network model for ECG signal classification. Comput. Biol. Med. **96**, 189–202 (2018)
21. Srivastava, N., et al.: Dropout: a simple way to prevent neural networks from overfitting. J. Mach. Learn. Res. **15**(1), 1929–1958 (2014)
22. Sellami, A., Hwang, H.: A robust deep convolutional neural network with batch-weighted loss for heartbeat classification. Expert Syst. Appl. **122**, 75–84 (2019)

23. Ioffe, S., Szegedy, C.: Batch normalization: accelerating deep network training by reducing internal covariate shift. arXiv preprint arXiv:1502.03167 (2015)
24. Kingma, D.P., Ba, J.: Adam: a method for stochastic optimization. arXiv preprint arXiv:1412.6980 (2014)
25. Abadi, M., et al.: TensorFlow: large-scale machine learning on heterogeneous distributed systems. arXiv preprint arXiv:1603.04467 (2016)
26. Chetlur, S., et al.: cuDNN: efficient primitives for deep learning. arXiv preprint arXiv:1410.0759 (2014)
27. Hannun, A.Y., Rajpurkar, P., Haghpanahi, M., et al.: Cardiologist-level arrhythmia detection and classification in ambulatory electrocardiograms using a deep neural network. Nat. Med. **25**(1), 65 (2019)

Author Index

Printed in the United States
By Bookmasters